MARGARET DRISCOLL

Web-
BASED TRAINING

Using Technology
to Design Adult
Learning
Experiences

Jossey-Bass
Pfeiffer
San Francisco

Copyright © 1998 by Jossey-Bass/Pfeiffer

Jossey-Bass/Pfeiffer is a registered trademark of Jossey-Bass Inc., A Wiley Company.

ISBN: 0-7879-4203-0
Library of Congress Catalog Card Number 98-25314

Library of Congress Cataloging-in-Publication Data

Driscoll, Margaret

    Web-based training : tactics and techniques for designing adult learning
    p. cm.
    Includes index.
  1. Employees--Training of--Computer network resources. 2. Employess--Training of--Computer-assisted instruction. 3. World Wide Web (Information retrieval system). I. Title
    HF5549.5.T7 D75 1998
    658.3'124'02854678--ddc21   98-25314

Printed in the United States of America

Published by

JOSSEY-BASS/PFEIFFER
A Wiley Company
350 Sansome St.
San Francisco, CA 94104-1342
415.433.1740; Fax 415.433.0499
800.274.4434; Fax 800.569.0443

www.pfeiffer.com

Acquiring Editor: Larry Alexander
Director of Development: Kathleen Dolan Davies
Developmental Editor: Susan Rachmeler
Editor: Rebecca Taff
Senior Porduction Editor: Dawn Kilgore
Interior Design: Bruce Lundquist
Cover Design: Tom Morgan/Blue Design

Printing 10 9 8 7 6 5

This book is printed on acid-free, recycled stock that meets or exceeds the minimum GPO and EPA requirements for recycled paper.

Table of Contents

Acknowledgements

A number of people have contributed to this book by helping me refine my thinking and pushing me when I needed pushing. Their contributions are like the field of adult education—expansive and connected in unexpected places.

This book began as part of my doctoral work at Teachers College under the guidance and patience of Dr. Jeanne Bitterman, my advisor. My research was often like a white-water rafting trip with patches of rough water, then calm water. I never felt alone on my journey because my AEGIS colleagues, Dianne Goss, Yvonne Thayer, Janet Mackin, Roberta Senzer, Joanne MulQueen, and Joan Buckley were always there.

Dr. Victoria Marsick and Dr. Stephen Brookfield, who know the river well, were also generous guides who provided additional direction at critical turns.

The strength of this book is its foundation in the experience and practical insights of educators, trainers, and consultants. These professionals were willing to share stories of successes and failures and to make recommendations to help other training professionals undertake projects using this new technology.

I own special thanks to Brandon Hall, Vince Eugenio, Burt Parcels, Greg Stone, Rob Schadt, Linda Barrille, Brian Duelm, John O'Connor, Ray Melcher, Paul Gilbert, Becky Hallden, Gary Baum, Mike Glass, Charlotte Corbet, Nora Busby, Patricia LeSaux, Anne Walker, Melioria Dockery, Bob Conway, Jim Kilmurray, Tom Keating, Bill Hertzel, Carolyn Lightner, Eric Cohen, Joe Lansing, John Curry, Bonnie Rae Jenson, Julie Mull, Robert Parson, Denis Finnegan, Melody Stowe, Tom Yokum, Jack Jurris, and Kay Bell for providing me with feedback and a sounding board for my ideas.

Thanks to Nora Driscoll for the distraction-free working space at her law office and innumerable hours of listening. After countless weekends in her office, I know nothing about law, but I suspect that Nora knows a great deal about adult education and Web-based training. Bob Geary, my editor, offered solid recommendations, asked good questions, and provided professional advice that shaped the final product.

The University of Massachusetts Boston has been an enthusiastic supporter and a resource during the research and writing of this book. Special thanks to Anthony

v

Martin, John Murphy, and Paul Paquin of the Learning Center for their technical assistance and support.

This book is dedicated to my mother and father, Jane and Nicholas Driscoll, and my academic mentors, Dr. Fredrick Pula and Dr. Marilyn Pula.

Margaret Driscoll
Boston, Massachusetts
January 1998

Introduction

This book will help you plan, develop, and deliver Web-based training programs for adults in the workplace. It provides recommendations, techniques, and models; it does not focus on technical skills, but rather it helps you, as a trainer, to understand your role in the process.

Audience for the Book

Web-Based Training is a step-by-step guide for training managers, instructional designers, course developers, and adult educators who have experience developing conventional classroom and self-paced instructional programs but are developing their first Web-based training. Training managers will find the book helpful for integrating Web-based instruction into a training plan for their organizations. Instructional designers will gain insight into the strategies and techniques unique to Web-based training. Experienced Web-based developers will find ways to improve their existing programs.

It is assumed that the reader is familiar with training concepts and terminology, such as needs assessment, objectives, and audience analysis. There is no review of basic training vocabulary or concepts nor of technical Internet skills, such as using browsers, writing programs, or creating graphic, video, or audio media. Mastery of the latter is not a prerequisite to designing a Web-based training program. Some resources for building technical skills are listed in Appendix D at the end of the book.

What the Book Covers

It is important that workplace training have a firm foundation in *principles of adult education and instructional design*. The primary focus of this book is applying those principles to training programs designed for delivery on the Web. Designing programs requires guidance from an educator to ensure that the learners' needs are addressed.

It is important that the developer know *when to use Web-based training programs and how to develop adult learning experiences*. Such programs differ both from traditional classroom training and from advertising and informational sites. Developing Web-based training requires more than an understanding of hypertext markup language (HTML), common gateway interface (CGI), or graphic user interfaces.

It is important that the developer know *what type of Web-based training to use*. This can make the difference between success and failure.

After reading this book, one should be able to do the following:

- Determine whether or not Web-based training is appropriate for a situation;
- Define the type of Web-based training that most effectively meets training needs;
- Apply principles of adult education to the design and development of the program;
- Manage the expectations of clients, users, and the development team;
- Plan programs that use elements of design and instruction effectively; and
- Know where to find other resources about Web-based training.

Web technology is continually improving and changing; each week new applications are developed and new functionality is added. Educators must focus first on the educational goals and then seek the tools that will help them meet these goals.

Sources for This Book

The suggestions, techniques, and models used in this book have come from instructional designers, course developers, and managers who have created Web-based training for adults in the workplace; from other books and articles; from personal conversations; and from information found on the Web itself. The quotes from anonymous practitioners in the boxes provide scenarios about success and failure gathered from qualitative research. Relevant books and articles are cited at the end of each chapter and in Appendix D.

Many excellent books are devoted to the topics of creating HTML files, writing Java applets, creating CGI scripts, managing Web servers, and other technical themes. Appendix D lists resources for exploring these topics. In addition, the reader is encouraged to search the Internet for the latest product information from vendors and to participate in listservs and news groups that provide practical information on technical problems and solutions.

 This icon indicates an exercise related to the content just covered. They are designed to encourage the creation of programs for adult learners. Do as many as possible.

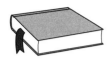

This icon indicates that a bookmark should be created in your browser. Bookmark sites will be referred to later.

This icon indicates a suggestion or idea from an experienced Web-based training developer.

This icon indicates that worksheets or forms follow.

This icon indicates materials included on accompanying CD-ROM.

How To Use the Accompanying CD-ROM

The CD-ROM been designed for use in conjunction with *Web-Based Training.* Following is an explanation of how to use the directories and documents on the CD-ROM.

What Is on the CD-ROM?

The CD-ROM has five folders that contain resources such as templates, sample presentations, job aids, and URLs.

1. **Document templates.** The *Document Directory* contains templates to guide you in the creation of design documents, scripts, and storyboards. These templates can be copied and then customized to meet your needs and used for multiple projects.

2. **Job aids.** The *Jobaids Directory* contains checklists, tables, and guidelines to help manage an initial Web-based training project.

3. **Presentation templates.** The *Present Directory* contains two presentations that can be used to educate the management team about Web-based training and to kick off a project.

4. **Worksheets.** The *Worksht Directory* contains copies of the worksheets that accompany the exercises in the book. Before starting an exercise, make a copy of the worksheet and use it to mark your answers.

5. **WWW Links.** The *WWWlinks Directory* contains complete URLs that provide hot links to professional organizations, e-forums, listservs, and vendors of Web-based training tools.

What Hardware and Software Are Needed?

The files found on the CD-ROM require that you have access to a PC running Microsoft® Word 4.0 and PowerPoint® 6.0 or higher. The following table outlines what you can expect from various versions of software.

Hardware

Minimum hardware configuration for Word® 4.0/PowerPoint® 6.0

Operating Systems	MS-DOS version 3. or later
Microprocessor	386 or higher
Memory	4MB required
Hard disk space	Microsoft® Office Standard 21 MB
Disk Drive	One 3.5 high-density drive, 2X CD-ROM drive or faster
Video adapter	VGA or higher resolution
Pointing device	Microsoft-compatible mouse

Software

Browsers	**Versions**	
Either browser will work	Minimum	Higher
Microsoft	Internet Explorer® 3.0	Yes
Netscape	Navigator® 3.0	Yes

Microsoft Office Applications		
	Minimum	Higher
PowerPoint®	Office 95 version 4.0	Yes
Word®	Office 95 version 6.0	Yes

Where To Obtain Browser Software?

Browser software can be purchased from a computer store or from the Microsoft and Netscape Websites. The terms on which Microsoft and Netscape provide their browser software are subject to change, so it is best to locate their Websites to become familiar with most current terms.

Microsoft Internet Explorer: http://www.microsoft.com

Netscape Communicator: http://www.netscape.com

Chapter 1

Advantages of Instruction on the Web

What You Will Learn in This Chapter

After completing this chapter, you will be able to

- Determine whether or not Web-based training (WBT) is the appropriate method for your program;

- Discuss the advantages and disadvantages of Web-based training;

- List the most common design flaws in Web-based training; and

- Identify the characteristics of well-designed Web-based training.

When To Use WBT

Web-based training is not the solution for every training problem, but it is appropriate for teaching certain skills and imparting particular kinds of knowledge, such as software applications, management skills, or business writing. The medium can also be highly effective to teach learners the skills needed to close a sale, diagnose a problem, or evaluate the merits of competing solutions.

Organizations that are considering Web-based training should have many or all of the indications shown in Figure 1.1.

Figure 1.1. Indications that WBT Is Appropriate

☑ Gap in learners' skills and knowledge.

☑ Need for cognitive skills.

☑ Learners have adequate computer skills.

☑ Organization has capacity to deliver.

Gap in Learners' Skills and Knowledge. Web-based training is a potential solution to a performance problem if the learners lack skills or knowledge. Like any training, it will not work if the performance problem is the result of factors other than lack of skill or knowledge.

Need for Cognitive Skills. Technically and theoretically just about anything can be taught on the Web, but it can be impractical. Consider the following types of skills:

- *Cognitive Skills.* Cognitive skills include solving problems, applying rules, and distinguishing among items. Tasks that require the manipulation of symbols and numbers are well suited to being taught on the Web, such as completing an income tax form. Cognitive skills are traditionally taught using text, graphics, and symbols and such instructional strategies as reading, writing answers, solving computational problems, and completing exercises. All are well suited to Web-based training.

- *Psychomotor Skills.* Psychomotor skills require a complex combination of physical movement and thought, such as operating a crane or driving a golf ball. These skills are difficult to teach in a WBT program, as they require an environment with coaching and detailed feedback. Given adequate funding and time, it is possible to design such a program.

- *Attitudinal Skills.* Teaching learners to change their opinions and, in turn, to change their behavior is challenging in any medium, but it is particularly challenging in Web-based training. For example, if the objective is to teach learners to care about the environment and, therefore, to choose to recycle, there is no opportunity to use reinforcement strategies available in the traditional classroom. The tools that allow trainers to develop simulations, conduct discussions, and facilitate group learning can be expensive and usually require that learners have access to powerful computers.

It is possible to teach psychomotor and attitudinal skills on the Web, but such programs are difficult to design and develop (see Table 1.1 for a summary). Based on the experience and recommendations of trainers, instructional designers, and course developers, psychomotor and attitudinal skill training should generally be avoided on the Web.

Adequate Computer Skills. The learners must have computer, browser, and Internet skills. Even learners with these skills must be carefully assessed, and the program must be matched to their skill level. Learners with novice-level computer skills do best in programs that simply run in the browser. Offer more technically advanced learners complex WBT programs with video and audio that require the downloading and installation of plug-in software.

Organization Has Capacity to Deliver. Organizations must have adequate hardware, software, and staff to support learners. Determine whether your organization has the technical infrastructure to connect to the Internet or the organization's intranet. Be sure that computers have sufficient memory and RAM; provide support staff to assist local and remote offices with network problems, hardware failures, and browser installation.

Table 1.1. Development and Delivery by Type of Skill

	Web-Based Training	
Types of Learning	**Well Suited**	**Not Well Suited**
Cognitive Skills: *Complete a tax form; balance a checkbook*	✔	
Psychomotor Skills: *Hit a golf ball; use a table saw*		✔
Attitudinal Skills: *Value diversity; choose to recycle*		✔

Some Potential Issues

Some problem areas that you should be aware of when planning programs are listed in Figure 1.2 and discussed below.

Inadequate Resources. Avoid Web-based training for psychomotor or attitudinal skills unless you have adequate resources. Designing Web-based training for complex psychomotor skills is expensive. Teaching them requires more than instructing learners to execute steps in a process; it requires opportunities for practice that brings together the mental and physical knowledge and skills required to act. A successful WBT program requires high-quality simulations, two-way video for coaching, and a network that can handle a large volume of traffic. For example, it is technically possible to develop a WBT program to teach newly hired warehouse workers to drive a forklift, but it would require substantial programming, editing, network bandwidth, and computer resources. Before starting a project like this, develop a detailed cost estimate and compare it to alternative training options such as on-the-job training, one-on-one training sessions, or a mentoring program. Even if the program could be delivered on the Web, does it make sense?

Inadequate Materials. Avoid using existing materials for a Web-based training program without redesign. Although existing courses are a good starting point for material, they will require instructional, graphic, and technical redesign to take advantage of the Web. Existing materials such as student guides, computer-based training programs, and videocassette programs were probably created with tools such as Microsoft's Word™ or PowerPoint™ and Macromedia's Director™ or Authorware™. If materials were created with these tools it is relatively easy to convert them to a Web-ready format.

Lack of Variety. Avoid using the same tool for every program. The four kinds of Web-based training methods will be covered in Chapter Five. Suffice it to say for now that it is not advisable to use a single software application or developmental tool to create

---

Figure 1.2 What Will Not Work with WBT

☑ Attempts to teach psychomotor or attitudinal skills without adequate resources.

☑ Using existing materials without redesigning them for the Web.

☑ Using one WBT tool as the solution for all problems.

all of your programs. Distinct software applications and tools are available for creating text-intensive learning, live instructional video, radio-like broadcast programs, and animation. Each of these offers wonderful training possibilities, but no single tool will be equally effective for solving all training problems. Use a combination.

WBT Within an Overall Training Plan

Think of Web-based training as an additional method for delivering instruction, along with videotapes, CD-ROM, and workbooks.

Select the appropriate combination of media, one that is easy for learners to use and that delivers the learning objectives. In some cases it is appropriate to deliver the entire class via the Web. In others, it is more appropriate to use the Web to complement instructor-led classes, for example, as a prerequisite for videoconference training or as advanced training for those who have completed internships or apprenticeships. Learn the unique advantages of this medium, and then use it judiciously. See Chapter Five for more information on this topic.

Moving Training to the Web

There are many advantages and disadvantages to moving training to the Web. The business and educational advantages and the disadvantages are explored on the following pages.

The role of Web-based training varies dramatically, depending on the needs of an organization. Below are strategies used by two different training departments.

Traditional instructor-led training does more than train people, it plays an important role in passing along the corporate culture and making people feel like part of the company. We didn't want to replace this with Web-based training. Instead, we use Web-based training as a way to provide continuous learning after a class and to keep the employees connected and talking.

In information systems there is so much training to be delivered that you can never get enough to stay current. We encourage people to sign up for courses on the Internet at Microsoft On-Line Institute™ (MOLI) or other places. These outside sources of Web-based training are a great supplement to our own Web-based training, classroom training, and professional seminars.

Advantages

As we face the challenges of living in the Information Age, with new knowledge generated at an ever-increasing rate and with the increasing demands of a global work force, we must adapt how we teach new skills, impart knowledge, and affect attitudes.

Information and job skills are changing so quickly that it is not practical to ask employees, business partners, and customers to attend traditional instructor-led classes. The advent of a global economy has led to employees scattered around the globe in satellite facilities. These realities point to the business and educational benefits of Web-based training, which are summarized in Table 1.2.

First, training at the desktop reduces travel and the lost productivity that occurs while a learner is in class. Educators can provide training when and how it is needed, when the skills are needed, not when the class is offered.

Second, Web-based training eliminates the need to install special computers or develop multiple versions of the training software for different platforms. Learners take training on a familiar computer system, and training programs are available to all users simultaneously.

Third, Web-based training eliminates the costs of duplicating, packaging, and mailing materials. Learners worldwide have access to information at the same time as learners at corporate headquarters.

Fourth, updating courses and making revisions from a central point ensures that changes are uniform and that learners have access to the most current training materials.

Table 1.2. Advantages of Web-Based Training

Business	Educational
Reduced travel expenses	Easy access
Use existing hardware	Use own computers
Reduced cost for print materials and CD-ROMs	Quick access
Control of revisions/updates information	Quick access to revisions and up-to-date
Utilize existing resources	Schematic drawings, reference manuals, databases, and technical experts on-line

Fifth, subject-matter experts, databases, engineering documents, videotapes, and diagrams can be reused for training purposes and selected to enhance the learning experience.

 A training manager working for a financial services organization initiated a Web-based training program to reduce expenses for new employee training and to make face-to-face training more meaningful.
We have had a flat budget in training for the last two years, so we have been searching for ways to deliver more training for less money. We used to conduct a two-week new-hire training program. This was a big percentage of our budget. We would fly new hires in, put them up, and entertain them for two weeks.

Using Web-based training we now deliver a week of new-hire training via the Web and a week of live face-to-face training. This reduces the cost of training and makes the face-to-face time more effective. The Web replaces things like lectures that can be read and offers self-paced exercises that can be studied without the new hires being part of a group or having a teacher there.

Disadvantages

The business and economic reasons for adopting Web-based training are easy to understand. It is also important to understand the disadvantages, as these may not be as obvious. See Table 1.3.

Substantial Technical Infrastructure. A clear disadvantage of Web-based training is the substantial technical infrastructure required to run programs. In addition to developing educationally effective training programs, designers must contend with computer system requirements, network capacity, and network access.

Table 1.3. Disadvantages of Web-Based Training
✔ Requires a substantial technical infrastructure
✔ Requires learners to adapt to new methods
✔ Requires team to design, develop, and deploy
✔ Requires management of resources beyond the training organization

Generally, Web-based training programs are able to be used from a variety of platforms such as UNIX™ work stations, IBM personal computers and clones, and Macintosh™ computers. Of course, this may not be true if developers use highly complex tools. Even ubiquitous Web browsers such as Netscape Navigator® and Microsoft's Internet Explorer® present subtle differences in how they display a page of text or a graphic.

Other technical infrastructure issues are network capacity and access. Training programs compete with other applications such as e-mail. Unlike workbooks that stand on their own, Web-based programs require access to the organization's network.

Yet another issue is network access. Learners must be able to log-in to an intranet or the Internet. Programs are limited by the kind of dial-in connections available. If learners are using a 28.8 modem, they may not have the capacity to download large files quickly. If learners are accessing the Internet from a corporate network, they may encounter security problems that prevent them from running Java code or downloading plug-ins.

New Learning Methods. Workbooks, videocassette programs, and job aids are familiar tools, but Web-based training is new for many learners. It requires learners to master using a browser, navigating nonlinear programs, and interacting with classmates using unfamiliar tools such as chat rooms or threaded discussions.

Required Range of Skills. Web-based training is labor intensive, requiring broad-range skills. Because resources are frequently in short supply, trainers have become adept at playing multiple roles, but Web-based training should not be designed, developed, and delivered by a single person. The design team should include graphic designers, network managers, server installers, end-user support personnel, and programmers. Managing a cross-functional team requires the coordination of schedules to accomplish project milestones in parallel. As the training group writes the program, the customer-support group may be talking with potential learners to determine if they have sufficient RAM and a current version of the browser software.

Management of External Resources. Another disadvantage of Web-based training is that it relies on external resources such as other organizations' websites, adequate hardware, and reliable access to the network. One is at the mercy of others. An external Website can be eliminated, leaving a hole in the program. Or a department may have no other use for a sound card, and so not have them installed. The trainer is also dependent on the information systems (IS) group to support end users and to keep the network running nights and weekends.

Well-Designed Web-Based Training

Web-based training is not simply a new format for instructor-led or self-paced training. Merely changing the format creates passive programs called "electronic page turners" that frustrate learners. These programs resemble books, presenting information in a linear format one page at a time.

Well-designed Web-based training takes new or existing content and uses the power of the Web to increase employee productivity. They are learner centered—designed to engage the learners, draw on their experiences, and meet their needs. Figure 1.3 is a comparison of the characteristics of well-designed and poorly designed Web-based training.

To assess the design of Web-based training, ask users how they feel about it. Must they search through nested menus? Are they distracted by busy screens with needless animation, flashing text, and graphics that do not contribute anything? Is the structure of the lessons clear? Can learners easily proceed through the lessons? Can they tell what to do first? Is it easy to find help or additional resources? Is the training effective?

Figure 1.3. Characteristics of Well-Designed and Poorly Designed WBT	
Good Design	**Poor Design**
Interactive	Passive
Nonlinear	Linear
Easy-to-use graphic user interface	Confusing graphic user interface
Structured lessons	Lack of structure
Effective use of multimedia	Dense text
Attention to educational details	Lack of attention to educational details
Attention to technical details	Lack of attention to technical details
Learner control	System control

Plan programs that involve the learners and allow them to interact with the system, other learners, and the instructor. Provide an opportunity for nonlinear learning, but take responsibility to guide the learner through the experience. Test the graphic user interface; examine the navigation, menus, and icons to be sure that they are clear and easy to follow. Provide structure so that learners know how to proceed. Use media judiciously to enhance the learning. Pay attention to both the technical details (free of "bugs") and educational details (clear objectives, opportunities to practice, and meaningful feedback) that are the hallmarks of a well-constructed program.

The first thing that you, the instructional designer, course developer, or manager, must do is determine whether or not Web-based training is appropriate for your purposes. Next, step back and think about how Web-based training fits into your overall training plan. If it appears to be an appropriate method, consider the advantages and disadvantages above.

Learning the characteristics of a well-designed Web-based training program is a great way to begin thinking about design issues. Complete the exercise at the end of this chapter and then proceed to Chapter Two for more guidelines.

PURPOSE: *This exercise will help you experience Web-based training as a learner.*

Set aside about an hour to explore training sites on the Web. Make a list of what appeals to you and what you do not like. Consider the types of learning activities, organization of content, structure of lessons, and use of resources and multimedia.

Suggested Readings

Barron, A., & Tompkins, B. (1996, May 12–13). *On-demand instruction with the World Wide Web*. Paper presented at Interactive 96, Atlanta, GA.

Driscoll, M. (1996). The good and the bad of Web-based training. *Multimedia Training, 3*(9) 6–7.

Filipczak, B. (1996). Training on internets: The hope and the hype. *Training, 33*(7), 24–32.

Lipp, K.A. (1996). Web-based training. *Service News, http://www.servicenews.com.*

Motter-Hodgeson, M. (1996). Bulla Gymnasia. In T. Dewar (Ed.), *Learning styles on-line* (Vol. 1). Calgary, Alberta: CyberCorp.

Polyson, S., Saltzberg, S., & Godwin-Jones, R. (1996). A practical guide to teaching with the World Wide Web. *Syllabus, 10*(2), 12–16.

Shotsberger, P. G. (1996). Instructional uses of the World Wide Web: Exemplars and precautions. *Educational Technology, 36*(2), 47–50.

Chapter 2

Principles of Adult Education

What You Will Learn in This Chapter

After completing this chapter, you will be able to

- Identify what is unique about adult learners;
- List the skills required to facilitate adult learning; and
- Integrate the principles of adult education into a Web-based training program.

Designing effective Web-based training (WBT) requires knowledge of the unique characteristics of adult learners and an understanding of the facilitator's role. It is easy to lose sight of the importance of the principles of adult education when caught up in the necessary tools and technology inherent in WBT approaches.

Adult Learners Are Unique

Adult learners are unique in that they have more life and work experiences on which to draw. They are motivated to learn as a response to problems and changes. The special characteristics of adult learners have been described by authors such as Knowles (1998), Brookfield (1990), Kidd (1973), Freire (1970), and Merriam and Caffarella (1991). Keep in mind the traits listed in Figure 2.1.

Figure 2.1. Characteristics of Adult Learners

☑ Have real-life experience.

☑ Prefer problem-centered learning.

☑ Are continuous learners.

☑ Have varied learning styles.

☑ Have responsibilities beyond the training situation.

☑ Expect learning to be meaningful.

☑ Prefer to manage their own learning.

Real-Life Experience. Adults bring a wealth of real-life experience to training that can be a resource for learning. Create interactions in which learners share their experiences with others.

Problem-Centered Learning. Adults are motivated to learn as a response to problems in their lives, so organize the content of training programs by problem area, rather than by broad subject. For example, offer a class in writing business letters rather than a course in business writing and grammar. Plan programs based on new skills to overcome difficulties that learners have experienced. For example, offer a course on tracking and managing budgets rather than one to learn spreadsheet applications. Use menus, exercises, and examples to highlight ways learners can use new skills and knowledge to solve real-life problems.

Continuous Learners. Adults are continuously learning to solve problems and negotiate changes in their lives. Daily challenges such as learning a new software application, completing a purchase order form, or planning a sales call are examples of learning opportunities. Web-based training is an excellent way to provide training at the time it is needed. Build on the learners' motivations to master new skills and knowledge as needed.

Varied Learning Styles. Adults prefer to learn in a variety of ways, and there is no one "correct" method of learning. Some prefer to read, some enjoy animation, and others appreciate the opportunity to participate in online discussions. Use the various tools and multimedia options available in a WBT environment to accommodate these learning styles.

Responsibilities Beyond the Training Situation. Adults have responsibilities and concerns beyond the confines of the WBT program that may affect their learning. Obstacles to learning such as family commitments, community responsibilities, and changes in the office environment may exist. Be aware of the personal and professional context in which training will be delivered. For example, learners in an office that is about to be downsized may not be interested in learning about the company's new database for tracking orders. Learners being asked to log in at home in the evening may not be able to give a program their full attention.

Meaningful Learning. Adults expect exercises and examples based on real-life problems, actual situations, and applications to which they can relate. Create interactions that are meaningful, and supplement the program with multimedia segments that add new perspectives. Web-based training programs can incorporate links to external experts, real databases, and live applications that make learning meaningful and relevant.

A company that publishes Web-based training programs for sale on the Internet talks about its philosophy for designing programs for adults.

Not all learners learn the same way. We create our Web-based training programs to appeal to three kinds of learners. If you like learning by example, we show you how to use the software by showing you an example. If you'd rather learn by following step-by-step examples, we have detailed steps; and if you prefer to learn by doing, we provide you the opportunity to learn by trial and error with feedback.

PURPOSE: *This exercise will help you apply principles of adult education in your WBT design work.*

Think about a training program that you have developed. Make a list of the design decisions that were influenced by adult learning characteristics. How did you address the variety of learning styles of your audience? What were the challenges of making the training "problem centered"? Did you allow the learners some degree of self-direction?

Self-Directed Learning. Adults prefer to plan their own educational objectives, determine the learning activities, and develop the evaluation criteria. Develop WBT programs that allow learners to sequence the content, select the mode of instruction, and assess their own progress.

Facilitating Programs for Adults

As you design WBT programs, think about how best to facilitate adult learning by using principles advocated by such authors as Knowles (1998), Brookfield (1986), Kidd (1973), and Cross (1981). The recommendations in Figure 2.2 are based on their principles.

Use Learners' Experiences. Use learners' experiences dealing with customers, supporting earlier versions of software, and identifying sales leads as foundations on which to build new knowledge. Integrate these experiences into your programs.

Develop Problem-Centered Programs. Create training programs that clearly relate new skills and knowledge to learners' needs. Programs that help learners solve problems are motivational. Use programs that feature menus organized by task and design exercises that feature transferable skills.

Involve Learners in Planning and Evaluating. Empower students to become self-directed learners. Ask them to help to define program goals, create exercises, and evaluate their own progress. Web-based training is well suited for collaboration be-

---

Figure 2.2. Principles for Effective Facilitation

☑ Use learners' experiences.

☑ Develop problem-centered programs.

☑ Involve learners in planning and evaluating.

☑ Develop interactive programs.

☑ Use multimedia elements in meaningful ways.

☑ Create a safe and respectful environment.

☑ Encourage exploration, action, and reflection.

☑ Nurture self-directed learning.

tween learners and the instructor because there is ample opportunity to communicate. Students can tell the instructor what they want to learn and what kind of resources they need. E-mail, listservs, and online bulletin boards facilitate two-way communication.

Develop Interactive Programs. Design learning experiences that require learners to become actively involved. Interactions can take the form of activities in which learners make menu choices, enter responses, or select modes of instruction. Sometimes the interaction will not require the learner to do anything observable, but just to think, perhaps about a new way to treat customers or an alternative way to troubleshoot software problems.

Use Multimedia Elements in Meaningful Ways. Graphics, videos, images, hypertext, and audio help learners understand concepts more easily. Multimedia provides learners with alternative ways to examine problems and learn new skills. Use multimedia elements to show things that cannot be adequately explained with a single media. For example, Pacific Bell provides a Web-based training program to teach customers about bandwidth and differences among various connections such as ISDN, T1, and 14.4 modem. Learners use an interactive animation sequence to understand the abstract concept of bandwidth. Avoid gratuitous multimedia such as sounds of cheering crowds for correct answers or animation sequences with a flashing "X" and thumbs-down symbol.

Create a Safe and Respectful Environment. Create an environment in which learners are valued as individuals and feel comfortable participating. Keep this principle in mind as you develop online forums, exercises, and feedback loops.

Encourage Exploration, Action, and Reflection. Encourage learners to explore new ideas and alternative ways of solving problems. Invite them to reflect on what they have learned by applying these ideas. Experiment with exercises that promote critical reflection. Design some individual and some group exercises.

Nurture Self-Directed Learning. Encourage learners to assume responsibility for continuing their education. Help them develop and apply skills for managing and assessing their own learning. Nurture the abilities and attitudes learners need to question their assumptions and to explore alternative ways of thinking.

The role of the facilitator varies depending on the goals of the program and the instructional strategies employed. A facilitator piloting a Web-based training program to teach consulting skills comments on the importance of involving learners and how his role varied.

The best part of the lesson for me was when the students were engaged. I know the things that I need to include more of next time: open-ended questions, short-answer responses, and to have students provide examples from their experience to summarize points.

PURPOSE: *Reflect on the overlap between the characteristics of good Web-based training design and the principles of adult education.*
Think about the characteristics of Web-based training described in Chapter One. What do these characteristics have in common with the principles of adult education presented in this chapter?

Use the following worksheet to reflect on the application of the principles of adult education in Web-based training.

Adult Learning Worksheet

Directions: Review the lists that follow and answer the questions at the end of the worksheet.

Principles of Effective Adult Education Facilitation	Principles of Effective Web-Based Training
Use the experiences of learners.	Interactive *(learners choose sequence, respond to quizzes, participate in online conferences)*.
Develop problem-centered programs.	Nonlinear *(learners select and sequence their lessons and access resources on the Web)*
Involve learners in planning and evaluating.	Easy-to-use graphic user interface *(intuitive menus, easy-to-understand icons, background colors and text provide clues)*
Develop interactive programs.	Structured lessons *(clear guidance and directions for each lesson)*
Use multimedia elements in meaningful ways.	Effective use of multimedia *(text, graphics, video, sound, and animation convey content)*
Create a safe and respectful environment.	Attention to educational details *(clear objectives, adequate practice, and meaningful feedback)*
Encourage exploration, action, and reflection.	Attention to technical details *(free of "bugs" and the links to other web sites work)*
Nurture self-directed learning.	Learner control *(to select navigational paths, sequence content, determine level of detail, and select presentation mode)*

1. What are the similarities between the lists?

2. What are the differences?

3. What challenges exist to developing Web-based training programs for adults? Are there conflicting principles? If so, what are they?

Suggested Readings

Brookfield, S. D. (1986). *Understanding and facilitating adult learning.* San Francisco: Jossey-Bass.

Brookfield, S. D. (1990). *The skillful teacher.* San Francisco: Jossey-Bass.

Cross, K. P. (1981). *Adults as learners.* San Francisco: Jossey-Bass.

Freire, P. (1970). *A cultural action for freedom.* Cambridge, MA: Harvard Educational Review and Center for the Study of Development and Social Change.

Kidd, J. R. (1973). *How adults learn.* New York: Association Press.

Knowles, M. S. (1998). *The modern practice of adult education: From pedagogy to andragogy.* Englewood Cliffs, NJ: Prentice Hall.

Merriam, S. B., & Caffarella, R. S. (1991). *Learning in adulthood.* San Francisco: Jossey-Bass.

Moore, M. G., & Kearsley, G. (1996). *Distance education: A systems view.* Belmont, CA: Wadsworth.

Chapter 3

The Web-Based Training Process

What You Will Learn in This Chapter

After completing this chapter, you will be able to

- Diagram the Web-based training (WBT) process;
- Describe a systemic model for design of instruction; and
- Define four types of Web-based training.

A complete Web-based training project has three phases: *design, development,* and *delivery.* This book deals primarily with the design phase, but touches on the development and delivery phases as they relate to design. Figure 3.1 lists the elements of each phase.

An Instructional Systems Design

Instructional systems design (ISD) is a process for developing instruction. Many models exist, ranging from simple to complex. All provide step-by-step guidance for developing training. The ISD approach acknowledges a relationship among *learners, instructors,* and *materials.* Instructional designers develop materials using an iterative process to relate the three components optimally. Figure 3.2 provides an overview of the steps in the ISD model as modified for developing Web-based training programs.

Figure 3.1. The Complete WBT Process

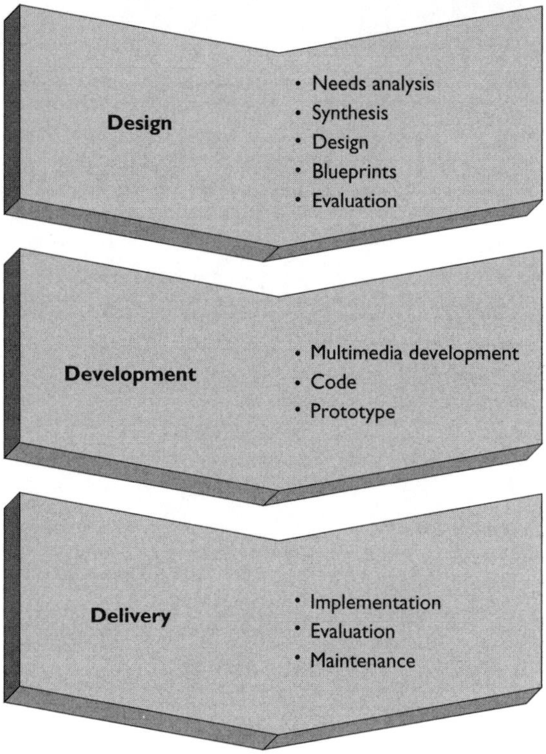

Design
- Needs analysis
- Synthesis
- Design
- Blueprints
- Evaluation

Development
- Multimedia development
- Code
- Prototype

Delivery
- Implementation
- Evaluation
- Maintenance

Figure 3.2. Systemic Model for Design of WBT

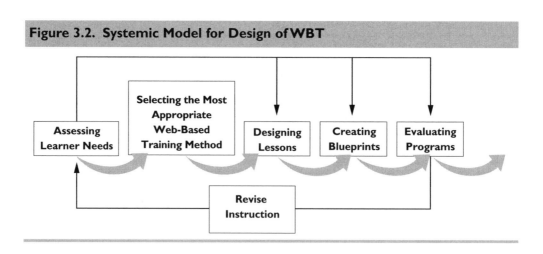

Developers who use the instructional systems design (ISD) model understand how learners, instructors, and materials are related and that they are dependent on one another. Changes to any one of these components affect the entire system and the outcome of training.

Systemic Design

Web-based training requires that developers take a systemic as well as a systematic view. They must understand how WBT impacts the entire organization. Successful WBT programs require all parts of an organization to work together to develop, deliver, and maintain them.

A systemic view includes an understanding of the technical infrastructure issues, such as network capabilities at remote locations, department-level plans to purchase computers, and corporate decisions to standardize browser software. The organizational impact of WBT can be seen when it is broadly distributed. For example, it may be integrated into customer support through online tutorials and promoted in the marketing department as a tool for differentiating the company.

Figure 3.2 depicts Web-based training design as a looping process. It requires the designer to revisit each step whenever there are changes to the audience, purpose, environment, or other parameters of the project. Figure 3.3 further illustrates what takes place at each step and the iterative nature of the SDI model.

The stages of the ISD model are discussed below. Each is also described in greater detail in succeeding chapters.

Assessing Learner Needs

During this stage, the scope of the project, the educational goal, the intended audience, and the delivery environment are defined. Designers determine whether Web-based training is appropriate for their needs.

Selecting the Most Appropriate Method

Based on the results of the needs analysis, the designer selects one or more of the four kinds of Web-based training shown in Table 3.1. These types are discussed in more detail in Chapter Five and outlined in Appendix E.

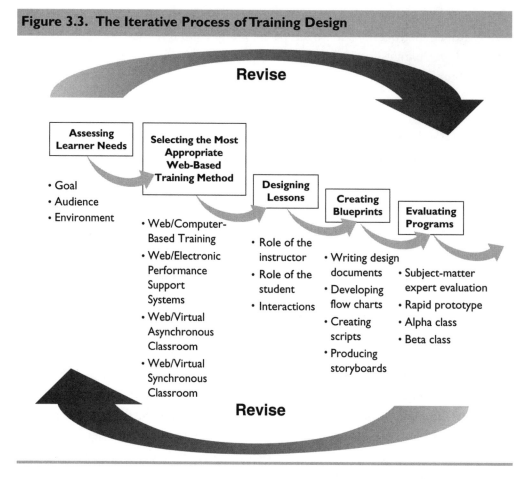

Figure 3.3. The Iterative Process of Training Design

Revise

Assessing Learner Needs

- Goal
- Audience
- Environment

Selecting the Most Appropriate Web-Based Training Method

- Web/Computer-Based Training
- Web/Electronic Performance Support Systems
- Web/Virtual Asynchronous Classroom
- Web/Virtual Synchronous Classroom

Designing Lessons

- Role of the instructor
- Role of the student
- Interactions

Creating Blueprints

- Writing design documents
- Developing flow charts
- Creating scripts
- Producing storyboards

Evaluating Programs

- Subject-matter expert evaluation
- Rapid prototype
- Alpha class
- Beta class

Revise

Table 3.1. Types of Web-Based Training

Type	Description
Web/Computer-Based Training (W/CBT)	Individual learning that features drill and practice, simulations, reading, questioning, and answering
Web/Electronic Performance Support Systems (W/EPSS)	Just-in-time training focused on problem-solving, scientific method, experiential method, project method
Web/Virtual Asynchronous Classroom (W/VAC)	Non-real-time group learning that employs experiential tasks, discussions, and team projects
Web/Virtual Synchronous Classroom (W/VSC)	Real-time collaborative group learning that uses discussions, problem solving, and reflection

Designing Lessons

At the design stage, a general plan is created that will guide the development of a detailed plan at the blueprint stage. During the design stage, the following steps are necessary:

- Define interactions that assist in the transfer of skills and knowledge;
- Plan feedback loops that correct, direct, and affirm; and
- Structure and sequence resources.

Creating Blueprints

Based on the lesson design, detailed blueprints are created to document interactions, feedback loops, and information structures. In addition, the blueprints contain detailed administrative tracking requirements and complete audio and video scripting.

Evaluating Programs

After the design is complete, a series of evaluations is conducted to test the WBT materials for accuracy, effectiveness, and clarity. Web-based training programs that require an instructor are reviewed to identify possible enhancements to his or her role and group interactions.

Traditional Classroom versus Web-Based Training

The steps used to develop a Web-based training program are very similar to those used to developing traditional classroom programs. Table 3.2 provides a comparison of the steps.

Think about an instructor-led training program you have designed. How were the steps for developing that program similar to the steps required for developing a Web-based training program? Use this personal analysis to focus on the steps that you need to reinforce during your next design.

Table 3.2. Comparing Traditional Classroom and WBT Programs

Traditional Classroom Training	Web-Based Training
Assess learner needs: Define goals, objectives, audience, and environment in which training will take place.	*Assess learner needs*: Define goals, objectives audience, and environment in which training will take place.
Select traditional classroom training as most appropriate method.	Select WBT as most appropriate method of instruction.
Determine how to present instruction: Choose instructional strategies.	*Select appropriate WBT methods*: Choose type(s) of training that will meet learners' needs.
Create course outline: Define instructional strategies (case studies, simulations, lectures, and discussions) to meet learners' needs.	*Design lessons*: Define interactions and instructional strategies (Internet relay chat or participation in a listserv) that assist in the transfer of skills and knowledge.
Create design document: Write a document that defines how information will be presented, what role the learners and instructor will play, and how the program will be evaluated.	*Create blueprints*: Document interactions, feedback loops, and information structures.
Develop and select training materials: Create overhead transparencies, student workbooks, and directions for activities and select videos.	*Develop Website*: Create Web-based training materials as a team (see Chapter Four).
Evaluate program: Review materials and course at each step as they evolve from draft stage to pilot stage.	*Evaluate program*: Conduct a series of reviews to test the materials for accuracy, effectiveness, and clarity and recommend improvements.

Suggested Readings

Dick, W., & Carey, L. (1996). *The systematic design of instruction.* New York: HarperCollins.

Romiszowski, A. J. (1988). *The selection and use of instructional media.* New York: Kogan Page.

Rossett, A. (1987). *Training needs assessment.* Englewood Cliffs, NJ: Educational Technology Publications.

Rothwell, W. J., & Kazanas, H. C. (1992). *Mastering the instructional design process: A systematic approach.* San Francisco: Jossey-Bass.

Chapter 4

Assessing Learner Needs

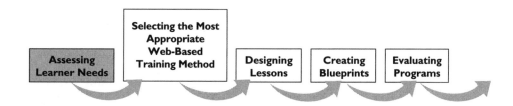

What You Will Learn in This Chapter

After completing this chapter, you will be able to

- Determine whether training is needed;
- Define the program goals, audience, and environment; and
- Determine who should be on the WBT team

Conducting a Needs Assessment

A needs assessment is a process whereby data is gathered to establish whether training is required and what type. The goals of a needs assessment are as follows:

- Determine whether training is needed;
- Define the goals of training;

- Define the audience;
- Define the environment;
- Select the training method or methods; and
- Establish a team.

Determine Whether Training Is Needed

To determine whether or not training is necessary, ask questions to discover if poor employee performance is caused by a gap in skills or knowledge. Consider factors such as a poor work environment, a lack of employee motivation, or the absence of incentives.

- *Environment.* Do employees have the equipment they need and is it reasonable to perform the required tasks with the given staffing levels?

- *Motivation.* Are there extrinsic rewards such as bonuses or recognition programs and are workers intrinsically motivated by the work itself or by contact with customers?

- *Incentives/Compensation.* Is the compensation equitable when compared to that of employees in other divisions? When compared to people doing the same job at other companies? Are sales quotas and margins adequate to promote the desired outcome?

Problems of performance that are related to poor work environments, lack of motivation, or the absence of incentives will not be resolved by training. Conducting training programs rather than correcting environmental issues, improving motivation, and providing adequate compensation can result in greater worker dissatisfaction by inferring that the problems are related to a lack of skill and knowledge.

Figure 4.1 relates an example of a performance problem based on factors other than lack of skill or knowledge.

There are several ways to collect data for analysis of training needs. Table 4.1 shows three methods and gives the advantages and disadvantages of each. These methods can be used alone or in combination. How they are used depends on the needs, the budget, and the organization.

Interviews. Interviews involve talking to people about their jobs. Interviews can take many forms. One of the most common is simply meeting with the employee. Interviews can also be conducted over the telephone, online, or in focus groups.

Figure 4.1. Performance Problem Unrelated to Lack of Skill or Knowledge

Last year, a manufacturing firm noticed a large number of data-entry errors in the order-processing department. Management's first inclination was to assume it was a training problem, but when the instructional designer researched the situation, she noticed that the orders received via facsimile were often illegible and that there was no process for clerks to use if they couldn't read them. Consequently, clerks would enter what they "guessed" the order said. Training would do little to reduce errors in this situation. A better solution was for management to install quality facsimile equipment and to design a process for clerks to verify illegible orders.

Table 4.1. Data-Collection Methods for Needs Assessment

Method	Variations	Advantages	Disadvantages
Interview	• Face-to-face • Telephone • Small group	• Provides rich data • Allows non-observable parts of a job to be understood • Enables questions to be adapted as needed	• Requires substantial resources to conduct • Possibility of lack of candor • Requires strong interview skills
Questionnaire/ Survey	• Paper-based • Online	• Easy and cost effective • Familiar data-gathering tool • Survey large numbers	• Requires skill to develop • Risk of low response rate
Observation	• Task analysis • Site visits • View videotapes • Mystery shop	• Detailed data on rule-oriented and sequential processes • Captures real steps of the process	• Does not capture thinking tasks • Requires that tasks have discrete beginning and end

Interviews have some clear advantages. One is the richness of data, the detailed information about a job. Because the information is so detailed, the interviewer can gain insights into people's attitudes and opinions as well as learn about procedures. An interviewer can ask questions about parts of a job that cannot be observed by asking something like "What are the characteristics of a good sales representative?" or "What frustrations do you experience dealing with difficult customers?" Interviews are flexible and adaptable. The questions or the approach can be adjusted quickly to engage in further exploration of an issue that comes up.

Interviews also have built-in disadvantages. One is that they require skill to develop guidelines, conduct the interviews, and analyze the data. A second disadvantage is that interviewees may not be entirely forthcoming about problems they experience. Even with assurances of confidentiality, some may be reluctant to discuss their jobs and gaps in their skills and knowledge. Conducting good interviews also requires an interviewer with the ability to make interviewees feel comfortable, to ask open-ended questions, and to analyze the data. For more information on conducting interviews, see the list of resources at the end of this chapter.

Questionnaire/Survey. Questionnaire and survey are often used interchangeably to describe a data-collection method that asks respondents to complete some kind of form, whether on paper or via a computer, or filled in by an interviewer.

Surveys are cost-effective and easy to administer. Compared with interviews, surveys are less labor-intensive and do not require skilled data gatherers. It is easy to distribute paper-based or online forms to large numbers of employees. Because employees are familiar with survey forms and know how to complete them, they require little assistance.

A disadvantage is that questionnaires and surveys can be a challenge to develop. Questions must be clear and written in a way that will provide answers to what is really being asked. Employees must respond in large enough numbers to gain a representative sample of the group. Zemke and Kramlinger (1992) and Rossett (1987) provide detailed guidance about developing questionnaires and surveys.

Observation. Data can also be gathered simply by watching employees perform the task. This is a simple way to document the steps in a process or the rules for making decisions. Other kinds of observation include conducting task analysis, leading a detailed time-motion study, and reviewing videotapes of employee performance. Yet another variation is mystery shopping, that is, acting as a customer to observe employees' performance.

The main advantage of observation is that it accurately captures the rules and the sequence of steps for any task. Because the observation takes place in the actual work environment, it reflects how the job is being performed and not the ideal performance described in a manual.

Observation can be time-consuming and disruptive to those working. Also, the process is limited to documenting jobs that are observable and those with clear beginning and end points. Observation may require that an interview or a survey also be conducted to identify aspects of the job that are not observable.

One or more of these techniques should be used to determine whether a performance problem can be solved by training or whether it is caused by other factors. When performance problems are the result of a gap in skills or knowledge, training is a good solution. The next step in this case is to define the goals of the training to fill the gap.

Define the Goals

To define the goals of a training program, first write a brief statement that describes what learners will be able to do after their instruction. The goal statement should describe how the gap in skill and knowledge identified earlier will be remedied.

Be clear about what learners will be able to *do.* You will use the goal statement later during the evaluation stage to measure the success of the program. If the training has been successful, learners will be able to do what the goal statement says.

Use the following questions to help define the goal:

- Why is training being offered?
- What should learners be able to do after attending training?
- Under what conditions will learners be expected to demonstrate their new skills?

The sample goal statements in Figure 4.2 give specific goals that should result from the training. Notice that all of the statements relate to the Series 5000 Laser Printer, but *what* the learner will be able to do is different in each goal statement.

Define the Audience

Gather information regarding how much learners already know about the topic being presented. Be careful not to train people to do things they already know how to do. On the other hand, do not assume they know the basics. Material that is too basic will bore learners; material that is too advanced will discourage them.

Figure 4.2. Sample Goal Statements

- Field Service Engineers will be able to **repair** the Series 5000 Laser Printer in the customer's office.

- Field Service Engineers will be able to **evaluate** the condition of Series 5000 Laser Printers and recommend either a replacement or a repair option.

- Field Service Engineers will be able to **diagnose** the reasons for poor quality output from the Series 5000 Laser Printer.

A consultant talks about the importance of focusing on educational goals. *I was so frustrated working with these clients. They had a bunch of HTML pages, an animated GIF from their Website and leftover images from a multimedia CD-ROM project. They were bound and determined to use this stuff, even though it had nothing to do with the new program. When we identified the educational goal, things became easier to sort out. It was clear that a lot of the material from past projects was not relevant to this project.*

As soon as word is out that you are working on a Web-based training program, everyone is going to want to know what you are doing. Prepare a short goal statement that clearly describes what learners will be able to do. Test the clarity of your goal statement by reading it to a peer, a manager, and a member of the intended learner population. Do they understand the goal of training? Do they understand what learners will be able to do after participating in training? What questions were raised? Improve your goal statement, if necessary.

Gather information on learners' existing knowledge by interviewing a representative sample of learners, interviewing the learners' manager, or conducting focus groups. Do your homework. Prepare questions that will help you probe for a detailed description of the learners' proficiency level. For example, to determine how computer literate learners are, ask questions such as:

Figure 4.3. What Learners Already Know

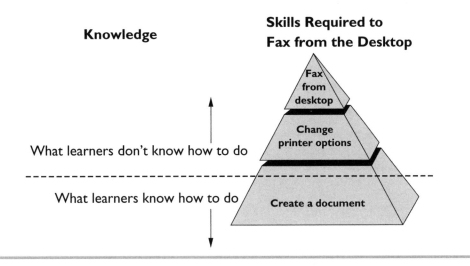

- Have you ever installed software on your computer? If yes, tell me about any challenges you faced during the installation and how you dealt with them.
- Which of the settings in the Microsoft Windows® control panel do you feel confident in your ability to adjust or change?
- Complete the following sentence: "When I have to use online help to solve a problem I. . . ."
- Have you ever changed the default printer you use?
- Have you ever sent a fax from your desktop?

Figure 4.3 illustrates the hierarchy of skills and prior knowledge needed to send a fax from the desktop. The dotted line shows where instruction should begin to avoid boring learners.

Determine how much knowledge learners have about computers. Do not make assumptions about their skill levels. Learners can have Internet and browser experience and still require help using certain functions. If assessing the skills of learners from a distance, use a survey or conduct a telephone interview. Be sure to make learners feel comfortable so that you obtain accurate information.

Use the following questions to help assess computer knowledge:

- Can you log-on to the system, to the service provider, to the Internet, and to the Web-based training site?
- Do you feel comfortable using the computer keyboard?
- Have you used a Web browser?
- Which of the following browsers have you used: Netscape Navigator®, Microsoft Internet Explorer®, America Online®?

Learners are sometimes unaware of what they do not know. If possible, create a simple checklist and ask a representative sample to complete the checklist over the phone. The checklist below is a sample of items to test computer skills through a hands-on exercise. Call a representative sample of learners and ask them to do the following things while they are on the phone with you:

1. Surf to a Website and describe what you see.
2. Create a bookmark or favorite place for a given uniform resource locator (URL).
3. Download the plug-in for RealAudio® and install it.
4. Use the bookmark or favorite place mark to return to the URL you saved earlier.
5. Follow a series of hypertext links and then use the tool bar or mouse to return to the initial page.
6. Send an e-mail.

Either ask questions or conduct a hands-on assessment to document the skill level of learners. The basic questions are essential. In some cases you must teach computer skills before beginning your Web-based training program.

Another consideration is learner preferences and attitudes toward Web-based training. If learners are veterans of old computer-based training programs that were text intensive, they may not be very enthusiastic. In the past, programs were boring "page turners" that were difficult to navigate. Some learners do not like using self-paced programs. They may prefer the interaction and social aspects of classroom training. Learning about learners' attitudes and preferences will help you plan an effective program.

> **An instructor talks about the importance of understanding learners' level of expertise with computers and the Web.**
>
> *I got this angry message about the poor design of my course. One of the students clicked on a link that took him from the Web-based course to a related document. The student continued to follow links for about an hour. His frustration grew as he hit endless cul-de-sacs and could not get back to the lesson. It never dawned on me that students wouldn't know when to quit linking and know how to get back to the course. Now I spend some time at the beginning of a course explaining how to use links and how to get back.*

Use the following questions to help assess learners' attitudes toward Web-based training:

1. Have you ever used a computer-based training program (CD-ROM, multi-media, or videodisk)? If yes, what did you like or dislike about it? What made the program enjoyable? What made the program effective?

2. When learning new skills, do you prefer to learn by yourself or do you like to be part of a group? Describe the best experience you have had learning new skills.

3. Have you ever taken a Web-based training course? Was the experience good or bad? In what way?

4. Would you like to participate in a Web-based training course? Why or why not?

Define the Environment

The most attractive feature of Web-based training is that it is delivered at the learner's desk. This feature is also one of the biggest challenges to designing training. Ask about the delivery environment before designing Web-based training. Answer the questions in Figure 4.4 when considering the environment for Web-based training.

Technical Capacity of the Network. Assess the general technical capabilities of the organization's network by meeting with the Information Systems (IS) group that supports your learners. Understanding the network and computer system will help

---

Figure 4.4. Environmental Conditions

☑ What is the technical capacity of the network?

☑ What role does the telephone play in the organization?

☑ What are the acoustics in the office?

☑ What kinds of social interactions take place?

☑ Does management support Web-based training?

☑ Are there peaks and valleys in the pace of work?

---

you understand the demands a Web-based training program can put on the network. Training programs can slow networks to a crawl because of large graphic and media files. Ask how the system deals with idle processes. Will it disconnect if a learner leaves for ten minutes to attend to a customer? Be sure to double check your assumptions regarding the capacity of your learners' computers. Does everyone have a color monitor and sound card?

Roles of Telephones. Evaluate the use of telephones in the organization by spending forty-five to sixty minutes observing. What is the lag time between calls? Do people forward their messages or use voice mail when they need to accomplish something? If people are continually interrupted with telephone calls, think about how this will influence lesson length.

Office Acoustics. Survey the office acoustics. If you plan to include sound in your training program, think about how it will affect others. Plan programs that will not compete with the office paging system and telephones. Determine the impact an audio track will have on co-workers who are answering phones or trying to concentrate.

Social Interactions. Notice the social interactions of the office, the nature of the teams, and the physical set-up. Is this the kind of office in which workers are continually interacting and sharing information, or is it a place in which people make appointments to meet? Does the office feature open work space and clusters of cubes, or long hallways lined with individual offices? The social interactions tell a great deal about how the program will be used. In an open environment, a Web-based training program might be used by teams or pairs of workers. In organizations with individual offices, learners may be more likely to work alone in a quiet atmosphere.

Management Support of Web-Based Training. Schedule interviews with managers to learn about their attitudes toward Web-based training. Do the managers plan to schedule time for workers to take training? Do the managers value Web-based training as highly as they value traditional, instructor-led training? Take steps to ensure the success of the program. Inform and educate managers of the value of Web-based training.

Pace of Work. Assess the pace of work by talking to managers and learners about peaks and valleys in the business cycle. Improve the odds that your program will be used and that it will be viewed as effective by creating a program that fits into the business environment. Avoid introducing Web-based training during the closing week of a fiscal period when everyone is rushing to process orders or close sales. Create lessons that are short enough to be taken between phone calls or before lunch. Understanding the pace of your learners' work environment makes implementation easier and the instruction more effective.

A trainer discusses delivery environment issues in his organization.

Everyone has a multimedia PC and can access the Web for training, but we have also set up learning centers. The learning centers are good because we manage the (computer) systems and know they are in working order, and we offer a place for learners to go if they want to escape the telephone and interruptions.

Selecting Training Method(s)

In the instructional systems design (ISD) process, the steps for determining if training is needed are defining a goal; identifying the audience; defining the environment; and selecting a training method. The latter process requires the developer to synthesize all of the data.

Developers have a range of methods from which to choose. The following list is just a small sample of training methods:

- Traditional classroom instruction;
- Educational satellite television;

- Self-paced workbooks;
- Videocassette programs;
- Videoconference programs;
- Audiocassette programs; and
- Web-based training.

A single training method or a combination of methods can be used. Obviously, Web-based training is not the solution to every training problem, but it is an appropriate strategy for teaching some skills and imparting particular kinds of knowledge. If Web-based training is not the best method, based on your analysis of needs-assessment data, be firm with clients and managers about your reasons for not recommending it.

At times developers receive a management directive to create a WBT program prior to conducting a needs assessment. This is a risky scenario, first because there is the possibility that the performance problem is not due to a lack of skill or knowledge and therefore cannot be corrected by any type of training. The second risk is that Web-based training may not be the optimal solution to the problem.

If needs-assessment data or a management directive does lead you to implement WBT, begin by establishing a team. The following section explores the roles and responsibilities of team members.

Establishing a WBT Team

Designing Web-based training is a team effort, starting with the needs-assessment phase. The team may include the learners, as well as those involved in the development and delivery of the course. It is important to identify the people who should be involved early in the process. Do not limit the team to instructional designers and subject-matter experts. Table 4.2 shows the members of the WBT development team and their involvement at each phase.

Developing Web-based training requires many team members with specialized skills. In some organizations people play more than one role, for example, the project manager may also be responsible for the instructional design and the system manager may act as the Webmaster and network specialist. The following paragraphs describe the major responsibilities of each role.

Project Manager. The project manager is responsible for leading the overall WBT effort, setting milestones, negotiating for resources, and communicating changes to the team. He or she has responsibilities at every phase of the project.

Table 4.2. Phases and Roles of Web-Based Training

Roles	Phases					
	Assessing Learner Needs	Selecting Most Appropriate WBT Method	Designing Lessons	Creating Blueprints	Developing Website	Evaluating Program
Project Manager	X	X	X	X	X	X
Instructional Designer(s)	X	X	X	X	X	X
System Managers	X	X	X	X	X	
Subject-Matter Expert(s)	X	X	X			X
Learners	X	X				X
Learners' Manager(s)	X					
Legal Counsel	X	X				
Editor(s)	X	X	X			X
Programmer(s)	X	X	X			
Graphic Artist(s)	X	X	X			X
Webmaster	X	X	X			
Instructor(s)	X					X

Instructional Designer(s). The instructional designer is responsible for conducting the needs assessment, choosing the most appropriate form of Web-based training, designing lessons, and developing blueprints. During the Website-development phase, the instructional designer must be available to clarify directions in the blueprints and to negotiate changes in the design necessitated by technical limitations or changes in time or funding. The instructional designer leads the effort to evaluate the program.

System Manager(s). The system manager provides technical guidance and support for the program. When the team is choosing the most appropriate form of Web-based training, the system manager provides insights into the organization's technical capabilities and limitations. As the instructional designer creates lessons and blueprints, the system manager reviews them to ensure that the network and software can support the design. During the site-development phase, the system manager provides the team with system resources, such as access to servers, passwords, and development accounts. During the evaluation phase, the system manager assists the pilot learners with network issues and installation of WBT software, plug-ins, and browsers.

Subject-Matter Expert(s). The subject-matter expert contributes to the needs-assessment phase by helping to define program goals. When the blueprints are ready for review, the subject-matter expert reviews the documents for gross omissions and inaccuracies. During the program-evaluation phase, he or she continues to identify omissions and inaccuracies as well as recommend improvements to the program.

Learners' Manager(s). The learners and their managers are involved at the beginning and again at the end. Both groups are expected to complete questionnaires and participate in interviews and observation sessions. When the program has been developed and is ready to pilot, the learners and their managers review the program and provide feedback.

Legal Counsel. The role of legal counsel is to review the design documents and program blueprint to ensure that there are no problems regarding copyright, use of trademarks, or improper use of proprietary information. For example, if the Web-based training program is using sections of a multimedia program developed by a third party, legal counsel will help the developer secure the copyright for use of the program on the Web.

Editor(s). Editors are responsible for the grammar, consistency, and clarity of the text used on Website pages. Reviewing the blueprint before it goes to programmers and graphic artists reduces the amount of rework during the development of the Website. Editors continue to make corrections and recommendations during the Website development and during the evaluation phase of the program.

Programmer(s). Programmers play an active role during the last three phases of development. As the blueprint is being developed, they review the design and make technical recommendations. For example, if the instructional designer wants to create an exercise that tracks learner responses and provides dynamic feedback, the programmer gives recommendations regarding how to accomplish this. During the development stage, programmers are responsible for developing HTML pages, creating Java applets, and developing interactions using tools such as mBED™ or Macromedia's ShockWave™. During the program evaluation phase, the programmers make the necessary iterative changes from the pilot.

Graphic Artist(s). The responsibility of the graphic artist is to help translate the lesson designs and storyboards into Web pages. The graphic artists provide creative direction and style. The images, navigation, and layout of screens developed and agreed on during the blueprint phase are put into production during site development. The graphic artist works with programmers to create Joint Photographic Experts Group (JPEG) and GIF images to be included in HTML pages. They design the images programmers use to create maps for navigation. After the evaluation phase, the graphic artist makes changes to the Web pages as needed.

Webmaster. The Webmaster is responsible for maintaining the Web server and the site on a day-to-day basis. During the blueprint stage, he or she estimates the server capacity and hard drive space required to support the program. During the Website development phase and the program evaluation phase, the Webmaster puts pages on the server or grants access to the team as needed.

Instructor(s). Instructors are responsible for delivering asynchronous and synchronous (real-time) programs. They are involved in the program evaluation phase

---

Review your needs-assessment questions and make a list of the people in your organization who can answer them. Think about people who might not be obvious sources of data. Gather information for the intended learners and those associated with the learners, such as customers and staff members in other departments.

to identify any delivery problems and may make recommendations for timing and sequencing in a synchronous class.

Summary

Before selecting an appropriate training method, it is essential to determine whether a performance problem is due to a lack of skills and knowledge. If the problem is caused by a lack of tools, poor morale, or inadequate compensation, training will not correct it.

During the needs assessment, determine what the gap in skills and knowledge is and write a goal statement that clearly spells out what training will accomplish. Next, assess how much the learners already know about the topic being presented. When considering Web-based training, take special note of the learners' computer skills and the environment in which the WBT program will be delivered. Reflect on the information you have collected about learners, the program goal, and the learners' environment, then select the method or methods for delivering instruction. If Web-based training is not appropriate, be prepared to explain your reasoning to management.

Based on the needs assessment, Web-based training may be an appropriate solution for delivering an entire program or it may be the right method for delivering part of a program. When you are ready to begin, establish a team to help you.

Chapter Five describes four kinds of Web-based training and explains how each is used. Understanding the options enables you to select the type of Web-based training that best meets your needs.

Suggested Readings

Dick, W., & Carey, L. (1996). *The systematic design of instruction.* New York: HarperCollins.

Romiszowski, A. J. (1988). *The selection and use of instructional media.* New York: Kogan Page.

Rossett, A. (1987). *Training needs assessment.* Englewood Cliffs, NJ: Educational Technology Publications.

Rothwell, W. J., & Kazana, H. C. (1992). *Mastering the instructional design process: A systematic approach.* San Francisco: Jossey-Bass.

Zemke, R., & Kramlinger, T. (1992). *Figuring things out: A trainer's guide to needs and task analysis.* Reading, MA: Addison-Wesley.

Chapter 5

Selecting the Most Appropriate WBT Method

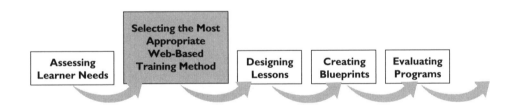

What You Will Learn in This Chapter

After completing this chapter, you will be able to

- Determine the kind of learning to be achieved;
- Differentiate among four types of Web-based training; and
- Select the appropriate type of Web-based training for your purposes.

Determining the Types of Learning

The goal statement developed during the needs-assessment process is the starting point for determining the types of learning your program must accomplish. Decide which of the three types of learning presented in Chapter One best describes the kind of learning your program will provide. Use the questions in the second column of Table 5.1 to help you.

It is important to classify goals, as Web-based training is better suited to teaching cognitive skills than to teaching psychomotor or attitudinal skills.

In real training situations, of course, it is rare to find a goal that can be defined exclusively as one type of learning. Many situations require learning in two or more domains. For example, learning to sell life insurance may require both cognitive and attitudinal skills or learning how to assemble and use a meat slicer requires both cognitive and psychomotor skills. The key to identifying the types of learning required is to divide the goal into distinct parts. Classify the skills needed for each part as *cognitive, psychomotor,* or *attitudinal.* Develop strategies to deliver instruction for each part of the goal.

Use objectives to help break a goal into manageable pieces. Use the methods described by Robert Mager (1975) to define the behavior, condition (if appropriate), and criteria that learners must demonstrate to prove they have mastered the goal.

Table 5.1. Indicators of Types of Learning

Types of Learning	Indicators
Cognitive Skills Examples: • completing travel expense forms • memorizing and applying mutual fund terms and concepts	Does the goal require the learner to • memorize terms and concepts • apply rules • distinguish among items • analyze or synthesize data • evaluate information • solve problems
Psychomotor Skills Examples: • giving an insulin injection • using a table saw	Does the goal require the learner to • engage in mental and physical activity • use muscular actions • practice the skill
Attitudinal Skills Examples: • choosing to value diversity • sensitizing employees to sexual harassment issues	Does the goal require the learner to • change attitudes • reflect on his or her values • explore alternative perspectives Will the goal require time to be achieved? Is the goal difficult to observe or measure in behavioral terms?

For example, if the goal is to teach learners how to write a newsletter, it can be broken into objectives such as the following:

Learners will be able to

- Develop a profile of reader interests;

- Describe three strategies for finding story leads;

- Write a feature story free of spelling and grammatical errors; and

- Lay out a newsletter using desktop publishing software.

Psychomotor. Psychomotor skills require repeated practice and feedback for mastery. They are not suited for delivery via Web-based training. If a goal calls for a combination of cognitive and psychomotor skills (such as teaching a diabetic patient to give himself or herself an insulin injection), you may want to use a combination of Web-based training and face-to-face tutorial sessions. Cognitive skills (such as procedures for preparing the injection and disposing of used syringes) could be delivered via the Web. Psychomotor skills required to giving an injection would be taught in a face-to-face tutorial session that provided opportunities for practice, coaching, and feedback.

Attitudinal. Teaching learners new attitudes requires the instructor to build on what the learners already know, both directly and indirectly. Neither direct methods, such as giving praise, rewards, and recognition, nor indirect methods, such as modeling appropriate behavior, is suited for Web-based training. Again, a combination of methods might be appropriate, for example, to teach managers to value diversity in the workplace Web-based training and a mentoring program could be combined. The Web could be used to teach information about cultural differences, equal-opportunity regulations, and the company's philosophy about diversity. Direct methods, such as praise, rewards, and recognition, could be used by a mentor in a face-to-face situation. Indirect methods, such as role modeling and leading by example, would require identifying local managers to serve as role models.

Cognitive. Cognitive skills are best suited to delivery via Web-based training because they can be communicated to learners using language, text, numbers, and symbols. The cognitive domain includes intellectual skills such as memorizing terms and concepts, problem solving, applying rules, distinguishing among items, analyzing and synthesizing data, and evaluating information. If the skills and knowledge you seek to teach require these intellectual skills, Web-based training is appropriate.

Deciding that the goal or pieces of the goal are in the cognitive domain is a good starting point for selecting Web-based training. The next step is to selecting the most appropriate type of Web-based training by examining the kinds of cognitive skills required to achieve your goal.

Bloom, Hastings, and Madaus (1971) identified six levels of intellectual abilities and skills that could be used to classify cognitive objectives (see Figure 5.1). The levels range from simple knowledge to complex evaluation. Understanding the different levels is important because the intellectual skills and abilities required influences the selection of a Web-based training method.

Knowledge. Knowledge can be defined as the recall of specific and isolated bits of information, methods, sequences, and principles. Teaching couriers the map symbols, such as icons for interstates, railroads, airports, and bridges, is an example of teaching knowledge.

Comprehension. Comprehension is the ability to use knowledge without necessarily relating it to other material or seeing its fullest impact at the time. Teaching a field technician to assemble a computer without helping him or her to understand how the power supply, CPU, operating system, and other components are related is an example of teaching comprehension.

Application. Application is the ability to abstract information such as rules, general methods, and procedures, and to apply them. Teaching telephone representatives to use checklists of questions to resolve simple problems without scheduling a repairperson to visit a customer is an example of teaching application.

Figure 5.1. Bloom's Taxonomy of Educational Objectives in the Cognitive Domain

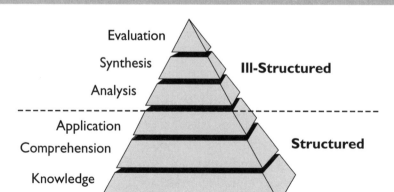

Analysis. Analysis is the ability to break down an item into its constituent elements or parts. Teaching loan officers to examine a loan applicant's financial data and to identify the applicant's financial liabilities and assets is an example of teaching analysis.

Synthesis. Synthesis is the ability to put together elements and parts to form a whole. Teaching product managers to develop marketing plans that incorporate market data, competitive information, and personal experience is an example of teaching synthesis.

Evaluation. Evaluation is the ability to apply judgment about the value of materials or methods for a given purpose. Teaching college admissions officers to determine which courses are granted transfer credit is an example of teaching evaluation.

Highly Structured and Ill-Structured Problems. The dotted line shown in Figure 5.1 divides learning opportunities into structured or ill-structured. The skills associated with knowledge, comprehension, and application can be characterized as structured. There are clear right and wrong answers, performance is observable and measurable, and the application of knowledge varies little from situation to situation. Examples of structured situations are teaching learners how to use word processing software, apply a 15 percent discount, and withdraw money from an automatic teller machine.

Analysis, synthesis, and evaluation are characterized as ill-structured learning opportunities. They involve applying skills and knowledge to problems that are complex and require a combination of concepts, principles, and theories to resolve. The application of ill-structured knowledge also requires that learners apply knowledge to situations that differ from case to case and to problems for which there is no single right answer. Examples of ill-structured problems are analyzing the benefits and limitations of outsourcing work, designing a Website for e-commerce, and developing a treatment plan to manage HIV.

Training problems can be envisioned as falling along a continuum ranging from structured to ill-structured. Where a training problem falls along this continuum will influence the choice of WBT delivery methods.

Selecting the Most Appropriate Type of WBT

To choose among the four kinds of Web-based training, reflect on the goal. Determine the learning domain that best describes the goal, that is, cognitive, psychomotor, or attitudinal. If the goal is in the cognitive domain, determine the level of intellectual skills and characterize it as being a structured or ill-structured problem.

Use the following questions to help define the instructional needs of your program and the most appropriate type of Web-based training:

- Are the instructional goals and objectives measurable?
- Will the learners benefit from working alone or in teams, groups, or pairs?
- Is there a single right answer to the problems?
- Will the learners' experience be a resource for the lesson?
- Do the learners need to interact with one another?

Table 5.2 summarizes the purpose and types of learning associated with the four kinds of Web-based training.

Table 5.2. Characteristics of Web-Based Training

	Web/Computer-Based Training (W/CBT)	Web/Electronic Performance Support Systems (W/EPSS)	Web/Virtual Asynchronous Classroom (W/VAC)	Web/Virtual Synchronous Classroom (W/VSC)
Purpose	To provide learners performance-based training with measurable goals and objectives	To provide learners practical knowledge and problem-solving skills in a just-in-time format	To provide group learning and communication in a different time, different place computer environment	To provide collaborative learning in a real-time environment
Types of Learning	Highly structured problems that require transferring knowledge, building comprehension, and practicing application of skills	Ill-structured problems that require analysis and synthesis of elements, relationships, and organizational principles	Less structured problems that require application, analysis, synthesis, and evaluation	Ill-structured problems that require the synthesis and evaluation of information and shared experience

Web/Computer-Based Training

Web/computer-based training (W/CBT) is similar to traditional multimedia computer-based training (CBT) programs. In W/CBT learners engage in self-paced programs that use multimedia. Interactions take the form of branching decisions that are either controlled by the learner or by the program, based on responses. These programs are most frequently used to meet structured learning goals related to transferring knowledge, building comprehension, and practicing the application of skills.

Characteristics of W/CBT Table 5.3 provides a summary of the learning characteristics of Web/computer-based training. The hallmark of this kind of training is the design of the program. Web/computer-based training is taken by individual learners working at their own pace. The programs address structured problems and are designed to teach knowledge, comprehension, and application skills that can be assessed by observation of measurable outcomes. Because W/CBT programs teach subjects with measurable objectives, it is expected that learners will complete all of the lessons to master the objectives.

> **Example.** A needs assessment was conducted to determine the kind of training required for field service engineers at a computer company that planned to release a new software program. The new software was sub-

Table 5.3. Learning Characteristics of W/CBT

Characteristic	Description
Self-Paced	Learners engage in learning at convenient time and set own pace for completing lessons and modules.
Individual Learning	Learners work alone to master skills. W/CBT is well suited for drill and practice of repetitious skills.
Highly Structured	Topics with clear right and wrong answers are well suited to W/CBT. Developers can predict the answers and provide clear feedback, reinforcement, and remediation.
Discrete Units of Instruction	Teaching measurable objectives makes it desirable to divide the content into lessons and modules. Learners are expected to complete discrete units of material to demonstrate mastery of the objectives.

ject to change until the week before it was shipped to customers. The field service engineers had to learn to use the software before it shipped so that they could answer questions and support customers. The engineers worked from home offices and in small regional offices located across the United States and Canada. Because the company provided service seven days a week, twenty-four hours a day, the field service engineers worked in shifts. They were not always busy, but their schedules were unpredictable.

Web/computer-based training was selected to deliver the training. Field service engineers were able to learn the program from home and from regional offices, eliminating the need for them to travel to a central training location. It also allowed the engineers to complete the training at their own pace. Because learning to use software is a highly structured topic with clearly right and wrong answers, the W/CBT program provided clear feedback, reinforcement, and remedial help. Last-minute changes to the software and the related changes to the training were not a problem. The training department was able to make changes to the program to reflect the latest version of the software.

Comparison. Web/computer-based training is similar to traditional computer-based training in many ways. Both delivery methods are designed for individual learners and are well suited for teaching cognitive skills related to knowledge, comprehension, and application. Table 5.4 summarizes the key differences between the two delivery methods.

Web/computer-based training differs from traditional computer-based training because W/CBT draws on the resources of the World Wide Web and proprietary information found in company databases. In addition, information located on the company's intranet can be used. In traditional CBT programs the resources are limited to those included on the CD-ROM.

Another difference is the number of options for communications between the learner and the instructor. Web/computer-based training offers tools such as e-mail, to communicate with the instructor, or link to an online bulletin board. Some Web-based training software programs track learners' progress. They inform the instructor of learners' quiz scores and notify him or her if a learner fails to log-in for an extended period of time. In general, traditional CBT programs offer better tools for scoring the learners' performance, but these programs lack the network

Table 5.4. Comparison Between Traditional CBT and Web/CBT	
Traditional CBT	**Web/CBT**
Resources are limited to what is included on the CD-ROM.	Resources can include proprietary company databases as well as information on the World Wide Web.
Communication between learner and instructor is not highly integrated.	Communication between learners and instructor can be seamlessly integrated.
Updates and modifications require the CD-ROM or disks to be revised, mastered, pressed, and distributed.	Program can be easily updated and modified.
Rich multimedia options for video, audio, and images are available. Robust tools for creating sophisticated interactions and exercises and tracking learners are available.	Rich media such as video, audio, and images can cause congestion on networks. Limited ability to create sophisticated interactions and exercises and track learners.

connections required to send that information back to a central database for tracking purposes.

Web/computer-based training offers developers the ability to update programs easily, instead of creating a new CD-ROM master, scheduling a press run, or distributing a revised disk. Web tools and technology can be used to create rich media such as video, audio, and images. Additionally, the computers used by learners are being upgraded continually, making it possible for developers to create sophisticated programs for powerful multimedia computers.

Current Web tools and technology are constrained by bandwidth limitations that prohibit developers from using rich media such as video, audio, or graphics that require large files. Large files cause network congestion and take a long time to download or paint on the learner's screen. But, this situation is changing rapidly as new tools are created to compress large files, greater bandwidth becomes available, faster modems are installed, and old computers are replaced. These improvements will make it possible for Web-based training developers to create more sophisticated programs with rich media.

> **A professor who teaches instructional technology recommends that trainers become connoisseurs of WBT programs before developing their own.**
>
> *It is outrageous to think that you can design training programs in a medium in which you have never learned anything. I ask all of my students to choose a topic, any topic, and to try to learn about it via the Web. After this experience they are sensitive to design issues.*

Web/EPS Systems

The Web and Internet make it possible to use high-tech job aids. Using the Web, a learner can find a Web page that provides step-by-step instructions for completing a travel expense form or directions to replace a computer mother board. Electronic Performance Support System (EPSS) applications offer several advantages over paper-based job aids. The most obvious is that they are available worldwide through the Internet and its communication links. Learners can access instruction just-in-time, avoiding what they do not need. Well-designed programs can link learners to experts, colleagues, threaded discussions, step-by-step instructions, training modules, and reference materials.

Characteristics of W/EPS Systems. Table 5.5 provides a summary of the characteristics of Web/computer-based training.

Table 5.5. Characteristics of Web/EPS Systems

Characteristic	Description
Learner determined	Learners determine how, when, and at what level of detail they will use the Web/EPS system.
Individual learning	Learners work alone to solve problems.
Ill-structured	Used to solve problems that require analysis, synthesis, and evaluation. Problems lack a clear right or wrong answer.
Just in time	Learners use W/EPS systems when and where needed, rather than in anticipation of future needs.

The ability to provide learners with training and information when and where it is needed distinguishes W/EPS systems from Web/computer-based training. In the latter, the learner is expected to complete all of the lessons and modules and hold the skills and knowledge for later use. Using a Web/EPS system, the learner does not access the system until the skills or knowledge are required, then decides how much information or training is necessary. There is a broad range. For example, a first-time learner may complete a lesson, read the documentation, and review tips posted to an online bulletin board before starting the task. On the other hand, a learner who has done the task previously may choose to scan the steps in the procedure to refresh his or her memory.

Web/EPS systems are ideal for helping learners with ill-structured problems that do not have simple right or wrong answers and problems that involve so many variables that it is impossible to anticipate all of the possible solutions.

> **Example.** A needs assessment was conducted to determine how to provide repair technicians with the skills and knowledge needed to install and maintain telecommunications equipment. Repair technicians located at four different regional offices were dispatched individually to make repairs on site. The skills and knowledge needed required technicians to solve problems they had not encountered before or for which they had not been trained. Because there were so many configurations and permutations of the equipment, it was determined that it would be impossible to teach technicians every possible repair scenario. The technicians' schedules and the breadth of knowledge necessary indicated the need for just-in-time training. Much of the information about repairing the equipment could be found in the company's technical manuals, engineering drawings, training materials, and repair bulletins. A less-accessible source of information was the experience and knowledge of senior technicians.
>
> A Web-based EPS system was chosen because it gave technicians access to rich resources when and where they needed them. Using this kind of training, technicians accessed instruction and information on-site by dialing in from laptop computers. They accessed documentation, scanned modules of online Web/computer-based training, sent e-mail to experts requesting help, and read notes files, where technicians had previously posted questions, recommendations, and responses to problems. A Web/EPS system eliminated the need for technicians to attend weeks of training to learn how to install every possible permutation of hardware.

Table 5.6. Comparison of Traditional and Web/EPS Systems	
Traditional EPS Systems	**Web/EPS Systems**
Updates require distribution of new software or media	Updates from a central point are available immediately
Communication with other learners requires separate tools	Communication with others can be integrated into the system

Comparison. Table 5.6 summarizes the differences between traditional EPS systems and Web/EPS systems.

One of the key differences between traditional EPS systems and Web/EPS systems is the technical implementation and use of networks. Traditional systems depend on software on the learner's computer to find steps, procedures, tips, definitions, checklists, and glossaries. In contrast, Web/EPS systems link learners to a central server, where information is easily updated and made available.

Integrated tools and the ability to connect learners to peers and experts are unique to this environment. Information contained in threaded discussions, online forums, news groups, and notes files is the equivalent of an electronic bulletin board. Users can post requests for information, recommendations, and answers to questions posted by others, creating a resource that grows over time.

Web/Virtual Asynchronous Classrooms

Like a traditional classroom, an asynchronous virtual classroom brings learners and instructors together to learn new skills and knowledge. The learners and instructor log on to the Internet at various times to work on assignments, read, and work on projects. The learners share a group learning experience but do not meet in real time. This application blends a variety of Web technologies, such as hypertext documents, online quizzes, multimedia, notes files, and e-mail to produce programs. The complexity and sophistication of the program are largely determined by the design and the hardware limitations of the learners.

Asynchronous virtual classroom programs are distinguished by their reliance on a variety of communication tools that allow peer-to-peer learning, group learning, and learner-instructor coaching. As a result of extensive communication and shared goals, a geographically dispersed class develops a sense of community, complete with norms for acceptable communication outside the virtual classroom.

Characteristics. Table 5.7 summarizes the characteristics that set Web/virtual asynchronous classrooms apart from other type of Web-based training.

The most important characteristic of Web/virtual asynchronous classrooms is the focus on group learning. Unlike Web/CBT and Web/EPS systems, which are designed for individual learners, Web/virtual asynchronous classroom programs are designed for groups. Organizations use this form of Web-based training because their goal is best achieved in a group learning environment. Learners work together to brainstorm ideas, analyze case studies, and solve problems, but they are not necessarily online at the same time. Learners log in at any hour of the day or night to contribute ideas, add insights to case studies, and present alternative solutions to problems.

Table 5.7. Characteristics of Web/Virtual Asynchronous Classrooms

Characteristic	Description
Group learning	Involves learners working with one another on projects, case studies, and exercises. Learners are encouraged to learn from one another as well as from the instructor, using collaborative learning strategies such as brainstorming, discussions, and problem solving.
Accessed at different times of day and night	Learners and instructor independently access the Web. Although learners and instructor are not online together, they participate in group learning activities such as projects, brainstorming, or case studies.
Problems/topics are somewhat structured	Topics best suited to this type of Web-based training are those for which the instructor and course developers can define the outcomes and anticipate most of the resources learners need. The role of the instructor is to provide flexible facilitation that supports learners' exploration of additional topics or new problems that arise as they explore the subject.
Learning is done in anticipation of need	Learners take training to fill a current or anticipated gap in skills and knowledge.
Requires more than one class meeting	Group work and projects require several sessions to complete.

Web/virtual asynchronous classrooms are well suited to problems or topics that are ill structured. They teach learners to apply guidelines, theories, and concepts to problems that are complex and varied and for which there is no single right answer. For example, a program to teach store managers how to increase sales, a program to teach human resource managers how to recruit and screen seasonal employees, or a program to teach physicians how to take a patient's medical history are appropriate for Web/VAC programs because they can be taught by providing learners with established guidelines, steps, procedures, and practices for real-world situations. The skills and knowledge taught require analysis, synthesis, and evaluation, and there is a range of correct or acceptable answers.

Learners participate in Web/VAC programs to fill a current gap in skills and knowledge or an anticipated need for new skills and knowledge. For example, a store manager faced with hiring summer workers may enroll in a Web-based class to improve his or her current recruitment practices. An assistant store manger may enroll in the same class because he or she anticipates the need for this knowledge.

Conducting a Web/VAC program usually requires more than one meeting. Because learners log in at their convenience to contribute, the program must be conducted over a period of time long enough to allow interaction, reflection, and feedback.

> **Example.** A training company that provides courses for corporate clients conducted a needs assessment to determine what additional training corporate clients were interested in taking. One of the training company's most popular courses was a two-day, hands-on, instructor-led course on basic Web-page design. A survey of learners who had completed the course revealed a desire for an advanced course. As part of the needs assessment, the company learned about problems with the original course. Learners complained that they were overwhelmed by the amount of information presented in such a short time. They also wanted more time to practice skills and reflect on what was learned. Learners reported that the strengths of class were the team projects and group collaboration.
>
> Attracting enough learners in a given geographic region for an advanced instructor-led course was a problem. The learners were concentrated on the West Coast and in the mid-Atlantic states. Many were employees of small start-up companies that could not afford to be absent from work or incur the travel expenses. In addition, the training company's sales staff identified a significant number of potential learners in Europe and Canada.

These facts led the company to offer the advanced course as a Web/virtual asynchronous classroom program. The needs assessment had highlighted learners' desire for learning as part of a group or team. Also, the limited number of learners in each geographic region made it easier to form a class without geographic barriers; travel costs were eliminated; and the class could be offered over an extended period of time, allowing learners to practice and reflect on what they had learned.

Webmasters from around the world used the asynchronous virtual classroom to learn advanced skills for designing and marketing Websites. Working in teams of three, they developed marketing home pages using the latest technology. Although the learners were never online at the same time, they shared responsibility for the final project. They communicated with one another and received coaching from the instructor via e-mail, notes files, and listservs. Due to the asynchronous nature of the class, each webmaster chose the day and hour that best suited his or her needs.

Comparison. The primary advantage of Web/VAC programs is their ability to bring together a geographically diverse class. Traditional classes are bound by geography. A Web/VAC program can enroll learners across the country or around the world in highly specialized classes that would not attract enough local learners to be viable.

Web/virtual asynchronous classes are not fixed by time. Traditional classes require learners to meet at a set time. Web learners log on at a time that suits their schedules. Table 5.8 provides a summary of the differences between traditional classroom instruction and Web/VAC programs.

Table 5.8. Comparison of Traditional Classroom Instruction and Web/VAC

Traditional	Web/Virtual Asynchronous Class
Geographically bound	Geographically open
Fixed in time	Independent of time

Web/Virtual Synchronous Classrooms

The most technically sophisticated Web-based training applications are virtual synchronous classrooms, in which the instructor and class are online at the same time (synchronously). Synchronous classroom tools consist of the following:

- Whiteboards
- Shared applications
- Videoconferencing
- Audioconferencing
- Chat rooms

Online whiteboards enable the entire class to write on them in turn. Shared applications, such as a spreadsheet, allow learners to work as a group to fill in cells, correct formulas, or modify column labels. Videoconferencing and audioconferencing are conceptually similar to traditional audio- and videoconferencing systems. Both allow learners to interact in real time and to hear and/or see the instructor and other class members. Chat rooms are a structured way for learners to carry on a dialogue by typing comments into a running discussion.

Characteristics. Web/virtual synchronous classrooms share some characteristics with Web/virtual asynchronous classrooms. Table 5.9 summarizes these.

Both synchronous and asynchronous Web programs bring learners together to learn as a group. Another similarity is the current or anticipated need for skills or knowledge that may not be as immediate as those that a Web/EPS system addresses.

Table 5.9. Characteristics of Web/Virtual Synchronous Classrooms

Characteristic	Description
Group learning	Learners work together on projects, case studies, and exercises. They are encouraged to learn from one another as well as from the instructor.
Anticipated need for knowledge	Learners enroll because they have a current or anticipated need for skills or knowledge.
Meets at fixed time	Learners and the instructor meet online at an agreed-on time.
Ill-structured problems	Topics best suited to this type of training involve many variables and complex issues. The problems do not have clearly right or wrong answers or are so complex that simple answers are not possible.

A major difference between Web/virtual synchronous classrooms and all other type of Web-based training is the requirement that the learners and the instructor be online at the same time. Learners participate in a live, instructor-led class. This requires that time zone differences be considered when scheduling classes (see Figure 5.2). For example, a ninety-minute class that starts at 4:00 p.m. Eastern Standard Time requires that learners on the West Coast log in at 1:00 p.m. Pacific time. Once online, the learners participate in class and interact with one another in real-time.

Like Web/virtual asynchronous classes, Web/virtual synchronous classes are well suited for ill-structured learning, complex problems that lack clear or simple answers. Web/virtual synchronous classroom programs enable learners to build new knowledge through active participation, dialogue with the instructor and other learners, and shared experiences and knowledge. For example, sales representatives can learn to

Figure 5.2. Take Time Zones into Consideration

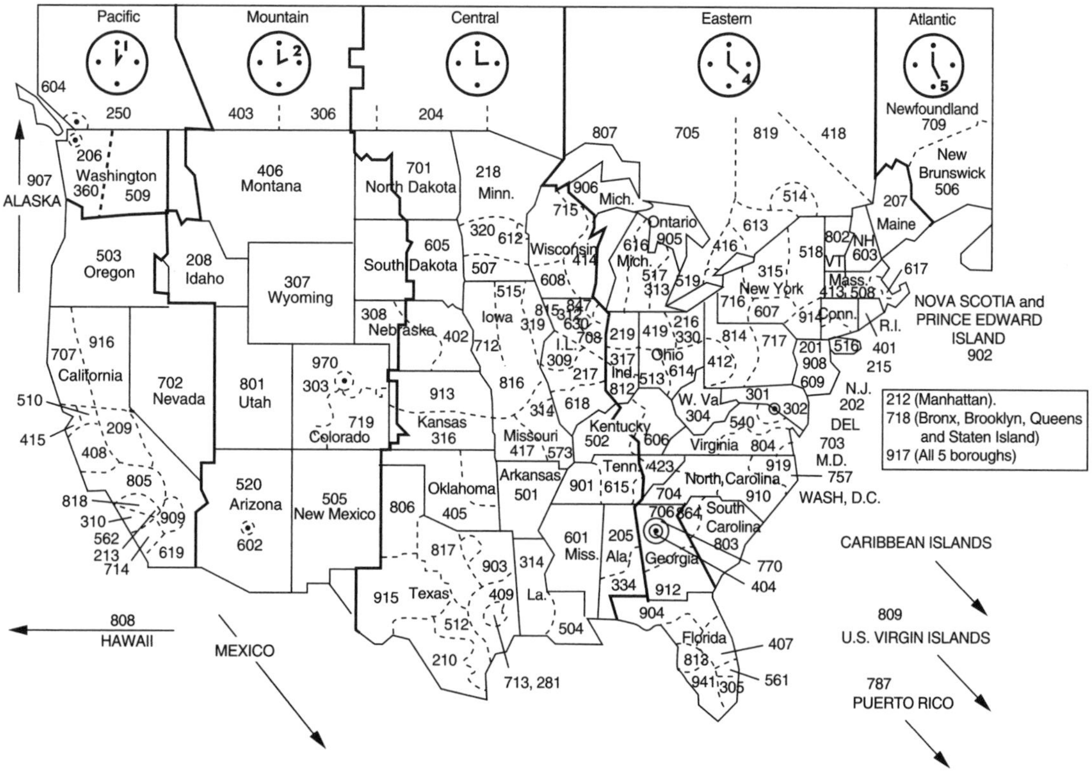

conduct a competitive analysis or identify decision makers during a sales call. As these topics do not have simple answers, they are well suited for group learning.

> **Example.** A company purchased a new software application to link its computers together. A needs assessment was undertaken to determine what kind of training was needed to use the new software. The systems managers were located in North America, the Far East, and Europe. Their managers were reluctant to release them or to pay travel expenses for training. The topics to be covered were impossible to identify with certainty. It was out of the question to fly systems managers in for an overview class and then again for a class tailored to address the options they chose to implement.
>
> A Web/virtual synchronous classroom was chosen because it enabled live interaction (audio) for real-time analysis, synthesis and evaluation of information, and application sharing. The spread of time zones created hardship for at least one geographic region each time; therefore the meeting times were shifted each time. The savings in travel expense and the ability to participate in an international class in real-time overcame the occasional hardship created by differences in time zones.
>
> During the class, systems managers were introduced to software options and encouraged to ask questions. In some cases, learners were able to test what they had learned on their local system and share with others. They worked in teams to determine which options were best suited for their needs. They also learned to install and customize the new software through application sharing. A trainer observed and coached them to provide direction and feedback.

Comparison. Web/VSC programs can be very similar to traditional classroom instruction; Table 5.10 provides a comparison.

Table 5.10. Traditional Versus Web/VSC Programs	
Traditional Classroom Instruction	**Web/Virtual Synchronous Classroom**
Geographically bound	Geographically open
Resources limited	Vast resources

Establishing a shared vision regarding Web-based training can be a challenge. *I was asked to initiate a pilot program* [Web-based training] *for my company. At the first meeting, I was getting direction from everybody. It was clear we were not talking about the same things. Some people were describing "information" or "reference material" online; other people were talking about desktop videoconferencing; and others were talking about just putting our CD-ROMS on the intranet. It was clear that unless we could all look at the same concrete examples we would never share a vision about the program.*

PURPOSE: *This exercise is designed to help you reflect on the differences among Web/computer-based training, Web/electronic performance support systems, Web/virtual asynchronous classrooms, and Web/virtual synchronous classrooms.*

Set your browser to the Web-Based Training Information Center at the following URL: http://www.filename.com/wbt/index.html

Locate the list of online learning classes and sample three to five of them. Use the Analysis of Web-Based Training Worksheet that follows to collect data about the courses.

Create four folders in your Netscape Navigator® bookmarks or four folders in your Microsoft Internet Explorer® Favorite Places.
Label the folders:

- Web/computer-based training
- Web/electronic performance support systems
- Web/virtual asynchronous classrooms
- Web/virtual synchronous classrooms

Use the folders to store examples of each of the four kinds of Web-based training to share with members of the development team or management. These sites can be a source for ideas and a resource for the entire team.

How closely Web/VSC programs mimic a real classroom depends on the kind of software chosen. If the software allows learners to see and talk to one another and to share an application, it is very similar to a real classroom. Software that only allows learners to type messages back and forth is obviously not as closely related.

Two key differences between a traditional classroom and all forms of Web/virtual synchronous classrooms are (1) the ability to draw a class from anywhere and (2) the ability to use resources that are located on the Web and on corporate intranets.

Analysis of Web-Based Training Worksheet

Program name:

Program URL:

Purpose of program:

Classify by type of learning:

The program is best
described as (circle one):   W/CBT   W/EPSS   W/VAC   W/VSC

Program name: _____

Program URL: _____

Purpose of program:

Classify by type of learning:

The program is best
described as (circle one):   W/CBT   W/EPSS   W/VAC   W/VSC

Program name:

Program URL:

Purpose of program:

Classify by type of learning:

The program is best
described as (circle one):   W/CBT   W/EPSS   W/VAC   W/VSC

Summary

The four types of Web-based training described above have been presented as distinct and separate. In reality, there are many variations of these types and many ways to use them in combination. Chapter Six presents instructional strategies for each.

Suggested Readings

Bloom, B. S., Hastings, J. T., & Madaus, G. F. (1971). *Handbook on formative and summative evaluation of student learning.* New York: McGraw-Hill.

Darkenwald, G. G., & Merriam, S. B. (1982). *Adult education: Foundations of practice.* Cambridge, MA: Harper & Row.

Elias, J. L., & Merriam, S. (1980). *Philosophical foundations of adult education.* Malabar, FL: Krieger.

Gagne, R. M., Briggs, L. J., & Wagner, W. W. (1992). *Principles of instructional design.* Fort Worth, TX: Harcourt Brace.

Heinich, R., Molenda, M., & Russell, J. (1989). *Instructional media and the new technologies of instruction* (3rd ed.). New York: Macmillan.

Keegan, D. (1993). *Theoretical principles of distance education.* London: Routledge.

Mager, R. F. (1975). *Preparing instructional objectives.* Palo Alto, CA: Fearon.

Moore, M. G., & Kearsley, G. (1996). *Distance education: A systems view.* Belmont: CA: Wadsworth.

Chapter 6

Designing Lessons

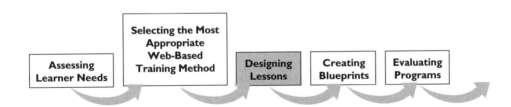

What You Will Learn in This Chapter

After completing this chapter, you will be able to

- Identify factors that limit instructional design on the Web;
- Define the roles of learner and instructor in Web-based training; and
- Identify the various interaction options for Web-based training.

Designing Within Set Parameters

Developers of Web-based training face certain limitations and must design within certain parameters. Figure 6.1 shows the four most common limitations they face.

Figure 6.1. Limiting Factors in Web-Based Design

☑ Repurposing existing courseware

☑ Financial or other resource constraints

☑ Technical limitations for design and delivery

☑ Business considerations

Repurposing Existing Courseware

Many developers are required to revise existing CD-ROM programs, PowerPoint® presentations, videocassette programs, and self-paced workbooks so that they can be used over the Web. This process is called "dumbing down" or "backward re-purposing" because the sophisticated interactions and media (video clips or large photo images) are often removed or reduced to make the files smaller and thus faster and easier to send over the Internet. Having to reuse an existing program limits the designer's options.

A developer talks about reusing content and media from a CD-ROM.
We had to strip out a lot of the cool graphics, animation, and interactions [that were in our multimedia CD-ROMs] *to put them on the Web. When people who knew the programs* [in CD-ROM format] *saw the Web stuff, they were not impressed. We call it backward repurposing because, compared to CD-ROM quality, it is a step backward.*

Financial or Other Resource Constraints

The financial and resource constraints for the design of Web-based training are the same as those that exist with conventional classroom programs, but the limitations are magnified because the tools can be expensive and time consuming to learn. In addition, developing programs is a resource-intensive effort, involving graphics artists, database developers, programmers, system managers, subject-matter experts, and instructional designers.

Technical Limitations

Technical limitations such as small bandwidth, limited functionality of tools, incompatibility of programs, and differences among browsers also constrain the designer's ability to create programs. Bandwidth, the capacity of a network to carry files from one place to another, is a major design consideration. If a network has limited bandwidth, sending large files such video files or image files may be a problem.

Any given tool or software program has limited features. No one software package will do everything, so one or more may be required. For example, a Web-based software program may be well suited for developing drill and practice exercises or quizzes, and it may offer an intuitive user interface, but it may be weak for tracking learner participation and managing communication with the instructor.

Another technical limitation is the ability to produce programs that can be viewed across all platforms, such as PC, Macintosh, and UNIX. Software may not run on all hardware. The choice of software that will run on all platforms is smaller than the choice of software exclusively for PCs.

Programs can also be limited by the functional differences among browsers such as Netscape Navigator®, Internet Explorer®, and America Online®. Browsers also have different versions, which makes matters more complicated. Learners may have access to browsers that display text only. Programs may have to be designed for the lowest common denominator—the oldest and least functional browsers.

Technical limitations for delivery also constrain design options. If your sales force is equipped with old laptop computers with slow modems, you will want to minimize the inconvenience of waiting for files to download.

Business Considerations

Business considerations such as corporate branding, corporate culture, new product release dates, and contractual obligations also limit design decisions. Programs connected to the corporate Website often require adherence to certain standards, such as where the corporate logo must be displayed, the size and color of text, and conventions for creating hypertext links to internal and external Web pages. Web-based training programs connected to new product releases are subject to volatile changes in content and to short development time frames. Contractual obligations with business partners or organizations that resell or provide third-party services can create further complexity. Also, programs must take into account both training provided to employees and training provided to external business partners.

An instructional designer talks about the challenges of developing within the corporate guidelines.

This program was a collaborative venture between our company and a partner company. Both company logos had to be on every page, and there were "rules" about the size and location of the logos. It limited our screen real estate, and it made designing the screens and navigation a challenge.

PURPOSE: *This exercise will help you identify the technical, legal, and organization issues before beginning to design Web-based training.*

Schedule a meeting with your webmaster or someone from your information systems department and ask about legal, organizational, and technical considerations for adding pages to the organization's site. Obtain any style guidelines for how to display the corporate logo and how the pages must be formatted. Find out what role legal counsel plays and the technical limitations, if any. Use the Web Audit Form on page 75 to plan your meeting.

During the developmental phase, the programmers will need to discuss detailed technical issues, such as directory structures, naming conventions, and how to access Web-server log files.

✓ Web Audit Form Worksheet

Questions	Notes
1. Who is responsible for setting up and maintaining the Website? If only one person can set up a Website, be sure to build time into the schedule. Anticipate changes and corrections.	
2. Are there style guidelines? Ask about the specifications or recommendations for menu depth, page length, fonts, and using the corporate logo.	
3. Who is responsible for legal issues such as copyright, trademarks, and libel? Does the corporate counsel approve Web pages? If there is no legal counsel, ask about internal review teams.	
4. Are there restrictions regarding inclusion of plug-ins, helper applications, downloading client software, creating ports, or processing forms? Programs of this type tax a server and require extra bandwidth if the WBT program will be accessed a great deal. They can also compromise network security.	
5. Is server disk space limited? Image and video files can take up a great deal of space.	

The remainder of this chapter presents strategies as they relate to the role of the instructor, the learner, and the desired interactions. The roles of instructors and learners, as well as the instructional strategies, differ among the four kinds of Web-based training.

The four kinds of Web-based training have been presented as distinct and mutually exclusive. In reality, a program may require a combination of several types of WBT. Figure 6.2 shows how a course on retirement planning has been divided among the methods.

The design of a WBT program is dependent on the purpose of the training. Like conventional classroom training, a range of exercises, assignments, and roles are used to achieve specific goals. For example, an exercise to help learners identify parts of a computer would be different from an exercise designed to help learners evaluate investments. A drag-and-drop exercise could be used to help learners memorize the names of parts of a computer. A more sophisticated exercise could be used to help learners understand the factors that influence the value of stock. Using an online calculator learners could change the investment period and the interest rate on screen, producing a series of graphs that illustrate investment growth.

Use the information collected during the needs assessment to guide the design. Frequently review who the learners are and what they will be able to do after completing instruction. Use an iterative process so that the design can be adjusted if there is new information about learners, a change in the goals, or a new context for training.

Figure 6.2. Sample Mixture of WBT Strategies

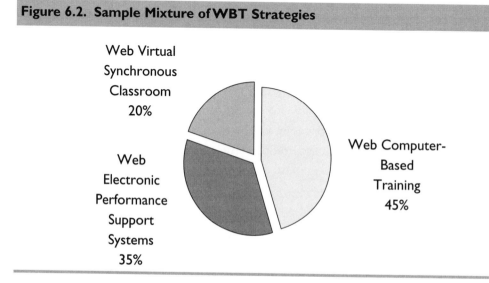

Web Virtual Synchronous Classroom 20%

Web Electronic Performance Support Systems 35%

Web Computer-Based Training 45%

An experienced trainer talks about the mixture of Web-based training modes used to deliver a management class.

Our first program was management skills. It had been a three-day class, you know, lecturettes, group exercises, questions and answers. Moving to the Web required that we redesign it so that students didn't have to spend three solid days in front of the tube. We broke it up and let the students have control over the pace. The lecturettes were turned into self-paced material (W/CBT), you know, hypertext documents. We gave groups the tools (e-mail, text-chat, and discussion forums) to do exercises (W/VAC). Once a week we had live instructor-led sessions using shared whiteboards and teleconference calls (W/VSC).

W/CBT Lessons

Web/computer-based training (W/CBT) is best suited to teaching clear, measurable objectives. Such applications as memorizing rules or learning to use software applications are well suited to this kind of training. Web/computer-based training can reduce the amount of time that an instructor spends working with learners.

Instructor Roles

"Instructor," in the case of Web/computer-based training, refers to two roles. First, the system itself has a role: It provides feedback, recommends the order in which to complete lessons, assesses learner progress, and directs learners to additional resources. A team of developers, subject-matter experts, programmers, and instructional designers crafts the role played by the computer. Second, a person also acts as instructor in the role of online facilitator, available to provide answers and resources beyond the scope of the program. The instructor can reply to e-mail messages, review test scores, assess participation, and proactively contact learners. Figure 6.3 lists the five roles that the instructor (system or online facilitator) plays in Web/computer-based training.

Controlling the Environment. The design team determines the amount of control learners will have of their environment: what kind of stimuli and feedback they will receive, such as drill and practice, structured menus, simplification of supporting documents, and simulations. The design team creates a safe environment for the learner to practice new skills by activating only certain functions of the software or providing structured menus that lead learners from one lesson to another only after prerequisite skills have been mastered. Developers can simplify and structure mate-

Figure 6.3. Roles of Instructor in W/CBT

☑ Controlling the environment

☑ Predicting what learners want to know

☑ Assessing outcomes

☑ Directing learning

☑ Communicating with learners

rials to make it easier for learners by adding a search engine to help learners find exactly what they need.

Predicting Needs. The design team predicts what learners want to know and determines the content, sequence, and depth of information. This is important because in an asynchronous environment there is little opportunity to make dynamic changes. In W/CBT programs, changes cannot be made in real time. The development team must anticipate learners' needs during the assessment phase. Learners' needs can be reflected in the design of menu titles, and the sequencing of topics can be problem centered, such as building applications, modifying applications, and customizing applications. Other strategies include layering and sequencing content to reflect learners' interests, for example, setting up links to system documents. Learners who want even more detail can be linked to system schematics.

Assessing Outcomes. The online facilitator and the system assess the learners' outcomes in two ways: (1) the system can judge a response and send feedback or (2) the online facilitator can judge a response and send feedback. In either case, the instructor provides assessment interactions. If the system provides feedback, the design team must decide how many attempts to permit and what type of feedback will be given after each. If the online facilitator provides feedback, the tools must be given to track scores and communicate via e-mail.

Directing Learning. Directed learning refers to activities that guide the learner through the program. They can be as simple as queuing or as complicated as competency assessment. With queuing, the system provides a recommended path through the program modules, and menu items are grayed out when completed. For competency assessment, the online instructor administers a pretest, then creates a customized path.

Communicating with Learners. Communication sets Web/computer-based training apart from traditional CBT. Learners have a continual link to the instructor. Programs may include icons to encourage learners to send e-mail to the instructor or learners can contribute to a threaded discussion and request additional resources. The instructor can also contact learners and check on their progress. More sophisticated programs have built-in features to track learner progress and alert instructors to the learners' test scores and attendance.

Roles of Learners

Figure 6.4 lists the four roles that learners play in Web/computer-based training.

Participating in Drill and Practice. The most familiar role for most learners is to do drill-and-practice exercises, read and respond to questions, participate in simulations, and take quizzes. These activities allow learners opportunities to practice new skills and to integrate them into existing skill sets. Learners are familiar with the corollary of these activities in classroom environments, so the role is easy to understand.

Directing and Managing Learning. Directing and managing their own learning is not a familiar role to many learners. WBT learners are asked to make choices about what topics will be taught, the order of presentation, and the depth. They are connected to a wealth of resources and have the ability to navigate among them. This can be a daunting responsibility for Web novices unfamiliar with self-directed learning. Programs should provide clear structure and direction for learners. It is best to recommend the order in which lessons should be taken, to provide guidance on how to use online resources such as search engines, and to include concrete examples.

Reflecting on Feedback and Experiences. The ability to reflect about and draw on experience is critical for learners. They need opportunities to explore, take action,

---

Figure 6.4. The Role of Learners in W/CBT

☑ Participating in drill and practice

☑ Directing and managing learning

☑ Reflecting on feedback and experiences

☑ Communicating with instructors

---

and reflect on outcomes. The goals of most W/CBT programs are highly structured with observable behavior, such as applying a discount, using a spreadsheet, or processing travel expense reports. This type of skill is best learned using activities with drill and practice, read and respond, and quiz taking. The design team must make a conscious effort to engage adults and draw on their life experiences. When possible, instructors should encourage adults to think about the wider implications of what is being taught. For example, if adults are learning the mechanics of how to use e-mail, ask them to reflect on broader issues related to e-mail—the ethical, business, and legal issues of this communication tool in the workplace. Ask them to consider rights of privacy, electronic chain letters, customer communication, and the practice of sending unsolicited e-mail to large numbers of people (SPAMMING). Draw on the life experiences of adult learners and make the programs more meaningful to them.

Communicating with Instructors. Learners are responsible for communicating with the instructor to ask questions or to ask for additional resources. Exchanges between learners and the instructor are opportunities for learners to manage their learning actively. If a Web/computer-based program does not meet a learner's needs, he or she can be directed to a more basic program or to URLs for other resources. Learners do not have to silently endure an inappropriate program.

W/CBT Interactions

The W/CBT designer must identify the cognitive level of skills needed, draft a goal statement that defines them in concrete terms, then select the type of interaction that will help build them. The most common kinds of interactions are reading and responding, communicating with the instructor, participating in simulations, completing tests, and engaging in drill-and-practice exercises. An instructor can devise many types of exercises to provide drill and practice: simple multiple-choice games or drag-and-drop exercises. See Chapter Nine for more details.

Purpose of Instruction

Web/computer-based training provides learners with performance-based training with measurable goals and objectives. Learning new material, comprehending information, and applying skills are well suited for this delivery method. Table 6.1 provides examples of goals and interactions for teaching word processing via Web/computer-based training.

A variety of software tools, utilities, and programs create interactions. They can be thought of along a continuum from simple to complex. The simple tools range from hypertext markup language (HTML) written without the assistance of WYSIWYG (what you see is what you get) editors to sophisticated programs such as Macromedia's Authorware® or Asymetric's ToolBook II®. Many programs are available.

On the World Wide Web, use a search engine such as AltaVista or Yahoo to locate samples of Web/computer-based training. Search using terms such as: online learning, quiz, objectives, and Web-based training. Use trial and error to find sites that offer online instruction. Does what you find meet the definition of Web/computer-based training? Do the sites direct learning? Is there adequate drill and practice or feedback? Can the learner communicate with the instructor? What things do you like about the sites you identified? Could the sites be improved? Did you enjoy learning from these sites?

Create a bookmark in your browser program and name it W/CBT.
Save the URLs for the examples of Web/computer-based training you have located. The programs will be helpful for illustrating concepts to your team and clients.

Table 6.1. Goals and Interactions for Teaching Word Processing

Goal	Level of Goal	Interaction
Identify the functions of each icon on a tool bar.	*Knowledge:* Recall specific and isolated bits of information.	Multiple-choice quiz, drag-and-drop labels
View documents in "normal," "outline," and "page layout" formats.	*Comprehension:* Use knowledge without necessarily relating it to other material or implications.	Software simulation
Open a file, check spelling, and print using tool bar.	*Application:* Apply abstract information in a concrete situation.	Launch a real application in a PC window and have the W/CBT running in a second window.

Web-Based EPS Systems

Web-Based Electronic Performance Support Systems (W/EPSS) are best suited for providing learners with practical knowledge to solve problems. Teaching field service engineers to configure networks is an effective use of this type of program. It is impossible for someone to learn how to configure every possible system, so by using W/EPS systems learners can find the resources they need to configure whatever is needed at the time.

Role of the Instructor in W/EPS Systems

The role of the instructor depends on what is discovered during the needs assessment and planned during design phases. Like the design teams that create system feedback and interactions in Web/computer-based training, the W/EPS design teams create systems that act as the instructor. Figure 6.5 lists the four key tasks that the design team performs.

Figure 6.5. Roles of Instructor in W/EPS Systems

☑ Identifying content

☑ Organizing and integrating content

☑ Choosing the environment

☑ Selecting media

Identifying Content. During the needs-assessment phase, the design team must identify the skills and knowledge needed to solve problems in a just-in-time learning environment. Then, the team develops the content from sources such as engineering specifications, user manuals, pre-release training kits, "bug" logs, third-party documents, ISO standards, or technical reviews.

Organizing and Integrating Content. Next, the materials from these diverse sources must be organized and integrated. The team sequences content according to themes such as audience or task. For example, a software troubleshooting program could be organized by level of user (novice, intermediate, expert) or by task or function (print, copy, and import). Because information from diverse sources will vary in quality, ease of use, and format, the team must integrate and edit it.

Choosing the Environment. The team also designs programs that use communication tools to meet the needs of learners. They develop forums, listservs, and notes conferences that allow learners to collaborate and build their own databases. Programs are designed for the environments from which the learners will log on to the system. Designers pay attention to the needs of those with slow modems or quiet workplaces.

Designers also create documents in both Web-viewable and printable format. Web-viewable documents take advantage of hyperlinks to enable documents to be viewed from a single screen, eliminating scrolling. Printable documents are in a single file, rather than in multiple HTML files.

Selecting Media. Media that enhances the message must be chosen. Materials designed specifically for W/EPS systems show learners how to do a task. Video or sound may be required. After selecting the right type of media (graphics, video, animation, or audio), consider technical factors such as bandwidth, disk space, and ease of updating. For example, learners could be taught to remove the back panel of a mainframe with a full-motion video that was detailed and realistic, but it would require a great deal of network bandwidth. To reach a broader audience more quickly, a simplified diagram that highlights how to align the hex-bolts might work better.

Roles of Learners

In W/EPS systems, the learners are responsible for all aspects of their learning (see Figure 6.6). This is the most self-directed type of Web-based training.

Figure 6.6. Roles of Learners in W/EPS Systems

☑ Choosing when to learn

☑ Managing and directing learning

☑ Selecting a mix of resources

☑ Participating in collaborative learning

Choosing When To Learn. In training by Web-based electronic performance support systems, learners do not study modules in anticipation of needing the knowledge or skills. Instead, they log on just-in-time, when needed and not before. Learners also choose whether or not to complete a module.

Managing and Directing Learning. Web/EPS programs include materials such as how-to modules, instructional videos, and reference manuals. Learners are responsible for selecting, sequencing, and completing material. Some learners may want to skim instructional modules and skip exercises and are free to do so because they are responsible for their own learning.

Selecting a Mix of Resources. Learners are free to choose the mixture of resources. A robust W/EPS system offers multiple formats. For example, a lesson on installing a new hard drive may have several options: access an online manual, look at a diagram, or watch a video clip. The learner not only chooses what information to access, but he or she also chooses the format. Learners are not expected to complete entire modules, lessons, or units, but to access the resources when and where they need them.

Participating in Collaborative Learning. A layer of communication distinguishes Web/EPS systems from traditional EPS systems. Learners choose to participate in collaborative learning such as Internet Relay Chat (IRC), notes conferences, listservs, news groups, and forums to share their experiences with others.

A manager talks about how his company prepares learners to use W/EPS systems.

We are serious about EPS systems on the Web as a solution. Our service engineers come in for a two-day class to learn how to use the system. If they are going to do their jobs, they'd better know how to use it.

Table 6.2. Sample Interactions in W/EPS Systems

Goal	Level of Goal	Interaction
Talk a customer through setting up printer.	*Application:* Ability to apply abstract information in concrete situation.	Access and read user's manual online.
Determine why printer function is not working.	*Analysis:* Breaking an item into its constituent elements or parts.	Access online checklist of common causes for printer failure.
Solve customer complaint about a printer.	*Synthesis:* Putting together parts to form a whole.	Search "bug" database and post note to listserv.

W/EPS System Interactions

Interactions in the W/EPS system environment are not physically interactive or structured. They do not require drill and practice. They are cognitive. Table 6.2 shows the application, analysis, and synthesis required to troubleshoot a printer software problem. Learners read, reflect, then act. Further information on interactions for Web/EPS systems can be found in Chapter Seven.

Troubleshooting a printer problem using a W/EPS program can be an effective method for learning to resolve problems. The learner in Table 6.2 must determine why the printer is not working, which requires research and thought. He or she uses the Web/EPS system to search for solutions and then acts to correct the problem. After taking action, the learner reflects on its effectiveness and why it worked, then connects that learning to other knowledge and experience. If the solution fails, the learner identifies other solutions. Through a series of actions, reflection, and more action, he or she can devise solutions and solve problems.

Purpose of Instruction

The purpose of a Web/EPS system is to provide learners with practical knowledge and problem-solving skills in a just-in-time format. The goals are to develop intellectual abilities through application, analysis, and synthesis.

Use one of the popular search engines to locate samples of **W/EPS** systems. Search using the term **Electronic Performance Support Systems, EPS,** or **online job aid.** Use trial and error to find sites that offer **W/EPS systems.**

How is the information organized (level of user/task)? Are there various media? Are the resources well integrated? Does this site offer an opportunity to direct and manage one's own learning? What features do you like about the W/EPS sites? In what way would you improve them?

Create a bookmark in your browser program and name it W/EPS. Save the URLs for the examples you have located. These programs will be helpful for illustrating concepts to your team and clients.

Web-Based Virtual Asynchronous Classrooms

Web-based virtual asynchronous classroom (W/VAC) programs are best suited to teaching groups of learners to solve less structured problems that have no simple or clearly right or wrong answers. Topics involve guidelines, concepts, and processes that help learners deal with messy real-world complexity. In addition, they require the application of skills and knowledge to problems that differs greatly from case to case. Some examples are designing an effective Website, writing a marketing plan, and developing a Java applet. They require learners to apply complex concepts such as demographic analysis, graphic design, and programming—solutions that vary from situation to situation. Web/virtual asynchronous classroom programs are also distinguished by the fact that the facilitator guides the instruction and the importance of group learning.

Roles of Instructor in W/VAC

The instructor in a W/VAC program has five responsibilities (see Figure 6.7) that are similar to those found in W/CBT and W/EPS systems.

Facilitating Learning. The instructor is responsible for facilitating group and individual learning, to create a safe and respectful environment. Learners should be

---

Figure 6.7. Roles of Instructor in W/VAC

☑ Facilitating learning

☑ Guiding instruction

☑ Providing resources

☑ Evaluating outcomes

☑ Communicating with learners

---

asked to send an e-mail message and to post a note to an online conference; this gives them practice and confidence for using the tools. The instructor should also demonstrate that learners' experiences are valued. Exercises that ask learners to introduce themselves and to talk about their experiences with the topic demonstrate that learners' experiences are valued. For example, learners' negative experiences using online help can be used to begin a discussion. In W/VAC environment, setting the tone for the group by using good "netiquette" such as proper greetings, signatures, and diplomatic and courteous responses is important. (See Appendix E, Netiquette.)

Guiding Instruction. The instructor provides a flexible outline and clear goals to guide the instruction. He or she encourages learners to direct and manage their own learning by refining the outline and helping to establish objectives. The instructor's role is to help learners recognize gaps in their knowledge and motivate them to explore related topics.

Providing Resources. Facilitating a virtual asynchronous class requires that both online and off-line resources be available for learners. It is helpful to draw on resources beyond those online. For example, managers learning to write a marketing plan may want to talk to engineers, industry analysts, and customers. Because the problems are complex, a mixture of resources beyond the Web may be required. The instructor should encourage learners to tap the experience and knowledge of experts, practitioners, and other learners, for example, by assigning learners to use e-mail to contact subject-matter experts. W/VAC programs may include listservs that provide opportunities to participate in worldwide dialogues and books, magazines, and newspapers.

Evaluating Outcomes. The instructor evaluates the outcomes of exercises, dialogues, and interactions. In addition, the instructor prepares learners to evaluate their own work. Learners submit assignments via e-mail, and the instructor responds with corrections or comments in a timely fashion. Monitoring the course listserv, suggesting new themes, and recommending new ways to approach a topic can be the responsibility of the instructor. If quizzes and multiple-choice tests are corrected using a software program, the instructor looks at item-analysis data to identify areas in which the class had difficulty. Test data also can be used to identify individuals who are having problems or not keeping up with assignments. The instructor provides tools such as self-scoring quizzes and reflection exercises to enable learners to assess their own progress.

Communicating with Learners. W/VAC programs provide communication tools to help learners share their experiences, ask questions, and engage in conversations with peers. Instructors should develop assignments that invite learners to share relevant experiences from work or home. Other assignments could include group projects that require learners to develop solutions, test them, and reflect on the outcomes.

Thus, the instructor has a range of tools to help learners to see problems from new perspectives. For example, an instructor teaching learners to write a marketing plan may suggest that they visit the Websites of potential competitors, read the archived notes posted to a listserv that serves the industry in which they plan to market their product, review a "zine" (online magazine) that addresses market issues, and examine data from the U.S. Department of Commerce. In addition, instructors can sponsor listservs and forums to showcase noteworthy learner work.

A training manager describes an innovative strategy to provide responsive facilitation for a W/VAC program.

We wanted to provide a very responsive environment for learners from around the world so they could take the class and know that no matter what time zone they lived in an instructor would respond to them in eight hours or less. For this course, we rotated the instructor's responsibility around the globe to be sure that there was always someone watching and waiting to respond to students twenty-four hours a day. This provided consistent response times.

Roles of Learners

In W/VAC programs, the learner is an active individual learner and group participant. The learner takes on the roles outlined in Figure 6.8.

Figure 6.8. Roles of Learners in W/VAC

☑ Managing and directing learning
☑ Participating in group learning
☑ Communicating with instructor and peers
☑ Reflecting on experience

Managing and Directing Learning. In W/VAC programs, learners should partici-pate in setting the agenda, defining the objectives, and assessing outcomes. The learners set expectations for the course and play a role in defining measurable out-comes to determine when course goals have been achieved.

Participating in Group Learning. Learners are assigned to groups that are small enough to allow each person to have an active role in group projects and to learn from personal experience as well as from the experiences of others. For example, a group project that requires learners to develop a customer survey would require learners to draw on their experiences, apply new information, and collaborate with group members. Projects that can easily be divided into neat sections and assem-bled at the end of the semester for submission as a group project should be avoided. They do not promote group learning.

Communicating with Instructor and Peers. Learners are encouraged to use all the communication channels available. To gain confidence with the tools, learners should start by sending e-mail messages to the group and to individuals. Later, learners should be introduced to listservs, e-mail, and forums. As learners master each new communication tool, they will understand its unique strengths and ap-plications. In addition to technical competence, learners should be encouraged to develop group norms and to build a safe environment for communication, indi-cated by prompt and tactful replies. Learners should be encouraged to present dis-senting opinion without attacking or ridiculing one another.

Reflecting on Experience. It is essential that learners reflect on what they have learned because the lessons are less structured than with other methods of Web-based learning and lessons often deal with messy real-world issues. Less-structured prob-lems and topics require analysis, synthesis, and evaluation and have no simple right or wrong answers. For example, learners enrolled in a course to learn how to design nonmonetary incentives have to deal with complex variables such as corporate culture, employee receptiveness, management support, and labor regulations. Learners should be asked to reflect on various solutions and how their application can differ from situation to situation. Learners should also be challenged to look at solutions from a new perspective, perhaps keeping an online journal and critiquing one another's work.

W/VAC Interactions

Interactions in W/VAC programs are unique in that they are designed for non-contiguous group learning. Learners are not working in isolation completing drill and practice exercises as in W/CBT, nor are they learning a skill to address an immediate need as in W/EPSS.

Purpose of Instruction

The purpose of W/VAC programs is to provide group learning that does not require learners or the instructor to be online at the same time. The goal of W/VAC programs is to develop application, analysis, synthesis, and evaluation skills. These abilities are well suited to delivery over the Web. Table 6.3 shows the relationships among goals, levels of cognitive skill, and types of interactions for W/VAC programs for home page design class.

Interactions in the W/VAC environment should take advantage of the Web's communication tools and the asynchronous nature of the environment. Like the range of tools available for Web/computer-based training, a range of tools is available for W/VAC programs, ranging from stand-alone tools to complex bundled packages.

Simple stand-alone tools perform a single function, such as providing e-mail, hosting a notes file, or managing a listserv. For each kind of tool, there are many commercial vendors. The tools in each category are distinguished by what they can do, how much they cost, and what kind of computer infrastructure is required to use them.

Complex bundled packages bring together the stand-alone elements such as listservs, forums, and e-mail. Packages such as Lotus' Learning Space® or WBT System's TopClass® use a single interface that brings together functions such as an e-mail address book for the class, access to a forum, and tracking information about learner status. Too many stand-alone and bundled packaged exist to mention here; these tools are continually changing to provide more functionality. The best place to learn about these tools is in current editions of the journals listed in the bibliography (see also Appendix A).

Table 6.3. Sample Tasks and Interactions in W/VAC

Goal	Level of goal	Interaction
Ask groups to design a home page.	*Application:* Ability to apply abstract information.	Collaborate on design of a home page.
Ask groups to analyze the sites listed on Netscape's "cool pick" list and identify the elements that make these sites "cool."	*Analysis:* Breaking an item into its constituent elements or parts.	Participate in discussion on listserv.
Ask individuals to incorporate some of the elements they identified as "cool" into their home pages.	*Synthesis:* Putting together elements and parts to form a whole.	View and critique one another's home pages and post a review to a notes file.
Ask each group to develop criteria for identifying effective sites.	*Evaluation:* Judgments about the value of materials or methods.	Send instructor e-mail with the criteria.

Web/virtual asynchronous classroom programs are a wonderful medium for promoting diverse viewpoints; exploring alternative ways of looking at problems; and teaching higher-level skills such as analysis, synthesis, and evaluation. In addition, the asynchronous nature of the medium should not be overlooked. The ability to think about problems and respond when one is ready, as opposed to when class is scheduled, encourages reflection.

On the World Wide Web, use a search engine to locate samples of W/VAC programs. Search using terms such as online learning, virtual classroom, and distance education to locate sites. Use trial and error to find sites that offer W/VAC.

What kind of group activities are planned? What kind of collaborative learning activities are used? Has a safe environment been established for presenting dissenting views? Are learners asked to reflect on their experiences? How could you improve on a site you have visited?

Create a bookmark in your browser program and call it W/VAC.
Save the URLs for the examples of W/VAC programs you have located.

Web-Based Virtual Synchronous Classrooms

Web-based virtual synchronous classroom (W/VSC) programs are best suited to group learning in a real-time environment. Like W/VAC programs, W/VSC programs are best suited for ill-structured problems. The live interactive environment and the rich communication tools enable learners to solve complex, messy, real-world problems. For example, a W/VSC program can teach teams of sales representatives how to conduct a financial analysis of potential clients or how to prepare a sales strategy. In these examples, there are no clearly right or wrong answers, but rather unique applications of skills of analysis, synthesis, and evaluation to the problems.

Roles of the Instructor

The instructor in a W/VSC program recommends a direction to the learners and may offer resources. The role of the instructor can be directive, as in W/VAC programs, or dynamic and collaborative, as in a symposium. Figure 6.9 outlines the responsibilities of the instructor in this collaborative environment.

Facilitating Learning. The instructor is responsible for facilitating both group and individual learning, and creating a safe and respectful environment. Because the instructor and learners are online in real time, creating a safe environment and correcting learners requires both technical and diplomatic skills. For example, if a

Figure 6.9. Roles of Instructor in W/VSC

☑ Facilitating learning

☑ Guiding instruction

☑ Providing resources

☑ Evaluating outcomes

☑ Managing live communication

learner is participating in an interactive relay chat room (a real-time dialogue conducted by typing back and forth) and is dominating the conversation or using language that is offensive, the instructor should intervene. What the instructor does is dependent on his or her diplomatic skills and/or the technical options available in the Internet reply chat program. In this case, the instructor could ask the learner to consider the impact his or her language might have on others. If the chat program were sophisticated enough to allow a moderator to control access privileges, the instructor could limit that learner's ability to participate in the chat session.

Guiding Instruction. A second role for the W/VSC instructor is guiding instruction. This role can range from directive to dynamic. In a directive environment, the instructor can create a detailed outline defining how the live, online time will be spent in five-minute increments. In a directive role, the instructor devises case studies, exercises, brainstorming activities, and lectures. The instructor is expected to know more about the topic than the learners.

In a dynamic environment, the role of the instructor is to act as a symposium leader, not directing the learning of the group but facilitating the process by drawing out the expertise of the participants. The instructor acts as a co-learner and allows the learners to guide the program. This is unique to the W/VSC environment, as learners can switch between receiving knowledge and providing knowledge. For example, in a W/VSC program using application sharing, a learner can take control and demonstrate to the class how to create a mail merge.

Providing Resources. The instructor also provides learners with relevant resources. Like the W/VAC instructor, this instructor can provide learners with access to pertinent Websites and online articles. Because Web/virtual synchronous classrooms can include live audio and video, the instructor can invite guest speakers to field questions or participate in debates.

Evaluating Outcomes. The evaluation of outcomes in W/VSC programs can take many forms. If the class is run in a directive manner, the instructor may evaluate exercises, dialogues, and interactions. In a symposium-like environment, the learners may take responsibility for evaluating their own work, in which case the instructor's evaluation is weighted the same as that of other learners.

Managing Communication. Managing communication is an especially important role because communication is limited to the time that the instructor and learners are online together. The instructor is responsible for providing all learners with an opportunity to ask questions and present their opinions. He or she must manage learners who dominate the conversation and draw out those who may be reluctant to participate.

Roles of Learners

In W/VSC programs, the learner is an active participant in a real-time class. The learners' responsibilities are shown in Figure 6.10.

Managing and Directing Learning. This is the primary role of the learner in W/VSC programs. The degree to which learners take on that role depends on the nature of the program. If it is led by an instructor, the learners will have little input into the goals, objectives, resources, and evaluation. If it is conducted like a symposium in which the learners and the instructor are equals, the learners will have more influence and may choose the order in which topics are presented, select topics for their group projects, and request in-depth information on selected subjects. If the class is run by the learners, they take total responsibility for the program, perhaps even revisiting the goals.

In W/VSC programs learners must actively participate. They are responsible for logging in on time and for staying until the end of the program. They are also expected to engage in group activities such as case studies and discussions. If a synchronous program involves answering questions, all learners are expected to participate.

Like W/VAC programs, W/VSC programs deal with ill-structured topics— messy, real-world topics that do not have simple answers. Because W/VSC programs take place in real time, it is important that learners listen to what others have to say. After the program learners should take time to reflect on the experience and consider alternative solutions and question their assumptions.

Figure 6.10. Roles of Learners in W/VSC

☑ Managing and directing learning

☑ Participating in group learning

☑ Reflecting on experience

W/VSC Interactions

Interactions in W/VSC programs are unique because they take place in real time. The logistics involved are challenging and often requires some participants to be up early or stay up late. Interactions should be well organized and carefully planned. Further information on interaction for W/VSC programs can be found in Chapter eight.

Purpose of Instruction

The purpose of W/VSC programs is to bring learners and the instructor together to participate in a collaborative learning experience. The goals of W/VSC programs are to develop intellectual abilities, characterized as analysis, synthesis, and evaluation. Table 6.4 shows the relationships among goals, levels of cognitive skill, and types of interactions in a financial context.

Use W/VSC programs to generate new ideas, make plans, and develop products. Ill-structured problems are ideal topics for this environment because they do not have readily available answers. For example, a program designed to teach financial planners about a change in the tax code, and how to help clients adjust their portfolios to avoid tax penalties, is an opportunity to generate new ideas. Financial planning and tax avoidance is a messy, real-world problem that requires solutions that differ from situation to situation. Learners in this example can take advantage of online conversations and the ability to share spreadsheet applications and white boards.

Table 6.4. Tasks and Interactions in W/VSC

Goal	Level of Goal	Interaction
Review the client's annual report and financial statement.	*Analysis:* Breaking an item into its constituent elements or parts.	Application sharing
Create sales strategy based on client's financial data, market trends, and past buying patterns.	*Synthesis:* Putting together elements to form a whole.	Web-based video-conferencing
Assess the strengths and weakness of various sales strategies.	*Evaluation:* Judgments about the value of materials or methods for a given purpose.	Web-based audio graphics

On the World Wide Web, use a search engine to locate samples of Web/virtual synchronous classrooms. Search using terms such as video-conferencing, distance education, synchronous learning environment, and real-time learning. Use trial and error to find sites that offer Web/virtual synchronous classrooms.

Create a bookmark in your browser program and name it W/VSC. Save the URLs for the examples you have located. Use them as a resource for the design team and the client. Think of your bookmarks as a high-tech scrapbook.

Summary

Designing Web-based training programs requires developers to consider many factors. The easiest to evaluate are practical considerations such as the need to repurpose existing course materials, the limitations imposed by financial considerations, and the boundaries created by the technical infrastructure. These factors are relatively easy to identify and plan for.

The more challenging factors to consider are the learning outcomes, roles of instructors and learners, and types of interactions available in Web-based training. Table 6.5 presents six levels of cognitive skills and abilities. The lower levels—knowledge, comprehension, and application—have clear right and wrong answers and observable outcomes. The higher levels—analysis, synthesis, and evaluation—deal with complicated problems that require unique solutions.

After the program's goal has been defined and the level(s) of cognitive skills and abilities established, it is time to consider the training options. Each type of Web-based training has specific benefits and limitations.

Web/computer-based training is well suited for teaching lower-level cognitive skills to individual learners. The topics best suited for this environment are structured and can be taught using drill and practice, simulations, reading, and questioning and answering. Skills and abilities related to knowledge, comprehension,

Table 6.5. Cognitive Skills and Abilities Required by Type of WBT				
	Web/CBT	**Web/EPS Systems**	**Web/VAC**	**Web/VSC**
Level of Skill	*Individual Learning*		*Group Learning*	
Knowledge	X			
Comprehension *Structured*	X			
Application	X	X		
Analysis		X	X	X
Synthesis *Ill-Structured*		X	X	X
Evaluation		X	X	X

and application that do not benefit from learning as part of a group or require that learning take place in real-time are best.

Web/EPS systems are well suited for teaching higher-level intellectual skills. In this environment, just-in-time learning allows learners working alone to solve unique problems that vary from situation to situation. This environment requires design options such as problem solving and experiential methods.

Web/VAC programs are well suited for teaching groups high-level intellectual skills. The problems and topics best suited to this environment are ill structured and benefit from being taught through group learning tools such as listservs, e-mail, and forums. This environment offers the advantage of exploring multiple right answers, examining alternative perspectives, and drawing on the experience of others.

Web/VSC programs are also well suited for teaching groups of learners high-level intellectual skills for solving ill-structured and messy, real-world problems. Learners in this environment work together in real-time to solve problems and create new knowledge. It is an excellent environment for drawing on the knowledge and experience of learners scattered around the country.

Each type of Web-based training has been presented as separate and distinct. In realty, there are many variations of these approaches, and different approaches can be used in combination. The mixture of interactions available distinguishes each kind of Web-based training. Chapter Seven provides an overview of the interactions available for Web/computer-based training, Web/EPS systems, and Web/VAC programs. Chapter Eight explores the interactions available for the Web/virtual synchronous classroom.

Suggested Readings

Akers, R. (1997). Web discussion forums in teaching and learning. URL: *http://sunsite.unc.edu/horizon/mono/DC/TECH-HTML/Akers.html*

Compton, C. (1997). Interactivity on the Web. URL: *http://www.nmis.org/AboutNMIS/Pape. . .teractive_web/interactiveweb.html*

Eastmond, D. V. (1995). *Alone but together: Adult distance study through computer conferencing.* Cresskill, NJ: Hampton Press.

Guzdial, M., Kolodner, J., Hmelo, C., Narayanan, H., Carlson, D., Rappin, N., Hubscher, R., Turns, J., & Newsletter, W. (1996). Computer support for learning through complex problem solving. *Communications of the ACM, 39*(1), 43–45.

Reeves, T. C., & Reeves, P. M. (1997). Effective dimensions of interactive learning on the World Wide Web. In B. Kahn (Ed). *Web-based instruction.* Englewood Cliffs, NJ: Educational Technology Publications.

Schwier, R. A., & Misanchuk, E. R. (1997, February). *Designing multimedia for the hypertext markup language.* Paper presented at the annual meeting of the Association for Educational Communications and Technology, Indianapolis, IN.

Soulier, S. J. (1988). *The design and development of computer-based instruction.* Boston: Allyn and Bacon.

Wagner, E. D., & McCombs, B. L. (1995). Learner-centered psychological principles in practice: Designs for distance education. *Educational Technology, 35*(1), 32–35.

Zane, L. B. (1995). Facilitating computer conferencing: Recommendations from the field. *Educational Technology, 35*(1), 22–30.

Chapter 7

Asynchronous Interactions

What You Will Learn in This Chapter

After completing this chapter, you will be able to

- Distinguish among different types of interactivity;
- List examples of asynchronous interactions; and
- Design asynchronous assessments, tests, and quizzes.

Defining Interactivity

Interactivity, as applied to Web-based training, is still an evolving concept. There are as many definitions as there are authors, as shown in Figure 7.1.

Given the variety of definitions, it is more useful for our purposes to identify the hallmarks of an interactive training program. Traditional interactive classroom programs and Web-based training programs have the ability to:

- Encourage reflection;
- Provide control;
- Direct attention; and
- Add dimension to content.

Figure 7.1. Definitions of Interactivity

- [the ability] to create a totally immersive experience (Mok, 1996, p. 127)
- [the ability] to interact with words, numbers, and pictures (Kristof & Satran, 1995, p. 1)
- the capability to access and manipulate text, sound, and images (Ambron & Hooper, 1988, p. xi)
- a reciprocal interchange between the learner and the instructional medium (Reynolds & Iwinski, 1996, p. 581)
- an instructional program which includes a variety of integrated sources in the instruction with a computer at the heart of the system (Schwier & Misanchuk, 1993, p. 6)
- a design concept involving a true exchange of information between user and program (Gayeski, 1995, pp. 2–4)

Encourage Reflection. Traditional classroom programs encourage reflection by asking students to keep journals, critique the work of others, and consider alternative solutions. Web-based training programs can encourage learners to reflect on their experiences and question their assumptions. Plan a brainstorming session that requires learners to consider a wide range of solutions to a problem. Encourage learners to draw on their life experiences and not discount any possible solutions. Such interactions with course content and peers can create meaningful adult-learning experiences.

Provide Control. In traditional computer-based and classroom programs, learners have varying degrees of control. In simple CBT programs, learners may control the order in which they study the lessons. In traditional classroom programs, learners may control or influence the topics to be covered and how the class will be evaluated. Web-based training programs can offer learners a range of opportunities to control the learning experience. Develop interactions that enable learners to control the path, rate, and depth of content.

Direct Attention. Traditional classroom programs direct attention and motivate learners by making content relevant and meaningful. This strategy is also pertinent for Web-based training, but the tools available to the instructor are different. Create interactive programs that engage learners in topics that are important to them. Develop programs that are learner-centered rather than content-centered. (Also see Chapter Two, Principles of Adult Education, for further suggestions.) Use tools such as e-mail, Internet relay chat rooms, listservs, and forums to tailor programs to learners' interests.

Add Dimension. In traditional classrooms, instructors add dimension to the topic by showing videos, inviting guest speakers, or taking field trips. The Web offers a range of tools to assist the instructor. Give learners opportunities to interact with multiple forms of media and to develop new perspectives.

Types of Interactions

Interactions make learning active rather than passive, and they provide learners and the instructor with feedback. It is important to develop a variety of interactions. Moore and Kearsley (1996) describe three kinds of interaction found in distance-education programs: learner-content interaction, learner-instructor interaction, and learner-learner interaction. Table 7.1 shows which types are associated with the various WBT methods.

All forms of Web-based training feature learner-content interactions, in which the learner is presented with material to study. This can be as simple as text to read, a video to watch, or a lecture.

Learner-learner interactions are communications among learners working asynchronously, as in W/EPS systems and W/VAC programs, or as part of a real-time group in W/VAC programs. The interactions can be as simple as e-mail messages, postings to online forums, or as complex as real-time audio-based conversations. Web/computer-based training does not use learner-to-learner interactions.

Learner-instructor interactions can include feedback on assignments, responses to questions, quizzes, suggestions, encouragement, and motivation. How this is accomplished depends on the type of Web-based training. In Web/CBT, interactions are usually e-mail exchanges between instructor and individual learner. In W/VAC and W/VSC programs, the interactions can be between individual learner and instructor or among groups of learners and the instructor. There is no learner-instructor interaction in W/EPS programs because, as the

Table 7.1. Types of Interaction Associated with WBT Methods

	W/CBT	W/EPS	W/VAC	W/VSC
Learner with materials	X	X	X	X
Learner with learner		X	X	X
Learner with instructor	X		X	X

name suggests, it is an *electronic performance support system* designed to be used without an instructor.

Asynchronous Versus Synchronous Interactivity

It is important to remember that interactions can be synchronous or asynchronous. *Synchronous* interactions only happen in Web/VSC programs. They take place in real-time, when the learners and instructor are online at the same time having direct contact. In contrast, *asynchronous* interactions take place at the learners' and instructor's convenience. Table 7.2 shows a matrix of possible synchronous and asynchronous interactions.

Other multimedia products, such as graphics, video, animation, and sound, can add richness to programs, but they do not add interaction, as shown in Figure 7.2. Simple text, graphics, images, animation, video, and sound meet only some of the criteria for interactive learning. They attract attention, but they are passive. A clever animation sequence or colorful graphics attracts the learners' attention, but does not

Table 7.2. Tools for Synchronous and Asynchronous Interactions

	Web/CBT	Web/EPS	Web/VAC	Web/VSC
Asynchronous	X	X	X	
• E-mail				
• Listserv				
• Online forums/ threaded discussions/ notes files				
• Quizzes/tests				
• Hypertext/media				
Synchronous				X
• Internet relay chat				
• Real-time audio				
• Application sharing				
• Videoconferencing				
• Quizzes/polls				

Figure 7.2. Noninteractive Multimedia Products

☑ Simple text

☑ Graphics

☑ Images

☑ Animation

☑ Video

☑ Sound

engage them in making decisions or immerse them in the program. However, these elements do improve training programs when used in combination with asynchronous and synchronous interactions.

Asynchronous Options

An asynchronous interaction creates a reciprocal interchange between the learner and the instructional material, instructor, or other learners. Asynchronous interactions do not require the learners or instructor to be online at the same time.

Asynchronous interactions may result in both immediate and delayed feedback. Immediate feedback happens when programs automatically score quizzes or link documents. Learners may experience delay in learner-to-learner and learner-to-instructor feedback. These interactions require time for the instructor and other learners to respond to listserv, forum, and e-mail messages.

E-Mail

Electronic mail enables learners to send messages over the Internet or intranet. The advantages and disadvantages of e-mail as an option are outlined in Figure 7.3. Many learners are familiar with e-mail and need little instruction. Like a private conversation, e-mail is an excellent way for the instructor and learner to communicate. Conversations can also be shared with others, if desired. See Figure 7.4 for some of the various possibilities.

In more complex e-mail interactions, an expert can reply to a question and the response can be shared with the entire class. For example, a learner may have a question that only an expert can answer. The learner can send an e-mail to the appropriate

Figure 7.3. E-Mail Advantages and Disadvantages	
Advantages	**Disadvantages**
Familiar tool	Penalizes poor writers
Private one-on-one	Competes for attention with other e-mail
Two-way communication	
Allows time for reflection	

expert and copy his or her instructor (see Figure 7.5). The instructor can also see a learner's question and the expert's reply, realize the answer is important for all learners, and forward the reply to the entire class. Figure 7.6 shows the steps used in the process of sharing an expert's reply.

E-mail is an excellent tool for learners whose first language is not English because they can take whatever time they need to read and comprehend e-mail exchanges. E-mail does have two major disadvantages. First, learners must possess strong writing skills. Those who lack grammatical skill, spell badly, or cannot express themselves in writing are at a disadvantage. Exchanges can be rambling and hard to understand. Second, e-mail messages can be lost among learners' other e-mail

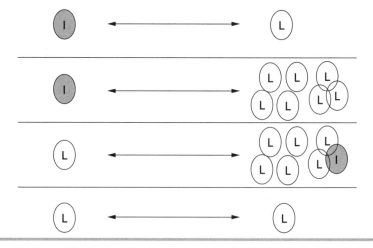

Figure 7.4. Possible E-Mail Interactions Between Instructor (I) and Learner (L)

Figure 7.5. Examples of E-Mail Interactions with Experts

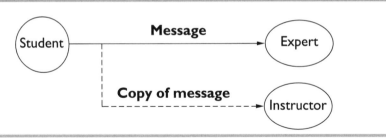

correspondence from work, family, and interest groups. E-mail messages related to class can stack up or, worse, be stored and forgotten.

To address this issue, let learners know that e-mail should be used for items that require immediate attention or response. Establish expectations about how e-mail should be used in the training program. See the checklist in Figure 7.7 for some guidelines.

Spelling and Grammar. E-mail is often used as a quick, informal communication tool. If learners are responsible for using it in a more formal way, let them know that grammar and spelling are important.

Figure 7.6. Examples of E-Mail Interactions

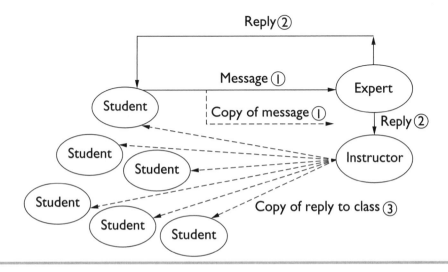

Figure 7.7. Checklist for E-Mail Usage

☑ Spelling and grammar

☑ Response times

☑ "Netiquette" rules

☑ Message length

☑ Type of interaction

☑ Type of document

Response Times. Set realistic expectations regarding how quickly e-mail messages will be answered. If instructors are traveling or teaching a traditional class, they may take several days to respond.

Netiquette Rules. Good manners on the Internet are not intuitive. Suggest that learners become familiar with netiquette (see Appendix F).

Message Length. Provide guidance regarding the length of messages and the kinds of information or questions that are appropriate for e-mail. Long e-mail messages are better posted to online bulletin boards or put into a directory and downloaded with file transfer protocol (FTP), which allows users to copy files to and from directories, and to work around file size restrictions imposed by some e-mail systems.

Type of Interaction. Complicated questions can be sent to a subject-matter expert. Questions that require a broader response can be posted to members of a listserv. Questions that do not require an immediate answer or questions of general interest should be posted to an online forum.

Type of Document. E-mail can include more than text. Learners can e-mail sound, video, animation, and graphics files as an attachment to their message (Figure 7.8). Such attachments offer perspectives not possible with words alone. Establish the kinds of files that are readable by the class, and be sensitive to the impact large files have on disk space and download times.

Figure 7.8. Sample E-Mail Attachment

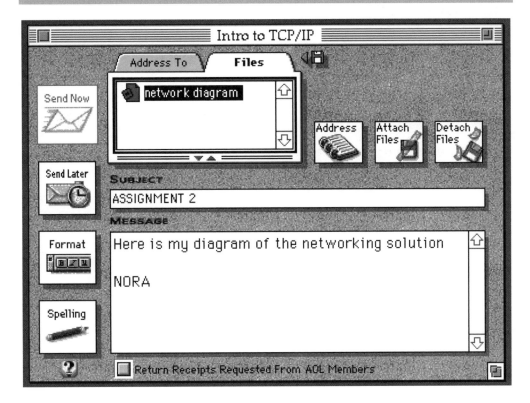

PURPOSE: *This exercise provides you with an opportunity to reflect on how e-mail is being used in the workplace.*

Complete the *E-Mail Worksheet* and think about the data you have collected. Draw some conclusions about the benefits and limitations of e-mail as a tool for interaction in Web-based training.

✓ E-Mail Worksheet

Directions: Enlist five to seven people who use e-mail at work. Ask each person the four questions below. Fill in their answers, then decide your own answer to the last question.

Questions

1. **How many e-mail messages do you receive a day?**

2. **How often do you read your e-mail?**

3. **How much time do you spend reading e-mail each week?**

4. **How would you describe your ability to send, save, receive, and respond to e-mail?**

Reflecting on E-Mail as an Interactive Tool

If you designed a Web-based training program for the people you interviewed, would you include e-mail interactions? Why or why not?

Listservs

A listserv is a software product that manages e-mail among a group of people. Using a computer server, the listserv maintains the people's names and electronic mail addresses. Learners send messages addressed to the list; the server forwards the messages to all other members (see Figure 7.9). Different lists can be established for members who share particular interests. Listserv messages are usually simple text (see Figure 7.10). Messages can be forwarded to the learner as they are received by the server or sent in batches.

Listserv products share many of the advantages and disadvantages of e-mail, as shown in Figure 7.11. Like e-mail, listserv messages are sent directly to the learner's account. There is a small learning curve for students to become active listserv participants if they are familiar with e-mail. Listservs enable learners to choose the topics or threads of conversations that interest them and to ignore or delete those that are irrelevant. Learners who choose to have the listserv journal, that is, send messages in batches, can review an index of the topics and read selectively. Others may prefer to receive messages one at a time and read only those that interest them.

Like e-mail, listservs are best suited for learners with good writing skills. Participating in an ongoing dialogue requires strong grammatical, spelling, and composition skills. The volume of messages generated by some listservs and the poor quality of responses can tire learners.

Listservs can be difficult to manage. Messages related to a given topic can dribble in over days or weeks. Conversations can also become entwined; comments from one thread or topic can blend with another, causing confusion. It is

---

Figure 7.9. Listserv Model

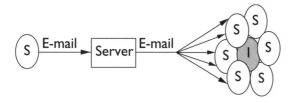

S = Students, I = Instructor

Figure 7.10. Simple Text Message from Listserv

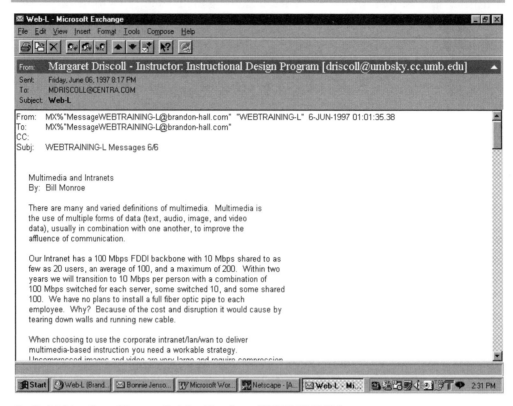

Credit: Multimedia and Internet Training Newsletter, WEBTRAINING-L.

Figure 7.11. Advantages and Disadvantages of Listserv

Advantages	**Disadvantages**
Messages sent directly to learners' e-mail accounts.	Penalizes poor writers.
Easy to participate with familiar tool.	Conversation threads become entwined.
Selectively follow conversations.	Quality and value of conversation varies.
Draws on experience of learners.	

also difficult to use the listserv as a resource if the messages are not archived or available in a central place.

The last issue is the quality and value of the conversation. Listservs can be moderated or not. Either can be problematic. Highly moderated listservs stifle dialogue because learners feel edited. Listservs that are not moderated can become dominated by a few learners or fall into disuse because no one is responsible for keeping the conversation moving or on track.

Use the interactive qualities of a listserv to create an ongoing conversation and to provide a means for learners to ask questions of one another. Many instructional design decisions must be made when using a listserv to add interactivity to a Web-based training program. Figure 7.12 provides a checklist for some of them.

Establish Norms and Standards. First, establish norms for what kinds of communication belong on the listserv versus private e-mail. For example, if learners want to discuss actual situations for a class, they should not use names or provide details that would make it possible to identify the parties involved. Detailed questions regarding specific cases should be limited to e-mail with the instructor or subject-matter expert.

Determine Whether To Moderate. Weigh the benefits and risks of a moderated listserv. Remember that you need not be the moderator; a learner or group of learners can be assigned the task.

Determine Who Will Be Included. Membership in the listserv can be limited to the class members or can include others in the organization who could add value.

Decide Whether To Participate in a Public Listserv. Relevant external listservs can be used to give learners an opportunity to interact with outside experts. This

---

Figure 7.12. Checklist for Effective Listserv Usage

☑ Establish norms and standards.

☑ Determine whether to moderate.

☑ Determine who will be included.

☑ Decide whether to participate in a public listserv.

☑ Decide whether to maintain after the class.

has the added benefit of providing a resource for dialogue and interaction after the class has ended.

Determine Whether To Maintain Listserv After the Class. If the information or topic is proprietary, an internal listserv can be maintained after the class has ended.

Figure 7.13 shows an internal listserv that has external membership. An internal listserv was created for learners to ask questions and share information. In addition, the membership of this listserv is open to all salespeople in the company. Salespeople working from their homes, as well as those in regional offices, benefit from the nationwide sharing of experience, skills, and dialogue.

Figure 7.14 shows the use of an external listserv. In this case, newly hired customer-service representatives taking a Web-based training course to learn to troubleshoot the company's new software product join a public listserv run by the customer (C) Users' Group. The Users' Group is an organization run by customers who want an outlet to share information, problems, solutions, and ideas. The listserv provides real problems for learners to solve during class and insights into issues customers find most frustrating.

Figure 7.13. Example of Shared Internal Listserv

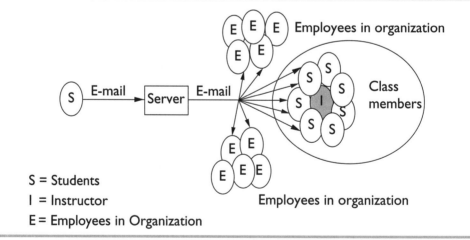

S = Students

I = Instructor

E = Employees in Organization

Figure 7.14. Example of Shared External Listserv

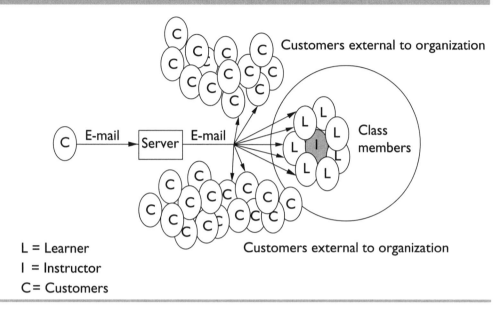

L = Learner
I = Instructor
C = Customers

PURPOSE: *This exercise is designed to help you reflect on your experience as a member of a listserv.*

Join a listserv devoted to training and development. Experience interactivity and dialogue with professionals interested in training.

Fill out the Listserv Reflection Worksheet about your experience.

Listserv Reflection Worksheet

Directions: Subscribe to Training and Development by sending an e-mail as follows:

To: *Subscribe LISTSERV@PSUVM.PSU.EDU*
Subject: Leave the subject line empty

In the body of the e-mail include the following:

SUBSCRIBE TRDEV-L (your name here)

After using the listserv for about three weeks, answer the following questions. Make note of specific examples.

Questions for Reflection

1. **Did you post or respond to messages? If not, why not? If yes, did you feel that your opinions were welcomed and valued?**

2. **Did you find the dialogue, questions, and comments informative? If not, explain. If yes, what kinds of messages were most interesting? In what way?**

3. **Was reading and responding to the TRDEV-L listserv convenient? If not, what made it difficult or inconvenient? If yes, what made it convenient?**

Online Forums, Notes Files, and Threaded Discussions

An online forum is a computer service where people can post messages, share solutions, ask questions, debate ideas, and read about topics of interest. Online forums are also referred to as notes files, notes conferences, threaded discussions, bulletin boards, news groups, computer conferences, and e-forums. Figure 7.15 is an example of a forum that allows learners to open a topic for discussion, called a "thread." Other readers can post responses to the threads or start new threads if appropriate.

Online forums, notes files, notes conferences, threaded discussions, bulletin boards, news groups, computer conferences, and e-forums technically refer to distinct kinds of computer-mediated communication. A blurring of the technical distinctions

Figure 7.15. Example of Online Forum

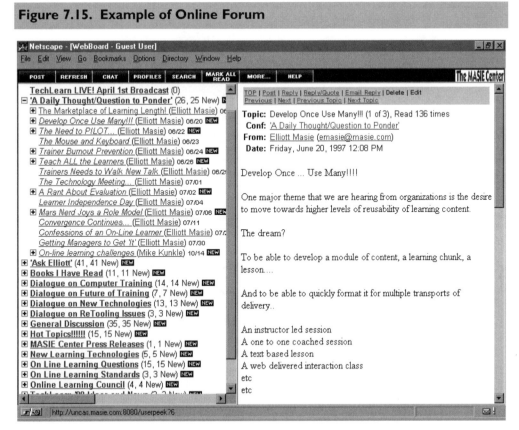

Credit: The Masie Center.

among them and common misuse of the terms has resulted in the terms being used interchangeably. Unlike e-mail and listservs, which deliver messages directly to the users' accounts, forum products require learners to log on to the forum. Figure 7.16 illustrates how learners connect to forums, notes files, and threaded discussions.

Forums do share many characteristics with e-mail and listservs. Before designing a program that uses a forum or threaded discussion, examine the advantages and disadvantages listed in Figure 7.17.

Forum posting can be read at the learners' convenience. Long documents and large graphic files can be posted to a forum and downloaded later. Selectively downloading information saves time and disk space. Because the conversation threads remain on the forum, learners can easily follow a conversation, engage in dialogue, and post replies at any time.

Figure 7.16. Model of Forum Connection

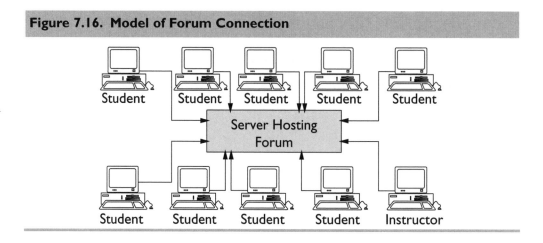

Figure 7.17. Advantages and Disadvantages of Using Forums

Advantages	Disadvantages
Long postings and large files do not take up disk space.	Penalizes poor writers.
	Learners must take the initiative.
Nonintrusive.	Requires that learners learn to use
Encourages dialogue.	forum tools.
Saves history of the conversation.	

Like e-mail and listserv tools, forum products require a certain level of writing ability. To benefit from reading one another's work, people must be able to communicate effectively. Forums also require a higher level of effort because learners must log in and identify new postings on a regular basis. The skills needed to participate are not difficult to learn, but may be unfamiliar to some learners.

To design effective forums, developers must understand the educational and logistical benefits and limitations of the technology. Figure 7.18 provides a checklist for designing effective forums.

Use Descriptive, Meaningful Titles. Ask learners to create titles that clearly describe the content. Meaningful subject lines help other readers determine if the posting is relevant.

Date Postings and Use a Dossier. Because postings are archived, it is important to date them and to create a document dossier that alerts other learners to the size and the kind of file that has been posted. For example, if learners are posting photos of themselves in a biographical forum, they should indicate that a large JPEG file is included. This alerts other learners to the possibility that the file will take time to open and what it contains.

Respect and Value Opposing Views. Create a respectful environment in which learners feel free to share ideas, present opposing views, and ask questions. Foster such an environment by making it acceptable to present dissenting views. Discourage the use of disparaging terms.

Figure 7.18. Checklist for Designing Effective Forums

☑ Use descriptive, meaningful titles.

☑ Date postings and use a dossier.

☑ Respect and value opposing views.

☑ Post notes only when they add to the discussion.

☑ Identify themes and patterns.

☑ Develop synthesis and evaluation skills.

Post Notes Only When They Add to the Discussion. Monitor class participation and encourage learners who are less forthcoming to post notes and to interact with others when they have something to add. Encourage meaningful participation by asking learners to answer specific questions, provide examples of how a process might be improved, list a relevant URL, or share an experience with a co-worker.

Identify Themes and Patterns. Recommend that learners analyze postings to identify themes, relationships, discrepancies, and patterns.

Develop Synthesis and Evaluation Skills. Plan assignments that help learners to synthesize and evaluate information they receive.

PURPOSE: *This exercise has been designed to help you reflect on the benefits and limitations of participating in a forum or threaded discussion.*

Choose a forum or threaded discussion or enter the URL shown below to join a forum related to EPSS.

http://www.epss.com

Use the worksheet that follows to reflect on the experience.

Forum, Notes Conference, and Threaded Discussion Worksheet

Directions: Locate a forum or threaded discussion of your choosing or enter the following URL: *http://www.epss.com*

Follow a conversation thread for several weeks, observe the interactions, assess the value of the dialogue, and evaluate the tone of the conversation. Make notes of specific examples of what you liked or did not like.

Questions for Reflection

1. **Did you post or respond to messages? If not, why not? If yes, did you feel that your opinions were welcome and valued?**

2. **Did you find the dialogue, questions, and comments informative? If not, explain. If yes, what kinds of messages were most interesting? In what way?**

3. **Was reading and responding to the forum or threaded discussion convenient? If not, what made it difficult or inconvenient? If yes, what made it convenient?**

Quizzes and Tests

Quizzes and tests are another type of asynchronous interaction. Online quizzes and tests enable the instructor and learners to assess progress or mastery of a topic. Design quizzes and tests that demonstrate respect for adult learners. Tests can make adults feel anxious and stressed. Show respect for learners, clearly explaining the purpose for testing. Explain that test scores are intended to help the learner assess progress and that they will not be shared with managers or that test scores are recorded anonymously and only class averages will be available to department heads.

In addition, provide feedback on tests quickly and make the feedback positive and respectful. Use automatic scoring mechanisms to furnish immediate scores and

Table 7.3. Types of Examinations in WBT

Format	Variation	Advantages	Disadvantages
True/False	Yes/No	Relatively easy to • construct • correct • administer	Guessing Not reliable indicator of depth of knowledge
Multiple choice	Fill in the blank Matching column Drag and drop	Relatively easy to • construct • correct • administer	Not reliable indicator of depth of knowledge Choices may be too close in meaning Difficult to write plausible choices
Essay	Short answer; Long answer	Relatively easy to • construct • administer Good indicator of depth of knowledge	Correction is subjective Penalizes weak writers Requires SME to correct
Application/ Job Task	InterConstructive	Measures job proficiency Good indicator of depth of knowledge	Time consuming to • construct • complete • correct

include a rationale of the test items that explains the right answers. Make feedback positive, identify the items learners scored high on and provide the correct answers for incorrect items. Avoid using sound effects such as buzzers or cheering crowds as feedback. Give learners an unlimited amount of time to complete the test, unless time is a factor in assessing competence.

Several test formats can be used to add interactivity to asynchronous Web-based training. Table 7.3 shows some of the test variations and the advantages and disadvantages of each.

True/False Questions

True/false and yes/no answers are best for testing simple recall, sequences, or patterns (see Figure 7.19). There are several advantages to using true/false in a WBT

Figure 7.19. Sample True/False Quiz

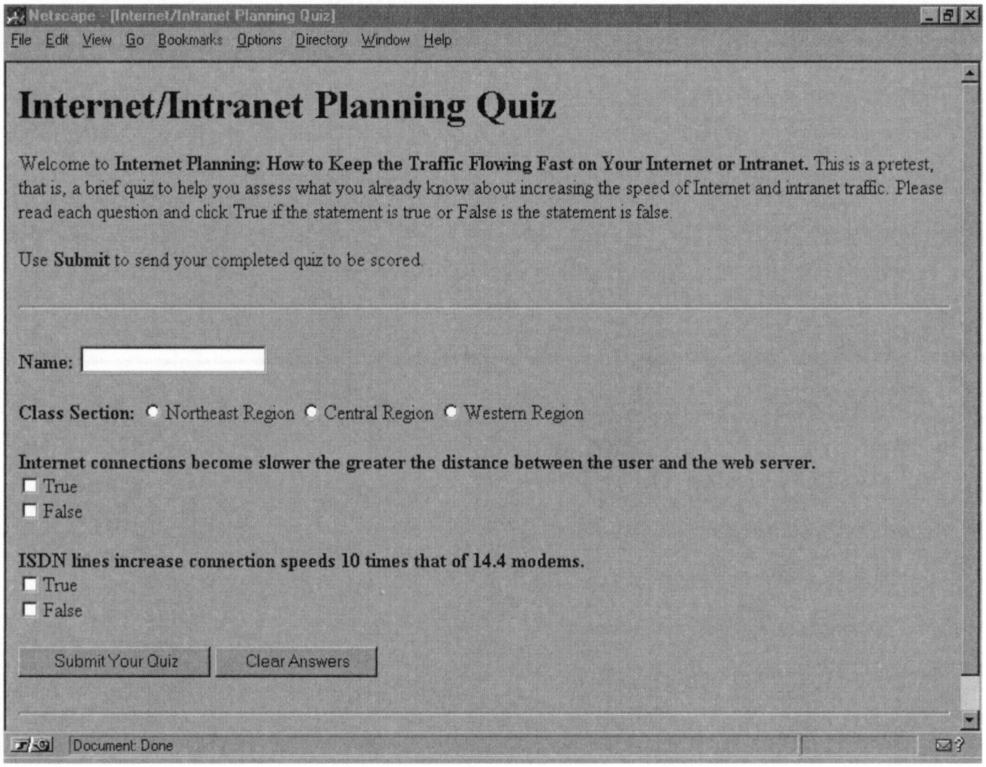

program. Questions are easy to develop; the answers can be scored by the system; and learners can receive immediate feedback on their performance. Learners can also obtain a detailed explanation of why an answer is right or wrong. In addition, learners understand how to take true/false tests, so the directions can be brief.

The same disadvantages that apply to the use of true/false tests in a classroom are relevant for their use in Web-based training. A learner can answer many questions right by guessing. The depth of knowledge that can be tested by true/false questions is limited. They should be reserved for testing recall of simple knowledge or for assessing knowledge and concepts. Figure 7.20 gives guidelines for developing true/false questions.

Provide Clear Directions. Explain how learners are to indicate true or false. Figure 7.19 shows a click box, but other variations could include typing the words, selecting a pull-down menu item, or turning on radio buttons.

Make Statements Simple. The statement (what learners are asked to evaluate as true or false) must be clear. Avoid asking multiple items, some of which are true and some not (see Figure 7.21).

Ask Questions in Logical Sequence. Ask questions in the order in which the content was presented in the lesson. Learners recall information better in a sequence similar to how it was learned.

Use Terminology from the Lesson. Use the same terminology in the quiz that was used in the lesson to avoid confusion. For example, if the lesson consistently used the term "Internet service provider," do not use the acronym "ISP."

Figure 7.20. Checklist for Effective True/False Questions

☑ Provide clear directions.

☑ Make statements simple.

☑ Ask questions in logical sequence.

☑ Use terminology from the lesson.

☑ Test breadth of the lesson.

☑ Allow learners to review their answers.

☑ Provide respectful and meaningful feedback.

Figure 7.21. Sample True/False Questions

Poorly Designed Question	**Well-Designed Question**
Computer input devices are keyboards, scanners, and printers	A keyboard is a computer-input device
___True	___True
___False	___False

Test Breadth of the Lesson. The quiz or test should assess the entire lesson; that is, test all the content you teach.

Allow Learners to Review Their Answers. Demonstrate respect for learners and be conscious of test anxiety. Allow learners to review their answers and change them, if necessary, before submitting them.

Provide Respectful and Meaningful Feedback. A score tells learners little. Develop feedback that provides more than the percentage right or wrong. Let learners know which answers were incorrect and why. Be respectful; proof any comments to guard against sarcasm.

Multiple Choice

Multiple-choice tests can take a number of forms, such as drag and drop, matching columns, and fill in the blank. These assessments are best for testing simple recall and for applying abstract concepts to a particular situation (see the example in Figure 7.22).

The advantage of multiple-choice tests is their ease of design and administration. It is relatively easy to develop questions that test learners' recall or to diagnose what learners have misunderstood. Like true/false tests, multiple-choice tests are a familiar format for learners, and the scoring and feedback can be done with a computer program.

The depth of knowledge indicated by a multiple-choice test is limited. Like true/false tests, these tests are best for assessing simple recall. The biggest challenge is in designing answers that are distinctive and plausible. Possible answers should not be too similar; each should be unique and meaningful, not silly. It is often difficult to come up with four wrong answers that are plausible. The easier it

Figure 7.22. Sample Multiple-Choice Questions

Network Multiple Choice Test

Congratulations on finishing the **Network Protocols Module!** Please read each question and use the pop-up menu to select the correct answer. Review your answers and make changes before submitting it for scoring.

Use **Submit** to send your completed test to be scored.

1. A twisted-pair ethernet is also called a:

    10BASE-T Network

2. A 32bps adaptive differential pulse code modulation is distinguished by its ability to:

    carry stable voice and non-voice sounds

3. Where are Packet-Switched Public Data Networks (PSPDNs) used?

    United States
    Central America   de facto network standard is:
    Latin America
    Soviet Block
    Asia
                    SUBMIT MULTIPLE CHOICE TEST

Figure 7.23. Checklist for Designing Multiple-Choice Tests

☑ Provide directions.

☑ Put all repeated words into a stem.

☑ Test one idea per question.

☑ Use a logical sequence for answers.

☑ Create plausible alternatives.

☑ Avoid using "all or none of the above."

☑ Create only one answer per question.

☑ Provide no clues inadvertently.

☑ Demonstrate respect for the learner.

is to eliminate possible answers, the easier it is for learners to guess the right answer. Figure 7.23 provides a checklist of design considerations for creating Web-based multiple-choice tests.

Provide Directions. Because multiple-choice tests can take many forms, such as drag and drop, pull-down menus, radio buttons, and click boxes, explain to learners how to indicate their answers (i.e., click, pull down, drag).

Put All Repeated Words into a Stem. Write clear and easy-to-understand stem statements. If possible, start with words like where, when, and what, which make clear the kind of answer you are seeking. Reduce cognitive loading, the amount of information that learners must keep in their heads. Put repeated words in the stem and not in the answer. Compare Figures 7.24 and 7.25 to see the effect of cognitive loading.

Figure 7.24. Sample of Poorly Written Multiple-Choice Question

1. Cyberbrand multimedia development tools
   * enable designers to develop cross-platform applications.
   * enable designers to repurpose existing CD-ROM content.
   * enable designers to reduce disk pressing times.
   * enable designers to integrate legacy files.

Figure 7.25. Sample of Well-Written Multiple-Choice Question

1. Cyberbrand multimedia development tools enable designers to
   * develop cross-platform applications.
   * repurpose existing CD-ROM content.
   * reduce disk pressing times.
   * integrate legacy files.

Test One Idea Per Question. Develop test items that assess a single idea and avoid complex multi-faceted stems. Figure 7.26 is an example of a needlessly complex stem.

Figure 7.26. Sample of a Complex Stem

" _____ is the network protocol used to _____."

Figure 7.27. Sample of a Simple Stem

"TCP/IP is the network protocol used to _____."

The question in Figure 7.26 is confusing, asks for two pieces of information, and may not accurately assess what the learner knows. A better stem statement is shown in Figure 7.27.

Use a Logical Sequence for Answers. List answers in a logical sequence, such as numerical, alphabetical, or temporal. For example, list modem speed choices from lowest to highest. See Figure 7.28 for a sample.

Create Plausible Alternatives. All answers should be plausible. When possible, create one correct and four incorrect answers. Learners' performance is more accurately measured when none of the answers can be eliminated because they are absurd (see Figure 7.29).

Avoid "All/None of the Above." There is little value in using "all of the above" or "none of the above." Learners who identify a single right or wrong answer can eliminate those alternatives. Using both items in the same list indicates that one of the answers is a throwaway and improves the odds for guessing.

Figure 7.28. Sample Sequencing

Poor Sequence	Good Sequence
3600	1200
9600	2400
2400	3600
1200	9600

| **Figure 7.29. Sample Plausible and Implausible Answers** |

1. Standards that result from many people doing the same things are called:

Poor Answers	**Good Answers**
standards de jure	standards de jure
standard and poors	industry standards
de facto standards	de facto standards
all of the above	ISO standards
none of the above	association standards

Create Only One Answer per Question. Avoid creating items that have several right answers or questions that require learners to choose the best answer from several that are correct. In multiple-choice tests, learners do not have an opportunity to explain why they chose an answer. Without understanding the learner's rationale for choosing an answer, it is difficult to objectively assess his or her understanding.

Provide No Clues Inadvertently. Review multiple-choice tests to identify any inadvertent clues you may have included, such as stem statements or answers that provide information that can be used to answer questions elsewhere in the test. An example is shown in Figure 7.30. In this case, learners can decode the acronym "CCITT" in the second question from the text in the first.

Demonstrate Respect for the Learner. Always demonstrate respect for learners. Provide scoring information that offers more than a score. Craft feedback that explains why an answer was not correct. Provide recommendations for finding additional information. Deliver feedback in a tone and format that will not diminish the learners or make them feel bad.

A consultant talks about the challenges of convincing a developmental team to rethink the tone of their program.

I was asked to review the first couple of modules of a Web-based training program for a fast-growing manufacturer. The corporate culture was young, confident, Web-savvy, and a little flippant. The development team was comprised of technically sophisticated trainers, subject-matter experts, and course developers. The program was technically outstanding: great graphics, wonderful tracking, and easy-to-use interface. Despite the technical strengths of the program, the most noticeable characteristic was the tone. The program was sarcastic at some points and patronizing at others. The tone was sarcastic when it reported out the learners' test scores. Learners who scored 0 to 30 on a quiz were told to "look for a new career." It was patronizing in an exercise where a box popped-up that read "come on, you can do it."

We talked about the intended audience, and how these kinds of things might make those learners feel. The group said that they liked learning from programs with this kind of feedback; it was funny. We talked more about how the intended audience would like attending an on-site class that was delivered with sarcastic feedback and patronizing support. The trainers were the first to acknowledge it would not be a good idea. After more consideration and with some reluctance, the team modified the tone.

PURPOSE: *This exercise is designed to help you reflect on the options for testing adult learning.*

Analyze one or more quizzes in WBT programs and assess their designs. Use the Quiz Evaluation Worksheet to evaluate a multiple-choice quiz.

Figure 7.30. Sample of Inadvertent Clue

1. The leading European standard setting body is:

   - The Comite Consultatif Internationale Telegraphique et Telephonique

   - European Computer Manufacturers' Association

   - Institute of European Electrical Engineers

   - German Ministry of Electronics

   - European Economic Commission Committee

2. Standards for telecommunications and networking are set by:

   - OSF

   - X-OPEN

   - CCITT

   - ECMA

   - ANSI

Quiz Evaluation Worksheet

Directions: Use a search engine such as Alta Vista®, Yahoo®, or Excite® to locate quizzes. Use the following terms to find examples:

- Sample course with demo quiz
- Sample quiz test
- Demo course test
- Online test demo
- Learning quiz
- Quiz question score
- Online test exam scoring demo

Answer the following questions and reflect on how an adult learner would respond to the quizzes you sampled.

Questions

1. **Were the directions clear?**

2. **Was the terminology used in the quiz the same as the terminology used in the lesson?**

3. **Were words repeated in the stem only?**

4. **Did each question test a single idea?**

5. **Were the answers sequenced in a logical order?**

6. **Was "all/none of the above" given as an answer?**

7. **Was there more than one right answer per question?**

8. **Were inadvertent clues provided?**

9. **Were the feedback and score meaningful?**

10. **Did the quiz demonstrate respect for adult learners?**

Essay

Essay questions merely ask a question and provide directions for answering it. (See the sample in Figure 7.31.) Essays are powerful assessment tools and should be used only after careful consideration and design.

Essay questions can ask for short or long answers. The advantage of these questions is that essays allow learners to demonstrate a greater depth of knowledge than true/false or multiple-choice questions. Essay questions are easy to write, and the format is familiar to most learners.

The disadvantage of essay questions is the amount of work required to correct them. Answers cannot be machine scored, and automated feedback is not possible. A subject-matter expert capable of providing an objective evaluation must correct responses. The value of this kind of interaction is based on the feedback that results. Essay tests may penalize weak writers. If a learner is not able to write well enough

Figure 7.31. Sample Essay-Based Question

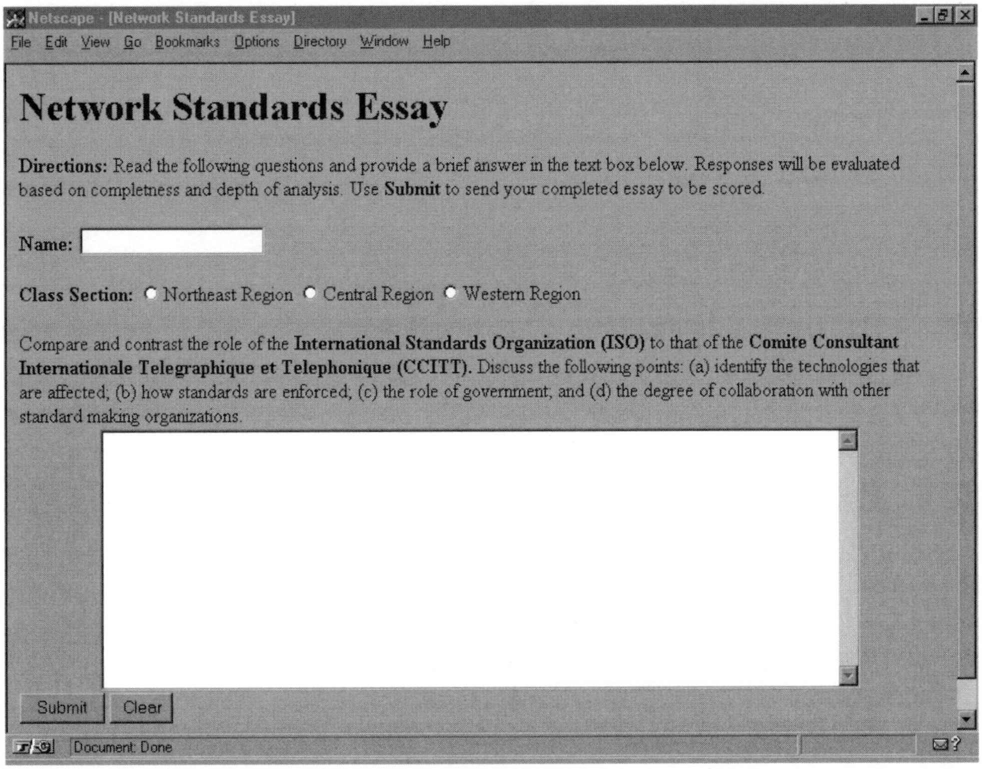

Figure 7.32. Checklist for Designing Effective Essay Questions

☑ Provide explicit directions.

☑ Encourage learners to respond to long essays with alternative tools.

☑ Test everything being taught.

☑ Find subject-matter experts.

☑ Plan respectful and timely feedback.

to respond to an essay, the exam may not provide a true measure of what he or she knows. Because of the labor-intensive nature of essay tests, carefully craft the questions. Figure 7.32 provides some guidance.

Provide Explicit Directions. Make it clear what you expect from learners. Let them know what you want them to compare, contrast, identify, discuss, relate, or evaluate. The more detailed the directions, the more succinct and focused the answers will be. Indicate if spelling, grammar, and composition are to be evaluated.

Encourage Learners To Respond to Long Essays with Alternative Tools. Short answers (no more than one screen in length) can be solicited online, using the browser's text editor. If the essay is longer and the learner needs to work on it over a period of time, provide alternatives such as an e-mail address to send a word-processing file or a directory where learners can store responses.

Test Everything Being Taught. Test the entire breadth of the course to determine learners' mastery of content. Essay questions should be broad enough to require learners to integrate all of the course content or there should be enough short-answer questions to sample the entire course.

Identify Subject-Matter Experts. Essay tests are time consuming to correct and require individualized feedback. If the course developer or facilitator is not a content expert, identify subject-matter experts and confirm that they will have time to correct tests. Ensure that evaluators share an objective standard for assessment. Create an answer key that outlines what should be included.

Plan Respectful and Timely Feedback. Provide guidelines for responding in a respectful manner. Recommend turnaround time on exams (e.g., three working days), and suggest that feedback be informative. For example, an evaluator should suggest additional readings, videotapes, or Web-based training programs that will help the learner understand what he or she is missing.

Application/Job-Task

The last type of test is an application or job-task assessment. This is a form of performance-based testing that requires learners to exhibit the skills they learned in class by performing them on the job or on a task that mimics the job. There are many permutations of this kind of assessment, ranging from simple to complex (see Figure 7.33).

A complex example would be to ask programmers to create and post a Java applet to the class Website. This is called "InterConstructive" testing. The Web is used as a repository, showcase, or arena for real-world testing or piloting. For example, a group of learners studying corporate communication can develop a

Figure 7.33. Sample Job-Task Interaction

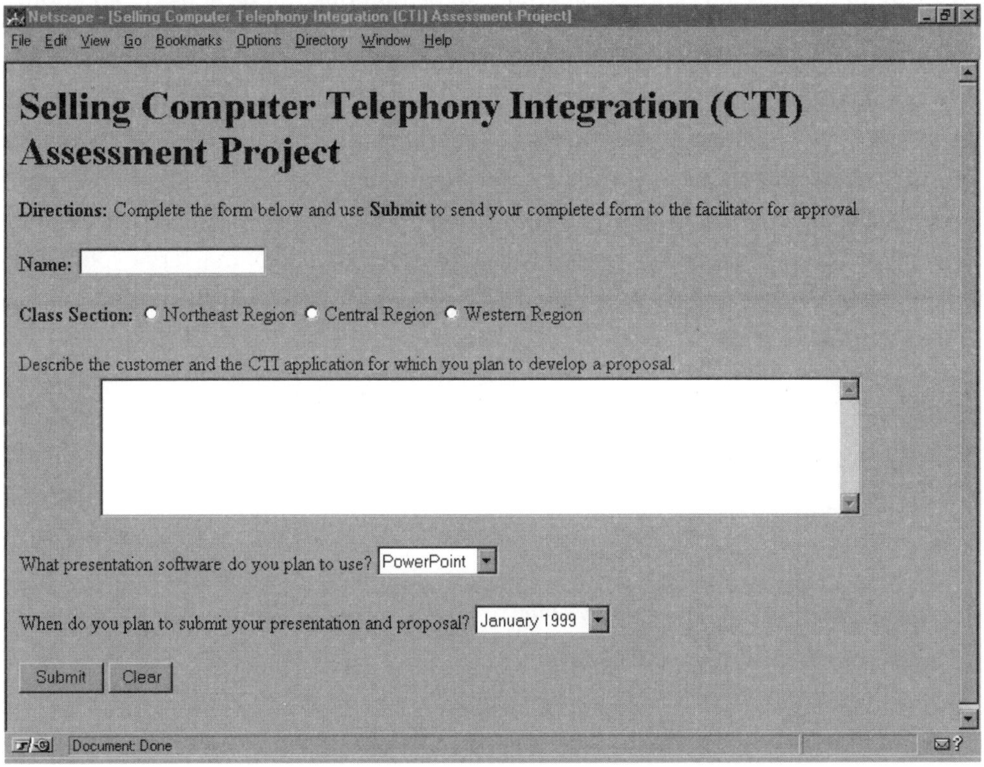

Netscape - [Selling Computer Telephony Integration (CTI) Assessment Project]

File Edit View Go Bookmarks Options Directory Window Help

Selling Computer Telephony Integration (CTI) Assessment Project

Directions: Complete the form below and use **Submit** to send your completed form to the facilitator for approval.

Name:

Class Section: ○ Northeast Region ○ Central Region ○ Western Region

Describe the customer and the CTI application for which you plan to develop a proposal.

What presentation software do you plan to use? PowerPoint ▼

When do you plan to submit your presentation and proposal? January 1999 ▼

Submit   Clear

Document: Done

"zine" (Web magazine) to demonstrate their ability to communicate with employees. Trainers learning to develop WBT programs can publish sample WBT modules on the Web.

Job-task assessment interactions are an effective way to test how well learners have integrated new skills and knowledge. The tasks should be closely related to the skills and knowledge required on the job in order to assess learners' depth of knowledge.

For traditional site-based training, an instructor can observe learners on the shop floor or at their terminals. In Web-based training, the assessment is limited to tasks that can be completed using the Internet or intranet. Because of the complex nature of the skills and knowledge being assessed, the tasks are often time-consuming to complete. Like the correction of essay questions, the evaluation of job-task performance is labor intensive. However, application tests can provide great value. Figure 7.34 outlines the key points to remember when designing them.

Use Only for Performance-Based Testing. Not every WBT program is a candidate for job-task assessment. For example, it would not be an adequate way to determine if a manager were able to conduct a performance review. Apply this kind of assessment to skills and knowledge that can be demonstrated by using an application and sending a file.

Provide Detailed Directions. Explain how you expect the learner to demonstrate mastery of the content. Describe the behavior accurately; use terms such as create, modify, incorporate, assess, compute, and diagnose. Inform learners of any special testing conditions, such as ability to refer to a textbook, use a diagnostic program, or work alone. Set performance expectations, that is, the degree of mastery expected (no errors, within + or − 5 percent, or free from spelling or grammatical errors).

Figure 7.34. Checklist for Designing Job-Task Assessments

☑ Use only for performance-based testing.

☑ Provide detailed directions.

☑ Provide adequate time to complete.

☑ Ask subject-matter expert to evaluate.

☑ Determine criteria for evaluation.

☑ Develop meaningful and respectful feedback.

Provide Adequate Time. Application- and job-task-based assessment takes more time than true/false and multiple-choice tests. Allow learners adequate time to work on the task. If possible, suggest how much time it should take to complete the project. Some learners will wait until the last minute and not allow themselves enough time, and others will exceed what is expected.

Ask Subject-Matter Expert To Evaluate. Identify subject-matter experts (SMEs) who are competent to evaluate projects.

Determine Criteria for Evaluation. Provide detailed criteria to help the SMEs deliver objective and consistent feedback. Set expectations with evaluators for providing feedback. Brief comments like "well done" and "nice work" do not provide much value. Ask the evaluator to comment specifically on which aspects of the assessment were well done. In addition, ask SMEs to point out what could have been done better.

Develop Meaningful and Respectful Feedback. Demonstrate that you appreciate learner efforts by providing adequate feedback. Suggest that SMEs explain the rationale for their comments and, when possible, direct learners to additional materials. Even learners who demonstrate a clear understanding of a task should be directed to more advanced or challenging readings, courses, or software.

Hypertext/Media

There is little agreement on the definition of hypermedia. In simplest terms, it is a product that connects media (text, audio, graphics, video, and animation) in a non-linear manner. The terms "hypermedia" and "hypertext" are often used interchangeably. Hypermedia is used here because it more accurately describes the applications in Web-based training. It is a powerful tool that offers many opportunities for interaction, but also has the potential to confuse learners. See Figure 7.35 for some advantages and disadvantages.

Figure 7.35. Advantages and Disadvantages of Hypermedia

Advantages	Disadvantages
Increases learner control	Hyperspace is disorienting
Develops associative thinking	Reading sequence is unpredictable
Creates connections to rich resources	Requires high maintenance

Hypermedia allows learners to control the pace, sequence, and depth of content. Learners choose what topics to examine and in what order. For example, learners can choose to review the introductory material quickly, then slow their pace to read a description or watch a narrated animation. Because the path through the content is not linear, each learner's path is unique. The unique path created by a learner is easier to remember because it is closer to the links in human memory. Hypermedia also creates links to rich resources within the organization's intranet and external links on the Internet.

The biggest problem with hypermedia is being "lost in hyperspace." Learners may get lost in complex hypermedia webs. Learners may find it difficult to orient themselves and may not be able to find their way back to the Web-based training. The second disadvantage is the unpredictable nature of how readers link to hyper-media elements. If essential information is located in a hypermedia link that is not selected, the learner will not master the objectives in that lesson. There is also a high degree of maintenance associated with links, especially external ones, because instructors have no control over when the information changes. Instructors cannot keep external Websites current or guarantee that they will be available. Maintaining links on an intranet is also a problem when other groups own them and are responsible for keeping the information current.

Figure 7.36 is an example of a course that uses hypermedia to navigate among modules. The bulleted items in the left frame are hyperlinks. The right frame shows the first page of the Welcome module. The icons and text in the right panel provide hypermedia links to a page listing the objectives, a page displaying schematics, and a video discussing product features. Icons show the learner what type of media each page contains.

Hypermedia is a valuable interactive product that offers instructors many opportunities to engage learners with layers of information. Figure 7.37 provides a checklist for developing hypermedia interactions.

Target and Profile the Audience. Determine how skilled the potential learners are in managing their learning in a nonlinear environment. Find out how familiar they are with navigating hypermedia: Do they know what a hypertext link looks like? and Do they know how to use a link and how to return to the WBT program after following a series of links?

Educate Users About Hypermedia. If they are not skilled, provide a section in the training program that explains how to use links and what kind of information they

Figure 7.36. Sample Hypermedia Interaction

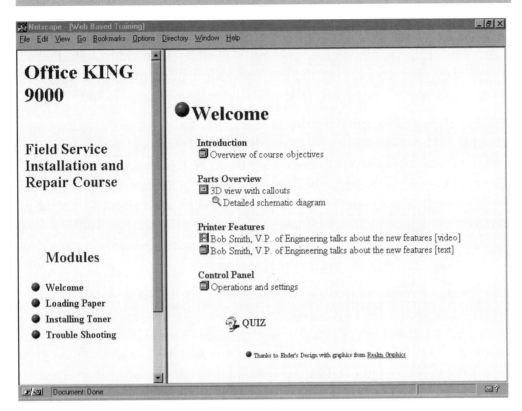

Figure 7.37. Checklist for Designing Hypermedia Interactions

☑ Target and profile the audience.

☑ Educate users about hypermedia.

☑ Collect information and establish links.

☑ Develop hypermedia and pilot the product.

☑ Keep design simple.

can access via the links. For example, is hypermedia used as a way to navigate the program or is it used to provide enrichment material?

Collect Information and Establish Links. If a Web-based training program is organized by objectives, design the hypermedia to educate, providing links that are related to the objectives. Do not abdicate responsibility to learners by asking them to figure out which links are essential and which are merely nice to know.

Develop Hypermedia and Pilot the Product. It is the developer's responsibility to create links between different pieces of course content. Links are established using a two-step process. First, create links based on the experience of the developer or subject-matter expert. Then test the links with the target audience, when possible in collaboration with potential learners and their managers. Check the effectiveness of links and pilot a sample section of the program. Get feedback from the target audience to assess if they understand the connections. Identify links that learners expect and add them if they are missing.

Keep Design Simple. Keep the design of hypermedia links simple. Put essential content in the body of the lesson; use hypermedia to provide enrichment or background information. Link information in logical groupings. Make the hypermedia structure clear to learners. When using icons or text clues, be consistent. Throughout the program, use the same symbol to represent help or indicate when an image is available, and use fonts and indents to suggest levels of detail. The icons shown in Figure 7.38 were used in the previous example in Figure 7.36. If hypermedia links take learners outside the Web-based training program, warn them that they are leaving the program and tell them how to get back. Figure 7.39 shows a simple linking model in which the learner moves back and forth between the lesson and the supporting hypermedia.

Figure 7.40 shows a more complex linking diagram. In this model, the learner moves back and forth between the lesson and the supporting hypermedia and among multiple links. With such complexity, the instructor should ensure that the learners do not become lost in hyperspace. Use navigation maps or color queuing to help learners stay oriented. For example, create a colored button for each module in a course and use the color as a way to remind learners what lesson they are in. Figure 7.41 is an example of a navigation map that provides learners with information about the elements in the Periodic Table. Learners click on an element to navigate to a page with more information.

Figure 7.38. Examples of Icons

Icon	Representing
	Text
	Video
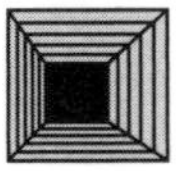	3D Image
	Schematic
	Quiz

Figure 7.39. Sample of Simple Hypermedia Links

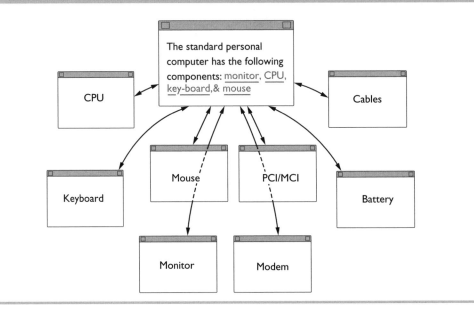

Figure 7.40. Sample of Complex Hypermedia Links

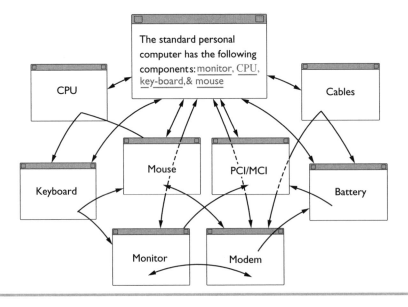

Figure 7.41. Sample Navigation Map

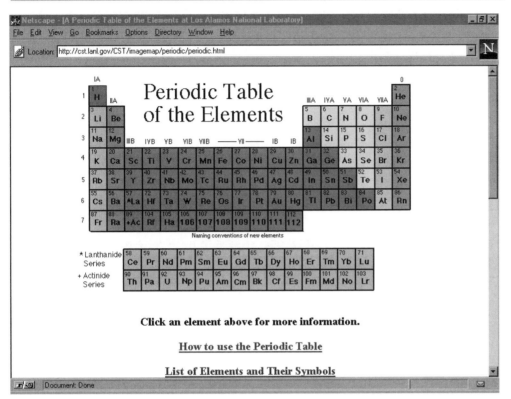

PURPOSE: *This exercise is designed to give you experience planning and creating a hypermedia flow chart.*

Think about how you would use hypermedia in a WBT program. How would you organize the hypermedia so the learner is not confused? How would you allow the learner to have control over the learning experience? Use the Hypermedia Worksheet to plan and create a simple hypermedia flow chart.

Hypermedia Worksheet

Directions: Develop a Web-based training course to teach job-search skills to recent college graduates. Use a sheet of blank paper to write your answers to the following questions and then draw a simple hypermedia interaction flow chart. A sample outline of one possible job skill is provided below.

Questions

1. **List the skills required to find a job.**

   After completing this WBT course learners will be able to:
   - Prepare a resume
   -
   -

2. **List the subskills, knowledge, and references that will help learners master the learning objective.**

   - Prepare a resume

        Explain the purpose of a resume

        Determine type of job sought

        Identify best type of resume (chronological, functional)

        Define what you can do for potential employer

        Write summary statement

        Assess job skills, knowledge, and talents

        Collect data on previous positions held (when, where)

        Gather data on training and educational accomplishments

        Write sample resume

        Understand resume-screening criteria

        Read article on evolution of resumes

        Prepare do's and don'ts checklist

   -
   -

3. **Create a hypermedia flow chart that shows the relationships between the content of your course and additional resource material on the World Wide Web. Figure 7.42 provides a sample of a simple hypermedia flow chart.**

Figure 7.42. Simple Hypermedia Flow Chart

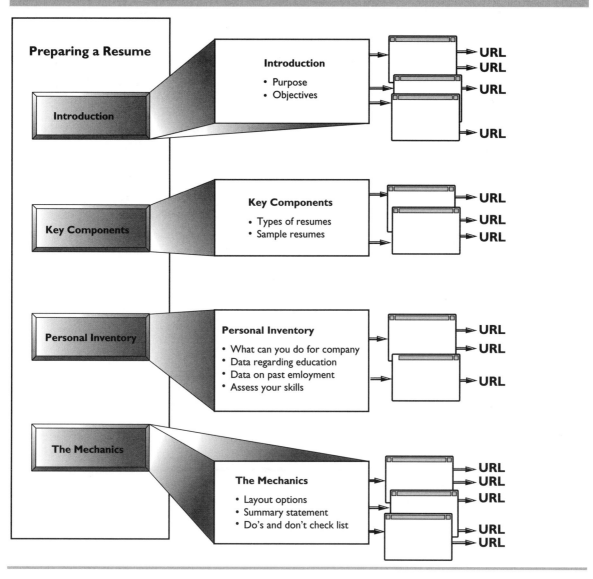

Suggested Readings

Ambron, S., & Hooper, K. (1988). *Interactive multimedia: Visions of multimedia for developers, educators, & information providers.* New York: Cobb Group.

Gayeski, D. M. (1995). *Interactive media.* Englewood Cliffs, NJ: Prentice-Hall.

Horton, W. K. (1990). *Designing & writing online documentation: Help files to hypertext.* New York: Wiley.

Jategaonkar, V. A., & Babu, A. J. (1995). Interactive multimedia instructional systems; A conceptual framework. *Journal of Instruction Delivery Systems, 9*(4), 24–29.

Kenny, R. F. (1995). Interactive multimedia instruction to develop reflective decision-making among preservice teachers. *Journal of Technology and Teacher Education, 3*(2), 169–188.

Kristof, R., & Satran, A. (1995). *Interactivity by design: Creating & communicating with new media.* San Francisco: Hayden Books.

Mok, C. (1996). *Designing business: Multiple media, multiple disciplines.* New York: Macmillan Computer Publications.

Parcel, B. (1997). *Testing 1, 2, 3.* Unpublished manuscript, Boston University, School of Education, Boston.

Park, I., & Hannafin, M. J. (1993). Empirically based guidelines for the design of interactive multimedia. *Educational Technology, Research and Development, 41*(3), 63–85.

Reynolds, A., & Iwinski, T. (1996). *Multimedia training: Developing technology-based systems.* New York: McGraw-Hill.

Schwier, R. A., & Misanchuk, E. R. (1993). *Interactive multimedia instruction.* Englewood Cliffs, NJ: Educational Technology Publications.

Chapter 8

Synchronous Interactions

What You Will Learn in This Chapter

After completing this chapter, you will be able to

- List the benefits of Web/VSC programs;
- Define four kinds of synchronous interactions;
- Explain the advantages of each; and
- Integrate synchronous interactions into Web/VSC programs.

Web/synchronous virtual classroom programs are the most technically complex type of Web-based training to implement and maintain. Generally, the tools used to create and deliver them require computers with newer processors, dedicated servers, robust bandwidth, and adequate technical staff to support developers and end users. Observing a W/VSC program can be a challenge because it requires you to seek out a demonstration or real class being offered at a fixed time. It is not possible to judge the benefits of W/VSC by looking at static HTML pages. You cannot assess the value of students interacting in real time, the synergy of sharing a white board to develop a solution, or the benefits of being able to hear the tone of a peer's voice or see facial expressions unless you are engaged in an actual program.

Because there is a great deal of overlap in what learners are able to accomplish in W/VAC and W/VSC interactions, the following section points out the unique benefits and limitations of each.

Web/Virtual Synchronous Classroom Programs

Synchronous interactions are only possible when instructor and learners are working together in real-time. It requires a set of tools that enable learners to see, hear, and/or share applications across the Internet. Before examining the tools and interactions possible in the synchronous environment, it is important to weigh the benefits and limitations of each.

Benefits

Live Group Learning and Immediate Feedback. The opportunities for live group learning and the immediacy of feedback are unique strengths of the Web/virtual synchronous classroom. The ability to bring a group of learners together for discussions, brainstorming, case-study analysis, debates, and project work in real time is only possible in this form of Web-based training. W/VSC programs allow immediate feedback on ideas, extension of suggestions, and building of consensus. Real-time interactions reveal the tone and personality of learners and create a greater sense of presence. Learners become part of a community, complete with norms and netiquette.

Just-in-Time Development (JIT). The JIT development and delivery capabilities of W/VSC are ideal for providing skills and knowledge for which learners cannot wait. Using tools such as Web-based audio conferencing, Web videoconferencing, and application sharing, corporations can deliver programs without long development cycles. For example, a software company can quickly provide sales representatives with the skills and knowledge needed to sell a new product. Using application sharing and live two-way audio, a program can be created in a matter of hours to demonstrate software features and to offer subject-matter experts to answer questions.

Range of Tools. The range of tools available in W/VSC programs makes complex topics manageable. Complex topics can be explained by directly using tools such as whiteboards, application sharing, text-chat, real-time audio, and videoconferencing. These synchronous tools can be combined with asynchronous tools such as video clips, text, images, animation, polling, and quizzing. Instructors and learners can illustrate their ideas and take the class in unanticipated directions. If the instructor discovers that a class lacks basic skills, he or she can digress to review basics with a whiteboard or a visit to a Website that provides fundamental skills. After all learners have the prerequisite skills, the instructor can begin teaching the topic.

Simple Classroom Metaphor. The simplicity of the classroom metaphor is a benefit of Web/VSC programs. This form of Web-based training is most like a real classroom, where learners and the instructor gather at the same time to share a learning experience. Unlike other types of Web-based training that rely on learners to be self-directed and motivated to log on and work alone, the virtual synchronous classroom provides a structured meeting time and the support and encouragement of live peers. The class cannot be put off like self-paced training.

Limitations

Limitations in Web/VSC programs can be classified as educational, logistical, and technical.

Educational Limitations. The educational limitations of W/VSC programs are the flip side of their advantages. Programs designed for individual learning or that employ passive instructional strategies do not work well in the virtual synchronous classroom. There is little value in bringing learners together if they are working on their own. Using passive strategies such as reading or viewing a video are of little value in this environment. The effectiveness of this technology is limited to instructional strategies that build on the synergy of live group interactions.

Logistics. Logistics can be a major limitation for organizations that want to offer programs to learners working in different time zones. For example, a class starting at 2:00 p.m. Pacific Standard Time would require learners in New York to log on at 5:00 p.m. Eastern Standard Time. Time-zone difference can become an even greater issue when they involve learners in Europe or Asia.

Technical. W/VSC programs require powerful networks and servers, multimedia computers, layers of software, and substantial technical support. Many of the software tools require powerful servers to host the programs and substantial bandwidth to accommodate video, audio, and application sharing. In addition, the computers used by learners may require sound cards, microphones, and color monitors. Because the software required to participate in a W/VSC is layered on network software, browsers, and operating-system software, substantial technical support may be required to install and troubleshoot programs.

The interactions described on the following pages are only possible in Web/virtual synchronous programs. They are described in general terms, as the specific functions and features of each vendor's synchronous tool and/or software package differ slightly.

Types of Synchronous Interactions

W/VSC programs are used to teach learners to solve unstructured problems such as how to design a database, how to evaluate chemicals for process manufacturing, how to plan computer-telephone integration, and how to develop strategies to enter a new market. The problems presented do not have a single right answer; rather they require learners to draw on their experiences, question one another's assumptions, and consider alternatives. As a result, learners create plans, develop unique solutions, and improve products and services. The instructor's role is as a facilitator who helps the group stay focused.

Four categories of tools provide synchronous interactions. They are shown in Figure 8.1. Synchronous tools are often used with the asynchronous tools discussed in Chapter Seven.

Select synchronous tools based on what is to be accomplished and balance that selection against what is technically reasonable for the organization.

Internet Relay Chat

Internet relay chat (IRC) is real-time, text-based conferencing via the Internet or an intranet. IRC "rooms" offer real-time communication between two or more people. They are similar to meetings or conference calls; the chats take place in the form of

---

Figure 8.1. Tools Used in Web-Based Training

Synchronous	Asynchronous
Internet Relay Chat	E-mail
Real-Time Audio	Listserv
Application Sharing/Whiteboards	Online Threaded Discussions/Forums
Videoconferencing	Hypertext/media
	Quizzes/Tests

Figure 8.2. Sample Internet Relay Chat Session

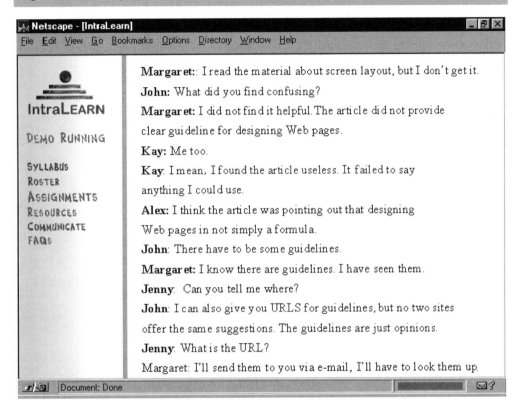

Credit: OnTour Multimedia Inc., IntraLEARN.

moderated discussions, private conversations, and question-and-answer forums. The IRC application shown in Figure 8.2 features a main menu in a panel on the left and the conversation on the right panel.

Advantages and Disadvantages

Consider the advantages and disadvantages of using IRC for synchronous interactions listed in Figure 8.3. Internet relay chat is an effective tool for creating peer-to-peer learning opportunities. Learners participate in discussion groups, brainstorming exercises, and problem-solving activities, and they learn from one another. IRC also levels the playing field; participants are judged by their contributions and not their physical traits. Try to select IRC software that allows learners to determine their online names rather than defaulting to using their log-in names. For example, some IRC programs use the learner's log-in name, such as "twood" and "zimm800," rather than Tom Wood or Zimmerman.

Figure 8.3. Advantages and Disadvantages of IRC

Advantages	**Disadvantages**
Creates peer learning opportunities.	Penalizes poor writers.
Equalizes participants.	Conversation can be disjointed.
Enables reflection.	Comments lack context and human
Creates audit trail.	emphasis.

A trainer talks about the value of having a user name that is meaningful.
Your name says a lot about you. In the chat room, people can pick any name they want. We recommend that they use their first or last name and maybe some indication of the office they are from, like Jameson-SF. This makes it easier to follow up on a comment or suggestion if you want to call the person later or look them up in the corporate phone directory.

Because the conversation in an IRC scrolls onto the screen, it can be observed as it progresses. Learners are encouraged to think about the conversation and to reflect on its evolution. Depending on the IRC software functions, the instructor can store the text in an online archive and refer to it later. This gives learners who were unable to attend the opportunity to read the conversation they missed.

Like all text-based learning tools, IRCs penalize poor writers. Learners who are not capable of expressing themselves clearly in writing are at a disadvantage. Because IRC programs take place in real-time, the interactions do not allow learners time to review their prose. Not only do learners have to be good writers, but they must also be fast typists, responding to a comment in a relatively short period of time; otherwise, the strands of conversation pass them by. Relay times—how long it takes a message to move across the Internet—can cause lags or delays and create disjointed conversations.

Internet chat rooms are not as much like real conversations as the name implies. There is a lack of context, as well as a lack of verbal and nonverbal clues. It is difficult to tell whether a chat room comment is meant to be funny, sarcastic, or serious. IRC comments do not benefit from an inflection of voice, a smile, or good timing.

PURPOSE: *This exercise provides you experience using Internet relay chat.* Think about the importance of experience and the role of dialogue in adult learning. Participate in and observe an Internet relay chat room. What are the benefits and limitations of this kind of interaction? Use the Internet Relay Chat Room Worksheet to reflect on the experience.

IRC Reflection Worksheet

Directions: Use a search engine such as Alta Vista®, Yahoo®, or Excite® to locate Internet relay chat rooms. Use the following terms to find IRCs: chat; Internet relay chat demo; chat room; chat room index; or IRC and chat room.

Follow the instructions to join a chat room that interests you. Spend twenty minutes participating in and observing that chat room. When you are done, reflect on the experience by answering the following questions:

1. **Did you enjoy the experience? If not, why not? If yes, what did you like about it?**

2. **How could you use this tool for training? What are its limitations? What are its benefits?**

3. **Would it be beneficial to have a moderator in the chat room? Why? If yes, what role would the moderator play?**

Guidelines for Internet Relay Chat

Use IRCs to draw on the experience of learners, build new knowledge, and solve ill-structured problems. The guidelines shown in Figure 8.4 can help you create effective IRCs.

Provide Clear Directions. Explain what you expect to result from the conversation. Provide a well-defined discussion topic, a brainstorming session with bounds, or a debate with clear expectations. Let learners know how long the IRC will last. (Will it take twenty or forty-five minutes?) Give every learner a chance to participate in the conversation. If possible, select the IRC group members to ensure that the group has a balance of participants. Mix experienced IRC participants with novices to create rooms that have a balance of senior managers and new hires; integrate staff from headquarters and the field.

Limit Number of Participants. Create groups of five to seven learners to give everyone an opportunity to contribute. Too few people and the conversation lags; too many people and the conversation becomes chaotic. Create a respectful and safe environment for participation and encourage observation as well as active participation.

Keep the Conversation on Track. Monitor the conversation or ask a learner to play the role of monitor. Keep the conversation on track by tabling items that become deadlocked. Capture issues for later that are sidetracking the conversation, and ask those who are observing passively what they think.

Ask for a Conversation Summary. Appoint a scribe to summarize the IRC chat. The report can be posted to a threaded discussion or sent to a listserv for review by the group. Use these kinds of exercises to develop learners' skills of analysis and synthesis.

Involve Learners in Setting Norms. Allow them to determine who should monitor and keep IRCs on track, what other IRCs should be created, and who should participate.

Figure 8.4. Checklist for Creating an IRC

☑ Provide clear directions.

☑ Limit number of participants.

☑ Keep the conversation on track.

☑ Ask for a conversation summary.

☑ Involve learners in setting norms.

Real-Time Audio with Visuals

Real-time audio is the ability to carry on a conversation with learners over the Internet or intranet. In most cases, real-time audio is used in combination with visuals. This enables the instructor and learners to talk to one another while sharing graphics, images, videos, and animation related to the topic. This kind of interaction is well suited for round-table discussions, question-and-answer sessions, guest speakers, and debates.

The functions of the audio vary from product to product. In some applications the audio works very much like a teleconference call. In others the audio works like a call-in radio program in which the instructor acts as the host and puts learners on the air. In yet others, the instructor can talk to the audience and the audience can type questions to the instructor in real-time and receive answers immediately. Figure 8.5 is an example of a Web-based training program that uses live audio with visuals.

As Figure 8.6 shows, there are several permutations of real-time audio with visuals. Audio can be heard via the Internet in three ways, and visuals can be broadcast from a single source or multiple sources.

Figure 8.5. Example of Real-Time Audio and Visuals

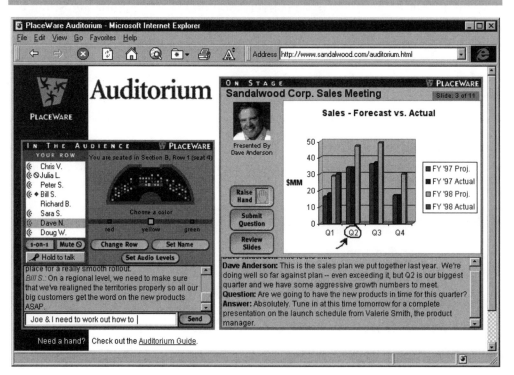

Figure 8.6. Mix of Real-Time Audio with Visuals   155

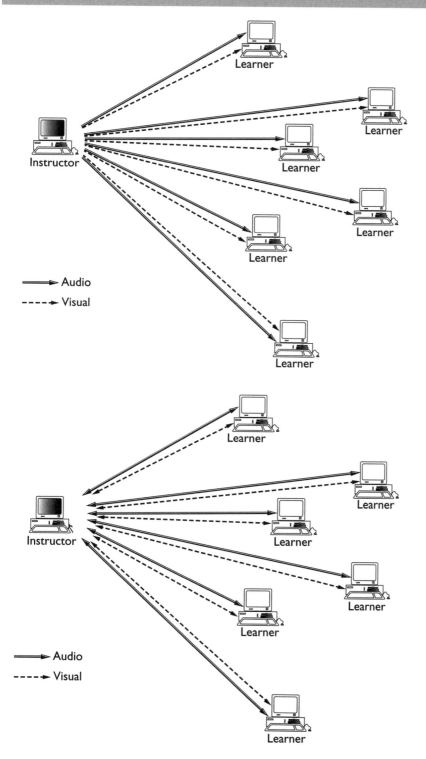

Figure 8.6. (continued)

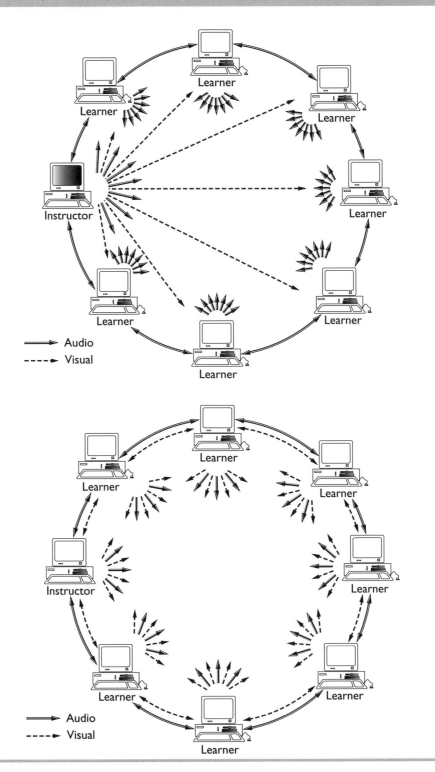

One-way audio is analogous to a radio show. Two-way audio is analogous to a walkie-talkie, and multipoint audio is similar to a teleconference.

Generally, visuals are broadcast from the instructor to learners' computers. Sophisticated and powerful software packages allow visuals to be broadcast from multiple sources. A sophisticated Web videoconferencing package allows learners to broadcast images, graphics, animations, and text from their computers to the instructor and other class members. As the technology evolves, the permutations continue to grow and the distinctions blur.

Advantages and Disadvantages

Like other tools for synchronous interactions, real-time audio with visuals has advantages and disadvantages, as shown in Figure 8.7.

One of the advantages of real-time audio with visuals is robust communication. Learners gain a deeper understanding of a topic when the information is delivered on two channels (auditory and visual). In this type of synchronous interaction, visual information is supported with interactive verbal messages that benefit from inflection, tone, and pace. For example, learners can see how an order form has been redesigned and hear how the changes will make it easier to track back orders.

Real-time audio does not penalize learners who are weak writers or poor readers. There are many variations on this form of interaction, such as round-table discussions, guest speakers, and debates.

Finally, real-time audio with visuals enables speakers to use graphics, images, and videos from anywhere on the Internet or intranet. Speakers can change the visuals that support their lessons on relatively short notice. Because the materials need not be shipped to other locations, they can be changed minutes before the course starts.

Real-time audio does have limitations. It requires a highly structured program format, such as radio programs with detailed scripts or outlines and the added

Figure 8.7. Advantages and Disadvantages of Real-Time Audio with Visuals

Advantages	Disadvantages
Robust communication.	Requires structured lessons.
Many variants (debates, guests).	Interactions are not intuitive.
Integrates Internet and intranet resources.	Needs management of two media.

complication of visuals. The instructor must be prepared to talk about the visuals, make transitions, monitor his or her timing, and manage interactions. Because visuals are usually sequenced in advance, it can be difficult to make changes during the program. Addressing new or unexpected issues can present a challenge because the program length is fixed and appropriate graphics to support unexpected topics may not be available. Again, the degree of structure or flexibility will depend on the software being used to deliver the program.

Managing learner-to-instructor and learner-to-learner interaction is not intuitive. In Web-based training there are no clues that a learner wants to ask a question or that a point was not clear. In a traditional classroom it is easy to see if a learner looks puzzled or to observe body language. It is an intuitive human response to stop and ask about the problem. The instructor must learn to proactively use tools built into the software to inquire about pacing, comprehension, and clarity of instruction.

Instructors must also be aware of other issues that can affect interactions, such as Internet lag times, learners who step away from their computers during class, and confusion caused by the interface. Learners may have a slow connection to the Internet and their responses may lag behind those of other learners. The instructor must be patient and not assume that the learner is not paying attention. Learners may log in to a class and then be called away, so be careful not to chastise a learner who is logged on and not responding. Also, the interface may confuse learners. Learners' interactions may be hampered by their inability to find the keys that control the microphone or volume or to signal the instructor that they wish to respond to a question.

If the software package being used does not offer tools to manage interactions and gather feedback, the instructor must continually seek this information by asking learners to summarize the points, provide examples, or provide nonexamples as a means of gathering feedback.

Guidelines for Real-Time Audio with Visuals

Figure 8.8 provides a list of guidelines for creating a sound Web-based training program using real-time audio with visuals.

Create an Advance Organizer. Give learners an outline of what to expect. This can be an overview or list of objectives that helps learners anticipate what to expect. Agendas, program guides, and course maps help orient learners.

Explain How To Interact. At the start of the program, review how interactions will take place, for example, how to use the "raise hand" button or yes/no buttons. Then ask learners to practice by signaling that they want to speak and introducing

---

Figure 8.8. Checklist for Creating Real-Time Audio with Visuals

☑ Create an advance organizer.

☑ Explain to learners how to interact.

☑ Plan five- to seven-minute segments.

☑ Use a variety of strategies.

☑ Have visuals support the audio.

☑ Create a respectful environment.

☑ Draw on audience experience.

☑ Bring the program to a clear close.

---

themselves. This is a good way to take roll call and to give learners a chance to interact in a safe environment. If you will call on learners randomly to respond to questions, make them aware of this.

Plan Five- to Seven-Minute Segments. Plan segments that are no longer than five to seven minutes. Real-time audio with visuals is a demanding medium, and learners can easily become distracted. Learners are also quick to assume they have been dropped from the network or are experiencing a technical failure if there are long pauses in the audio, the visuals do not change, and animations loop endlessly.

Use a Variety of Strategies. Real-time audio with visuals can become passive if no interaction is scripted into programs. If you must lecture, keep it short. Lectures are better delivered via text streaming audio, or sent via audiocassette before class. Figure 8.9 shows a sample scripting worksheet with time segments. Take advantage of having the class online together to provide interactions that draw from learners' experiences, develop critical thinking, and enable people to direct their own learning. Vary the strategies within a program to keep the lesson interesting (see Table 8.1).

Have Visuals Support the Audio. The audio portion of the program drives interactions in real time. Because audio interactions are not predictable, try to anticipate the topics, questions, and even side remarks. Prepare a series of visuals to support a number of possible directions in which the class might move. Visuals can include

Figure 8.9. Sample Scripting Worksheet

Elapsed Time	Time	Event	Audio	Visual
5	2:55–3:00 p.m.	Pre-class	Music	Title graphic with agenda
5	3:00–3:05 p.m.	Introduction	Instructor introduction and review objectives for class	Photo of instructor/ Text with objectives
7	3:05–3:12 p.m.	Check in	Ask participants to introduce themselves	Map of U.S., highlighting where each person is located
5	3:12–3:17 p.m.	Review of product features and installation requirements (Guest speaker: product manager)	Product manager delivers lecture	Presentation (text and graphics)
13	3:17–3:30 p.m.	Question and answer	Product manager fields questions	Picture of new products/ Whiteboard for product manager

text, pictures, maps, animation sequences, illustrations, and scanned images that can be viewed in a browser. How visuals are created and stored will depend on the software used to develop the program.

Create a Respectful Environment. Learners must feel free to share their experiences, ask questions, or present differing opinions.

Draw on Audience Experience. Encourage learners to talk about their experiences. Welcome learner questions and be open to hearing about both positive and negative experiences they have had.

Table 8.1. Strategies for Real-Time Audio	
Strategy	**Description**
Interview	Interview subject-matter experts for their perspectives or accounts of their experiences.
Role Play	Create a controlled environment in which learners develop skills such as interviewing or overcoming objections. Others can practice listening and analysis skills.
Debate	Use debate to provide a forum for opposing views.
Panel Discussion	Bring experts together and provide a moderator to ask questions.
Class Discussion	Invite learners to talk about a given subject in an open format.
Question & Answer	Invite learners to ask questions after panel discussions, interviews, or presentations.
Games	Create games to engage learners in competitive problem-solving situations or require learners to work in teams to find answers.

Bring the Program to a Clear Close. Web-based training programs that use real-time audio take place at specified times. Be aware of starting and ending the program on time. Bring the program to a clear end by saying something like, "Before we close, are there any more questions?" or "I'd like to take the last few minutes to talk about the assignment for next week." If you are unable to address all the learners' questions during the program, invite them to contact you after class via phone or e-mail.

A trainer explains the importance of adhering to the announced schedule.
We advertised a live WBT class to be delivered by a nationally recognized consultant. The promotional materials stated the class would begin at 10:30 a.m. and end at noon. Much to the consultant's disapproval, we started the class as scheduled with only three of the nineteen registered students logged on. At 10:45 most of the pre-registered students were logged in. At noon the consultant was only two-thirds of the way through his talk, and he was unhappy to see the students logging off.

After debriefing the instructor and reviewing the student evaluation forms, we learned a few things! First, students make appointments, schedule conference calls, and build their calendars around the advertised times. Second, consultants or any presenter must understand that on the Web you can't exceed your time. I'd say all-in-all, watch your time.

PURPOSE: *This exercise is designed to give you experience planning real-time audio with video interactions.*
Think about how a program could be crafted for adult learners to take advantage of audio and visual components. Script a program with one-way audio or with two-way audio. Create a script using the Real-Time Audio with Visuals Scripting Worksheet.

✓ Real-Time Audio with Visuals Scripting Worksheet

Directions: Review the sample script outline in Figure 8.9. Then develop your own script for a real-time audio with visuals Web-based training program.

Elapsed Time	Time	Event	Audio	Visual

Application Sharing/Whiteboards

Application sharing is the ability for learners to work collaboratively on a software application such as a spreadsheet, a PowerPoint® presentation, or a whiteboard. Like real-time audio, application sharing is frequently done in combination with other synchronous interactions such as text chat and real-time audio. Figure 8.10 illustrates a spreadsheet that can be shared by a group of learners working together. Each learner can add information to the appropriate cell, which automatically changes the bar chart and total.

There are two ways to use shared applications in Web-based training. The most straightforward is as a means of teaching how to use an application. For example, sharing a database program like Access®, an instructor can teach a new salesperson how to set up a customer database, sort records, and create fields. The second way to use

Figure 8.10. Example of Shared Application

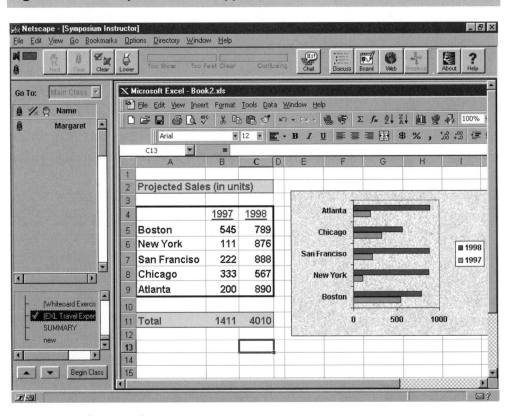

Credit: Centra Software Inc., Symposium.

Figure 8.11. Example of a Shared Whiteboard

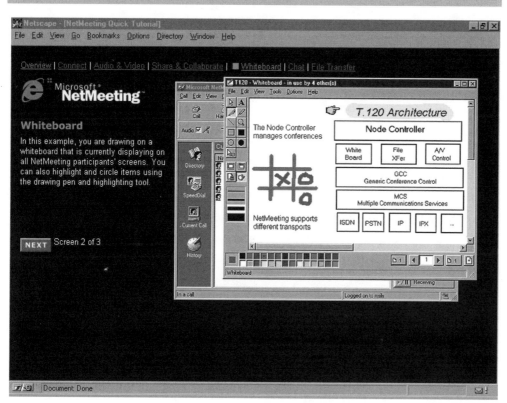

Credit: Screen shot reprinted by permission from Microsoft Corporation.

application sharing is to teach concepts and skills. For example, a shared database application like Access could be used to demonstrate how customers can be segmented by industry codes and targeted for specific marketing campaigns. In this case, the database is used to illustrate points, but students are not learning how to use the database.

A more generic shared application is the shared whiteboard, which resembles a regular whiteboard. On the Web, learners can write, annotate, draw, and paste items onto the whiteboard. It can be saved, posted to a threaded discussion, or e-mailed to the instructor (see Figure 8.11).

Advantages and Disadvantages

Shared applications are powerful tools that offer collaborative learning opportunities for a range of training needs. Figure 8.12 outlines the advantages and disadvantages of using this form of interaction.

Figure 8.12. Advantages and Disadvantages of Shared Applications

Advantages	**Disadvantages**
Mimics reality.	Requires layered knowledge.
Promotes collaborative learning.	Requires layering of technology (audio/text).

Working on shared applications enables the learner to practice skills similar to those required on the job. For example, learners can practice searching the company's database or receive coaching while using new software. Software skills can be taught in the context in which they will be used. The ability to provide an authentic experience is a big benefit of application sharing. Another benefit is the opportunity for collaborative learning. Learners can share what they have learned with peers.

The shared whiteboard is also an excellent tool for collaborative activities such as brainstorming, diagramming solutions, and outlining recommendations. Learners can work together to document their work, expand on themes, and summarize the outcomes of their working sessions. The ability to "pass the markers" and engage the entire group in drawing, annotating, and modifying an idea makes it an excellent tool for joint inquiry and problem solving.

Shared applications and whiteboards do have certain limitations and drawbacks. The most significant limitation is the necessary prerequisite knowledge. Learners must understand how the application works. The tools required for writing, erasing, and "passing markers" are unique to each vendor's software package. Learners must become familiar with the icons for the whiteboard tools (e.g., line, circle, bold, erase) and the rules related to taking turns. This presents a complex layering that can be confusing for some learners.

If the application is being used to teach concepts and skills, learners need a significant level of mastery. They must be fluent with the application before they can focus on the concepts and skills being taught.

The second major limitation of application sharing is the need to combine it with other technologies such as the telephone, real-time audio, and text-based chat. Layering these applications requires additional technical and logistical ability.

Guidelines for Using Application Sharing

Application sharing can be used for two main purposes: to teach learners to use a software package and to give learners access to a tool to help them learn another subject. Figure 8.13 provides a checklist for using shared applications to teach software skills.

Teach Problem-Solving Skills. Application sharing is best suited for teaching learners to use advanced features of a software application that require problem solving, assessment, or evaluation skills. For example, application sharing is appropriate for teaching learners to design word-processing templates or to create customized table wizards for a database. Reserve application sharing for problems that involve judgment, experience, and reflection. Avoid the use of synchronous interactions to teach basic cognitive skills (knowledge, comprehension, and application) such as the basics of word processing or spreadsheets. These are better delivered with W/CBT, computer-based training, traditional classroom training, or paper-based instruction. Basic application skills require the use of individual intellectual abilities. They require drill and practice, recall of information, memorization of processes, and the application of rules. There is no benefit from group learning nor live interaction with an instructor or peers.

Supplement the Application Sharing. Select a communication method to supplement application sharing—one that enables the instructor to explain what is happening. Depending on the tools chosen, the instructor can communicate with the learner via text-chat, telephone, or real-time Internet audio. Assess the impact that typing back and forth or holding a telephone receiver while typing will have on the quality of the learning experience. If you are using the telephone in combination with the Web, make conference call arrangements to bring learners together simultaneously.

Figure 8.13. Checklist for Using Shared Applications To Teach Software Skills

☑ Teach problem-solving skills.

☑ Supplement the shared application.

☑ Ask learners to work in teams.

☑ Provide problem sets and solutions.

☑ Limit class size.

Ask Learners To Work in Teams. Design exercises that take advantage of peer learning. Ask learners to work in pairs or small teams so they can share their experiences and help one another. This is a good way to build problem-solving skills and to develop skills of critical reflection and it reduces the need for the instructor to provide all the answers. In the process, the learners answer one another's questions and learn other skills.

Provide Problem Sets and Solutions. As you would for traditional classroom programs, you will need to create problem sets or exercises to provide a consistent and structured learning experience. Teaching software skills requires attention to detail and intense preparation. Develop problem sets that work flawlessly to illustrate concepts. It is also important to provide solution sets that enable learners to review the exercise after the live class ends.

Limit Class Size. Application sharing should be done with small groups to ensure adequate guidance and feedback. The exact size of the group depends on the complexity of the software and experience level of the learners. If all of the learners are new users of the application, the instructor must have a small group and a high level of interaction to provide adequate direction and coaching. On the other hand, programs that teach simple applications or provide an overview of new features in a familiar application can be taught to larger groups because they require fewer interactions.

Guidelines for Using Application Sharing as a Teaching Tool

Figure 8.14 gives some guidelines for using application sharing and whiteboards as teaching tools.

Assess Learners' Knowledge of the Application. Application sharing and whiteboards can be used to help learners understand concepts, analyze information, and

---

Figure 8.14. Checklist for Using Shared Applications or Whiteboards

☑ Assess learners' knowledge of the application.

☑ Explain how it will be used and time limits.

☑ Provide a practice exercise.

☑ Allow adequate time.

☑ Make applications available outside of class time.

---

develop models. First, however, learners must be familiar with the application itself. Before building application-sharing exercises, determine if learners know how to use the application.

Explain How It Will Be Used and Time Limits. Be clear about how the application or whiteboard will be used, when work will be accessed, how long will be given to work on it, and what the expected outcomes are. For example, explain that the class will use application sharing to manipulate existing data, that learners will be expected to turn in their work, and that they will capture whiteboards and post them to threaded discussions.

Provide a Practice Exercise. Plan a brief initial exercise to give learners practice. For example, ask learners to use the whiteboard to brainstorm five problems facing managers who travel and must access their voice mail and e-mail accounts from the road. This type of simple exercise gives learners experience and confidence using the whiteboard before they attempt more complicated tasks.

Allow Adequate Time. Allow adequate time for teams to work on shared applications and the whiteboard. Be sure to pilot the exercises and ask for feedback on the time allotted to shared applications. The time needed to complete an exercise will depend on factors such as network speed, the communication method used to supplement the application sharing, and learners' familiarity with the application.

Make Applications Available Outside of Class Time. If the tool you chose allows learners to work together at times other than during the synchronous class meeting, be sure to make this known to learners. Encourage them to meet synchronously outside of class to work on assignments or projects using application sharing or whiteboards.

Web-Based Videoconferencing

Web-based videoconferencing is the ability to transmit audio and video images to multiple learners via the Internet or intranet. Like real-time audio, Web-based video offers more than one environment. Figure 8.15 illustrates the two ways that Web-based videoconferencing can be delivered. The first diagram (Figure 8.15a) shows the instructor's video being broadcast one way to learners. The instructor cannot see the learners nor can they see one another, although they can hear one another. Figure 8.15b illustrates how the instructor and learners are able to see and hear one another in an environment similar to traditional videoconferencing. There

Figure 8.15. Two Ways To Deliver Web-Based Videoconferencing

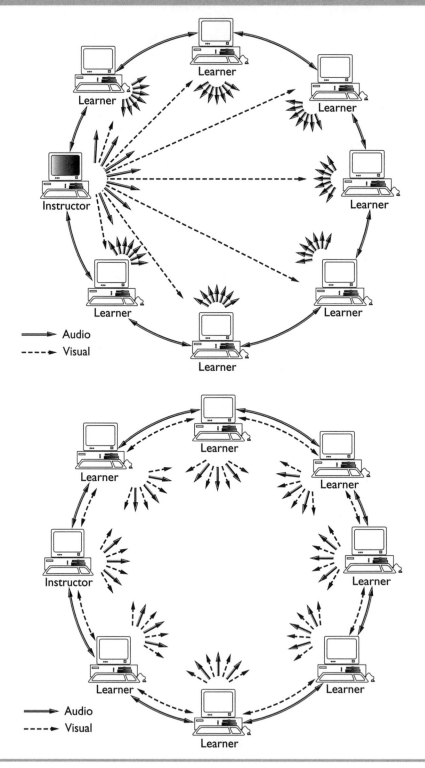

Figure 8.16. Example of Web-Based Videoconferencing

Credit: ILINC, LearnLinc.

are vendor-specific technical limits to how many learners can be connected at one time and how many sites can be viewed simultaneously.

Each Web-based videoconferencing software package provides slightly different features. The technology underlying these packages affects how the programs look, sound, and operate. Additional tools such as quizzing, sharing documents, and using prerecorded material are available. Figure 8.16 shows an example of Web-based videoconferencing product being used for training.

Advantages and Disadvantages

Figure 8.17 outlines the advantages and disadvantages of using multi-point Web-based videoconferencing for training. Like live classroom instruction, Web-based videoconferencing allows participants to see and hear one another. Learners communicate simply by talking, without text-chat or threaded discussion. Learners not only can hear others' voices, but they can see facial expressions and body language as well. In addition, a live videoconference can be supplemented with digital media

Figure 8.17. Advantages and Disadvantages of Web-Based Videoconferencing	
Advantages	**Disadvantages**
Mimics conventional classroom training.	Quality not as good as telephone or satellite-based.
Allows full video, audio, and document sharing.	Requires extra peripheral equipment.
	Not everyone is comfortable in front of a camera.

such as HTML pages, images, video clips, and animations, and with actual 3D objects such as paper-based graphics and artifacts using a document camera to digitize pictures, objects, and hard copy text. Digital cameras eliminate the need for scanning, creating, or preparing files in advance.

A limitation of Web-based videoconferencing is the poor quality of the image. It suffers in comparison with the quality of television or traditional videoconferencing programs. Because large amounts of information cross the Internet, the performance may not be as good as telephone or satellite-based solutions. As the technology improves, quality will be less of an issue.

Web-based videoconferencing requires that learners add a microphone, camera, and software to their computers. It is important to identify the resources needed to prepare the learners' computers because these devices add to the complexity of implementing a program. After the microphones, cameras, and software are installed, learners must take responsibility for focusing the camera and positioning the microphones correctly. Plan to spend a few minutes at the start of each program conducting a sound check and to adjust cameras.

Videoconferencing also presents a unique nontechnical dilemma: Many adult learners do not like to see themselves on screen and may be inhibited from talking. Start programs with an exercise that focuses on the content and not the learners. For example, ask learners to introduce themselves and to talk about the challenges that downsizing has created in their division.

Guidelines for Web-Based Videoconferencing

Figure 8.18 provides a checklist for creating a sound Web-based training program using videoconferencing.

Test System Prior to Program Date. Before running a Web-based videoconferencing program, conduct a test of the system. Ask the learners from each site to log

PURPOSE: *This exercise is designed to give you experience setting up a Web-based videoconferencing environment and participating in an informal videoconferencing session.*

Use a search engine such as Alta Vista®, Yahoo®, or Excite® to locate the free CU-SeeMe* software archive. Use the following terms to find the archive: CU-SeeMe, Cornell University CU-SeeMe, or desktop videoconferencing CU-SeeMe.

* CU-SeeMe is a free videoconferencing program copyrighted by Cornell University and its collaborators available to anyone with a Macintosh® or PC with Windows® and a connection to the Internet. CU-SeeMe allows you to videoconference with another site anywhere in the world. By using a reflector, multiple parties at different locations can participate.

Figure 8.18. Checklist for Creating Web-Based Videoconferencing

☑ Test system prior to program date.

☑ Prepare graphics in advance.

☑ Start on time.

☑ Familiarize learners with controls.

☑ Use a variety of interactions.

☑ Call on people by name and allow time for response.

☑ Limit the number of sites.

☑ Summarize key points.

☑ Conclude on time.

in and check the functionality and quality of the audio and video. Be prepared to provide technical assistance if learners are unable to connect successfully. Also, check the quality of the images that result from using the document camera and the quality of the microphones used by the instructor and learners.

Prepare Graphics in Advance. Before the videoconference, prepare graphics, text, video clips, and animations, and gather props to be shown during the program. The preparation required depends on the kind of software used to scan, digitize, compress, or render these items. Allow adequate time to develop and test digital media. Use a document camera to include paper-based graphics (i.e., hard copy printouts of

PowerPoint® slides, hand-lettered signs, pages of books), photographs, and maps. Test the legibility of these pieces before the class. One of the benefits of Web videoconferencing is the ability to use a wide range of images and objects to support a lesson.

Start on Time. Respect those participants who are on time by starting on time. Establish a process for providing participants who join in late the information they missed. You may want to provide them with copies of the graphics, a set of the instructor's notes, and an opportunity to stay logged in after class to talk to the instructor.

Familiarize Learners with Controls. Before using all the buttons and tools found on the interface, conduct an icebreaker activity to give learners experience using the controls. For example, ask participants to use the microphone to introduce themselves or ask them to raise their hands if they completed the pre-reading. Introduce the features slowly to allow learners time to learn how the buttons and tools operate. If the interface has features such as the ability to signal a raised hand, send the instructor a message, participate in a breakout room, and take a quiz, introduce the tools one at a time. Give learners adequate time and allow them to master one tool before introducing another.

Use a Variety of Interactions. As you did with multi-point real-time audio, combine a variety of instructional techniques in Web videoconferencing. Avoid the talking head syndrome; seeing the instructor's face adds little value to a program. Limit segments to five to seven minutes. Keep in mind that watching Web videoconferencing can be a passive experience. Use instructional strategies that engage the learner. All of the techniques presented in Table 8.1 for real-time audio also work for videoconferencing. Table 8.2 shows strategies unique to this mode of synchronous interaction.

Call on People by Name and Allow Time for Response. Depending on the system used, the display of learner names may not indicate which ones want to be called. During roll-call or an icebreaker activity, find out how learners want to be addressed. Allow time for your message to reach the learners' computers and time for the learners with the slowest connections to respond. Traffic on the Internet/intranet will cause lags in response time, so do not be quick to admonish participants for not answering.

Limit the Number of Sites. The number of sites able to participate in a program depends on the interaction level, technological limitations, and facilitation skills of the instructor. As the number of sites increases, interaction decreases. Highly inter-

Table 8.2. Strategies for Multi-Point Web-Based Videoconferencing	
Strategy	**Description**
Demonstrate	Use full-motion video to show participants steps in a process such as connecting cabling, replacing a computer board, or using a scanning wand.
Analyze	Perform a task and ask class members to critique it, such as counting cash. Ask learners to watch the demonstration and to explain what was done well and what could have been done better.
Monitor	Monitor learner performance, such as having them hold up parts of an engine as the parts are called out.

A instructor talks about creating a safe environment and naming conventions in a broadcast Web videoconferencing environment.

We used to let people choose any name they wanted. Then, students voiced concern that they did not feel comfortable speaking up in class because they couldn't tell who was really in the class. They didn't feel free to discuss their experiences or ask "dumb" questions because their boss or peers might be participating under a pseudonym. To create a learner-friendly environment, we now require students to use their real names.

active programs require adequate time for everyone to talk or respond. In other cases, the number of sites will be limited by the technology. Some videoconferencing programs allow a large number of sites to be connected if the program is one-way. Others allow a small number of sites for multi-point videoconferencing. The last factor limiting the number of sites participating is the skill of the instructor. As instructors become skilled at managing multiple sites, the number can be increased.

Summarize Key Points. As the program progresses, be sure to summarize key points. This is a good way to segue from one part of the program to another.

Conclude on Time. Be respectful of the learners' time and conclude the program as scheduled. If the program has not accomplished all of the stated goals, check with participants before extending the program. Consider scheduling another Web-based videoconference.

Technical and Logistical Considerations

The logistical issues related to planning synchronous interactions are not the focus here, but do address those issues before designing the interactions described in this chapter. First, assess the feasibility of synchronous programs for learners located around the world and ac ross the country. Consider local holidays, religious holidays, and time-zone differences. If the time-zone differences are irreconcilable, plan to run the program more than once. Next, consider the environment in which people will be learning (see Chapter Five). Think about the effect that microphones and cameras will have in the learners' work spaces. Determine how comfortable learners are talking to their computers and how supportive their managers are.

Technical issues are a major consideration when planning synchronous Web-based training programs. Software applications that enable real-time interactions vary in complexity and system requirements. Determine what kind of real-time interaction is needed, then work with the system manager to determine which applications best meet your needs. Avoid adopting technology that is not fully supported. Select tools that are easy for learners to use and will not require dozens of calls to the help desk for support. Explore the amount and kind of network and system-management resources required. Keep in mind bandwidth limitations, server resources, and end-user requirements. These technology requirements should not interfere with the organization's abilities to conduct business.

Summary

Web/virtual synchronous classroom programs are not appropriate for every situation, but they are the only solution when live interaction is essential. These tools foster synergy among learners, enable immediate feedback, and allow just-in-time development and delivery. Synchronous tools also enable instructional strategies not possible in other types of Web-based training, such as demonstrations, live debates, role plays, and discussions.

Four broad categories of synchronous tools are used to deliver live interactive programs: Internet relay chat, real-time audio with visuals, application sharing/whiteboards, and videoconferencing. These tools can be found as individual software applications or as bundled packages that bring together several synchronous and asynchronous tools. The descriptions presented in this chapter are general; each vendor's application varies slightly.

Synchronous and asynchronous interactions are the building blocks for developing Web-based training programs. Chapter Nine pulls together the needs assessment with the most appropriate Web-based training method, instructional strategies, and interactions.

Suggested Readings

Bradshaw, T. (1990). *Audiographics distance learning.* London: Wested.

Collis, B. (1996). *Tele-learning in a digital world: The future of distance learning.* New York: International Thomson.

Emery, M., & Schubert, M. (1993). A trainer's guide to videoconferencing. *Training Magazine, 30*(6), 59–63.

Gunawardena, C. N. (1992). Changing faculty roles for audiographics and online teaching. *American Journal of Distance Education, 6*(3), 58–71.

Lockwood, F. (1995). Open and distance learning today. In *Studies in Distance Education Series.* London: Routledge.

Mathis, G. A. (1988). *How to produce your own videoconference.* San Francisco: Knowledge Industry Publications.

Robinson, B., & Lockwood, F. (1996). *Achieving quality in open and flexible learning.* New York: Nichols Publishing.

Schieman, E., & Jones, T. (1992). Learning at a distance: Issues for the instructional designer. *Journal of Adult Education, 21*(2), 3–13.

Verduin, J. R., & Clark, T. A. (1991). *Distance education: The foundations of effective practice.* San Francisco: Jossey-Bass.

Chapter 9

Creating Blueprints

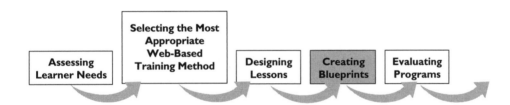

What You Will Learn in This Chapter

After completing this chapter, you will be able to

- Develop a design document;
- Draft a detailed program flow chart; and
- Create a script and storyboard.

The development of a Web-based training program is guided by detailed instructions in planning documents that constitute a blueprint for the program. Four kinds of planning documents are required to communicate the design of a lesson, as listed in Figure 9.1.

Figure 9.1. Required Documents for Development

☑ Design document

☑ Flow chart

☑ Script

☑ Storyboard

All forms of Web-based training need a design document; nonlinear forms (W/CBT, W/EPS, W/VAC) need a flow chart. Linear programs (W/VSC) need a script. All forms benefit from storyboards.

Design Documents

Design documents are detailed plans that provide the development team and client with a vision of the final product. Clients should review and agree to the specifications outlined in the design document before the development team invests time in creating storyboards or scripts.

Create design documents that are jargon-free, detailed, and easy to understand. Design documents will differ, depending on the client organization, program content, project size, length, and required sections. Figure 9.2 shows recommended sections and the types of content found in each section.

Introduction

Background. The introduction should set the context for the WBT program. Provide background information on the organization for whom you are developing the program. Inform the reader about why a distance-education solution is appropriate (i.e., geographically dispersed learners, just-in-time demand for knowledge).

Opportunity Statement. Draft an opportunity statement; explain how this program will enable an organization to improve productivity, reduce costs, limit legal liability, or increase profits. If possible, quantify the benefits of filling a skill or knowledge gap.

Audience. Describe the intended audience or learners. When possible, define learners based on job title and provide details regarding the expected entry-level

Figure 9.2. Outline of a Design Document	
Section	**Content**
Introduction	Background
	Opportunity statement
	Audience
	Goals/Objectives
Instructional Strategy	Presentation of information
	Learner participation
	Evaluation strategy
Navigational Map & WBT Outline	High-level graphic map/treatment statement
	Lesson outline for each unit
	• Title
	• Goal/Objectives
	• Length
	• Content
	• Learning activities
	• Evaluation
Resources	Design resources
	Development resources
	Delivery resources
Program Management	Timeline
	Roles and responsibilities
	Budget
	Risks and dependencies
Deliverables	Files
	Documents

skills and learner characteristics. It is important to document such assumptions before developing the program.

Goals/Objectives. Explain the goals of the program in easy-to-understand language. Create a goal statement that is clear and easy for a nontechnical person to understand. Include the objectives so the reader can understand what skills and

---

Figure 9.3. Sample Jargon-Free Goal Statement

Field service engineers in Europe, North America, and Asia will be able to install, customize, and troubleshoot the Office King 9000 laser printer.

---

knowledge the learner must master in order to achieve the program goal. It is up to the developer to decide how much detail to provide regarding goals. High-level objectives, called "terminal" objectives, may be adequate. In other cases, detailed, low-level objectives, called "enabling" objectives, may be required to fully explain the skills and knowledge required to achieve the goal. Figure 9.3 shows an example of a goal statement for a technical, Web-based training program.

Instructional Strategy

Presentation of Information. Provide an overview of the look and feel of the program. Explain how you plan to present the course content (i.e., text-based, role play, collaborative learning). If the presentation style is not one with which your clients or project sponsors are familiar, be sure to explain it. For example, if you are using experiential learning techniques, describe what that means.

Learner Participation. Provide details about how learners will participate in the lesson (i.e., self-paced reading, online dialogue with instructor, text-chat, Web-based videoconference with peers).

Evaluation Strategy. Discuss how you will assess learners' mastery of the content. If you plan to use asynchronous assessments such as tests and quizzes, see Chapter Seven.

Navigation Map and WBT Outline

High-Level Graphic Map. Navigation maps provide an overview of how the program is structured. They give visual pictures of the Web-based training outline, as seen in Figure 9.4. They are effective for nonlinear programs in which learners can select unique paths. They are appropriate for W/CBT, W/EPS, and W/VAC.

Treatment Statement. Web/virtual synchronous classroom programs take place in real-time and therefore have a more linear structure. For such a program, it is more informative to provide a treatment statement, a brief description of the program, such as the one shown in Figure 9.5.

Figure 9.4. Sample Navigation Map

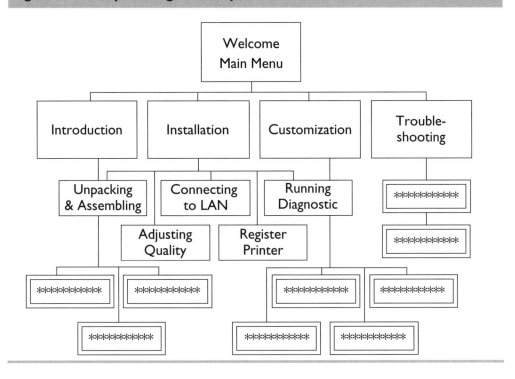

The more details provided in the outline section, the easier it will be to estimate the developmental requirements. In addition, clients benefit from a detailed outline because they understand what will and will not be included in each lesson.

Figure 9.6 depicts the hierarchy of the elements in a course. Each course has a number of lessons and each lesson has a goal and objectives. Plan to spend time analyzing and synthesizing the course content to develop the outline. Each lesson should

Figure 9.5. Sample Treatment Statement

This is a one-hour customer-service refresher training program. Bob Smith, VP of Customer Service, and Kathy Albright, recognized expert in customer service, host the program. It is a talk-show format with Bob Smith as the moderator and Kathy Albright as the guest. Learners are invited to send in questions via Internet text-chat while the program is being broadcast.

Figure 9.6. Hierarchy of Course Structure

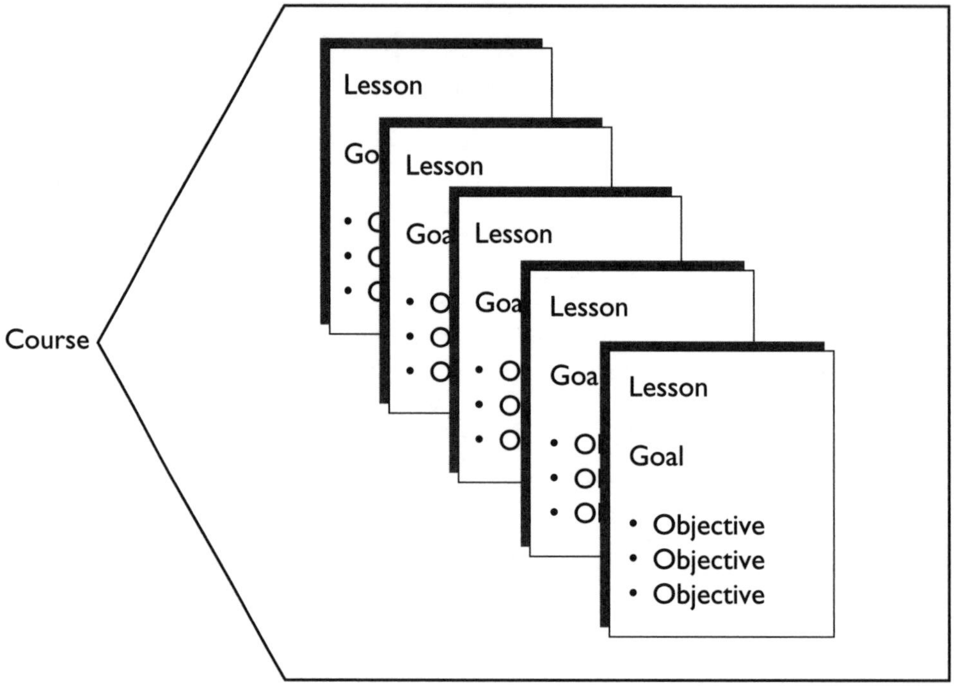

have a title, a goal statement, and five to seven objectives. Estimate the length of the lesson—how long it will take the average learner to complete the lesson. Outline the content that will be covered and, when possible, identify the source. Possible sources are user documentation, system specifications, and subject-matter experts.

In addition, include the learning activities that are compatible with the kind of Web-based training being delivered. For example, W/CBT is used to teach measurable skills and knowledge. Appropriate learning methods would be drill and practice, quizzes, question and answer, and reading. Table 9.1 shows the types of learning methods best suited to each kind of Web-based training.

Last, provide a brief description of how you plan to measure how much the learners have learned. Assessment or testing does not have to be in a traditional form; see Chapter Seven for more details on testing, quizzing, and nontraditional assessment options. If you choose not to test, inform the client and the learners, and explain why. Figure 9.7 is a sample outline for a simple lesson in a Web-based training program.

Table 9.1. Matching Learning Method to Training Type

	W/CBT	W/EPS Systems	W/VAC	W/VSC
Methods	Drill and practice, simulations, reading, question and answer	Problem solving, scientific method, experiential method, project method	Experiential tasks, group discussions, team projects, self-directed learning, discovery method	Dialogue and discussions, problem solving, and maximum interaction
Interactions	Multimedia, hypertext, hypermedia, simulations, application exercises, e-mail, listserv, and communication with instructor	Multimedia, hypertext, hypermedia, bulletin boards, notes conferences, modules of W/CBT, e-mail access to facilitator and peers	Multimedia, hypertext, hypermedia, bulletin boards, notes conferences, modules of W/CBT, e-mail access to facilitator and peers	Synchronous audio- & video-conferencing, shared , whiteboards shared applications, IRC

Resources

The resource section of the document is intended to clearly communicate the staffing and hardware and software resources required in each step of the process. Developing a Web-based training program requires a team of professionals, potentially drawn from many sources. In addition, special hardware and software may need to be ordered.

Design, Development, and Delivery Resources. Make separate lists for the resources needed to design, develop, and deliver the program. Remember, many of the team members, such as the system manager, Webmaster, and subject-matter experts, are drawn from other departments (see Chapter Four). Making separate lists for each phase of the project helps departments plan schedules and anticipate their

Figure 9.7. Sample WBT Outline

Office King 9000 Laser Printer Web-Based Training

Lesson Title	Time	Outline
OK 9000 Installation	8 min.	**Goal:** Field service engineers will be able to install the Office King 9000 (OK9000).

Objectives: After completing this lesson, field service engineers will be able to:

- Unpack and assemble the OK 9000

- Make network connections to LAN

- Run a diagnostic test pattern

- Adjust quality of output

- Register the printer with customer service

Content: The lesson will include:

- Unpacking and assembling directions

- Network connection diagrams

- Steps for running diagnostic test patterns

- Quality matrix (problem/recommended fix)

- Directions to send registration via Internet to customer service group at HQ

Learning activities: Activities include:

- Reading

- Internet chat room

- Responding to questions

- Problem solving using EPS Systems

Assessment: Multiple choice test, ten items

Figure 9.8. WBT Process and List of Resources		

List of Potential Resources

	People	**Equipment (Hardware, Software)**
Design	Instructional designers	Computers
	Subject-matter expert	Software to develop prototype
	Project manager	
Develop	Instructional designers	Computers
	Course developers	Servers
	Pilot subjects	Network access
	Graphic artists	Software to create
	Editors	• Audio
	Programmers	• Animation
	Facilitator	• Text
	Administrators	• Graphics
		• Video
Deliver	Facilitator	Computers
	System manager	Servers
	Local installation support	Network
	Help-desk staff	Software
	Webmaster	
	Programmers	
	Course developers	

level of involvement. Include a list of resources required to maintain the program; this will ensure that clients are not surprised in a few months when the program needs to be updated. Figure 9.8 shows the three phases of a project and identifies the resources needed in each.

During the development phase, establish a cross-functional team and equip it with the tools needed to create Web-based training. During the delivery phase, plan for the installation of browsers and additional applications, such as browsers plug-ins, and organize help-desk support. Identify the resources needed to keep the program accurate and functional after the initial roll-out.

Program Management

Timeline. Include a section in the design document that deals with project-management issues. Provide a timeline that lists the start and end dates for milestones, like the example in Figure 9.9. Break the tasks into manageable activities with clear beginning and end points. Activities that are too large may discourage members of the development team, because they take a long time to complete. Shorter activities give team members a sense of satisfaction and provide frequent opportunities to check progress.

Roles and Responsibilities. List the roles and responsibilities of team members internal and external to the organization. Make it clear who is responsible for tasks such as reviewing content, maintaining hardware, installing software, negotiating access to resources, and communicating with learners.

Figure 9.9. Example of a Project Timeline

Timeline for WBT Project

Activity	Start Date	End Date	Comments
Project kick-off meeting	January 12	January 12	Bob from Dallas office will participate via tele-conference.
Draft Lesson 1 content	January 13	January 23	
Draft questions for IRC	January 13	January 23	
SME reviews and signs off on Lesson 1	January 24	January 30	
Revisions to Lesson 1	February 2	February 6	
Graphics for Lesson 1	February 12	February 16	Icons developed for Lesson 1 will be used for all lessons.

Budget. Create a budget for the project that lists the expenses related to software, hardware, and staff. Review the list of resources to identify all the costs related to software, such as purchase and/or license fees and maintenance and support agreements. Determine hardware needs for the development team, such as computers with additional memory or graphics capabilities, servers, and modems. Decide who is budgeting for the hardware needs of learners, who may require sound cards, speakers, microphones, and high-color monitors. This expense may be the responsibility of the field organization or it may have to be on the WBT program budget. Review the expenses related to staffing the project at each phase. Will external consultants be needed to install servers, set up databases, or manage the installation of software and hardware in the field? Will internal organizations assess a charge-back fee to the project?

Risks and Dependencies. Create a section that discusses risks and dependencies. Let clients and team members know about risks—potential problems beyond your control. Risks can include failure to upgrade the end-user systems, last-minute changes in content, and lack of knowledgeable reviewers. Take time to identify when a success depends on things you do not control. Dependencies can include standardization on the latest version of Netscape Navigator® or employee access to the Internet on a 28.8 modem or higher.

Deliverables

Files and Documents. The final section of the design document lists the deliverables, that is, the items that will be given to the client at the end of the project. Deliverables can include files, documents, disks, CD-ROMs, digitized video clips, and film negatives. List and explain what they are to help the client understand the work required to develop a Web-based training program.

PURPOSE: *This exercise is designed to provide you with guidelines for collecting data and for reflecting on it before you create a design document.* Use the Design Document Worksheet to gather the data needed to develop a design document.

✓ Design Document Worksheet

Directions: Use this worksheet to reflect on design questions. When you have completed the worksheet, review it with the development team.

Introduction

Describe the organization for which the training is being developed. What gap in skills and knowledge will this program fill?

Who are the learners?

What is the goal of the program?

List five to seven objectives.

1.

2.

3.

4.

5.

6.

7.

Instructional Strategy

How will the information be presented (text, lecture, CBT)?

How will learners participate (answer questions, role play, discussion)?

How will you determine whether the learners have mastered the content of the course (test, quiz, performance-based assessment)?

Navigation Map/Outline

On a separate sheet of graph paper, sketch a navigation map.

On a separate sheet of paper create an outline for each lesson in your course. Be sure to include: title, goal/objectives, length, content, learning activities, and assessment of this lesson.

Resources

Before answering the following questions, see Chapter Four for a list of possible team members.

DESIGN PHASE

Who is needed to help you design the program?

What software, hardware, or equipment do you need?

DEVELOPMENTAL PHASE

Who is needed to help you develop and create the program?

What software, hardware, or equipment do you need?

DELIVERY PHASE

Who is needed to help you deliver and maintain the program?

What software, hardware, or equipment do you need?

Project Management

Create a timeline and list the major milestones for this project.

Activity	Start Date	End Date	Comments

What are the roles and responsibilities of each team member? *(List what you expect of each person iden-tified in the Resources section.)*

Create a line-item budget. List all expenses related to this project: software, stock images, music li-braries, consultants, and internal cross-charges.

Description of Item   **Cost**

_____

_____

_____

_____

_____

_____

_____

_____

_____

TOTAL

List the risks and dependencies (things that are beyond your control) so that others are aware of anything that may affect development dates, product functionality, and performance of the course.

Deliverables

What tangible items will be given to the client during the project (e.g., storyboards, pilot lessons, weekly reports)? Describe the items.

What are the final deliverables or items that will be given to the client at the end of the project (e.g., HTML files, images, master CD-ROM, Java or X-Active code)? Describe the items.

Program Flow Charts

Flow charts are highly detailed maps that illustrate how programs are organized. They are important tools for communicating the design of nonlinear programs. Use flow charts as maps to guide the development of W/CBT, W/EPS, and W/VAC.

Because flow charts require a great deal of analysis of content and detailed instructional design, they are developed after the specifications in the design document are approved. Creating a detailed flow chart prior to approval invites the risk of having to make major revisions. Figure 9.10 lists the benefits of creating flow charts.

Provide More Detail. Flow charts are highly detailed versions of the navigation maps included in the design document. Figure 9.11 shows how a piece of the navigation map shown in Figure 9.4 was expanded to create a flow chart.

Create Shared Vision. Flow charts offer the cross-functional team a shared vision of the final product. The visual representation of lessons provides a tool to analyze content overlap, variations in instructional strategies, and omissions. In addition, the flow chart helps identify potential problems.

Establish Measure. The flow chart is a yardstick against which to measure your work. Provide those who test your program with a copy of the flow chart and ask them to compare the functionality, navigation, and flow of the program to the flow-chart specifications.

Figure 9.10. Benefits of Creating Flow Charts

☑ Provide more detail than the navigation map or design document.

☑ Create a shared vision for cross-functional teams.

☑ Establish an independent measure of accomplishment.

Figure 9.11. Sample Flow Chart from Navigation Map

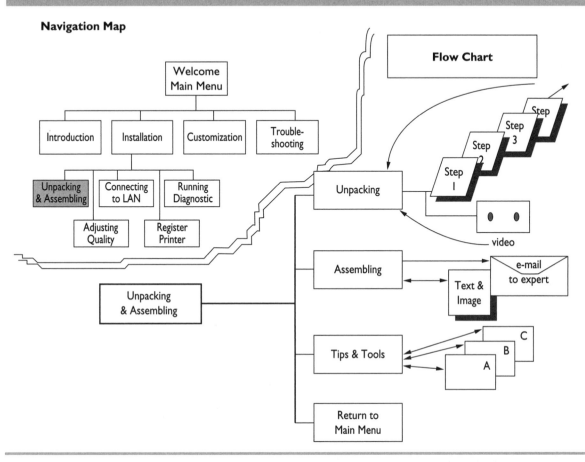

PURPOSE: *This exercise is designed to give you practice flow charting and an opportunity to analyze the design of existing Web-based training programs.*

Use one of the courses you bookmarked as an example of W/CBT, W/EPS, or W/VAC, or use a search engine such as Alta Vista®, Yahoo®, or Excite® to locate a Web-based training program. Use the following terms in your search: Web-based training, Web-based training example, Web-based training sample, Web-based training demo, Web-based instruction, Free Web-based training class, or Sample Class Web-based training.

Use a large sheet of flip-chart paper to create a flow chart of the navigation, lesson flow, and content hierarchy.

Use the Flow Chart Worksheet to reflect on your experience.

√ Flow Chart Worksheet

Questions

1. After creating the flow chart, did you see relationships among sections that you did not see before?

2. What were the easiest relationships to depict? What were the most difficult? Why were they easy or hard to depict?

3. Look at the flow chart you created and think back to one of the W/CBT programs you experienced and bookmarked in Chapter Six. Is there a relationship between the sections of the W/CBT you liked best and the flow chart? Were there places in the W/CBT in which you felt disoriented? Does the flow chart provide any clues about why you felt this way?

Program Script

A program script is a plan or set of directions for the Web/virtual synchronous classroom, a text-based document that outlines what will take place section by section. Nonlinear programs such as W/CBT, W/EPS, and W/VAC allow learners to take a number of paths and require graphic depiction to communicate the flow. A distinguishing feature of W/VSC is that learners and the instructor participate in a real-time linear experience. Figure 9.12 lists the benefits of creating program scripts.

Breaks Instruction into Clear Sections. The program script should have clear sections, such as an opening, information presentation, exercises, interaction, and closing. Distinctive sections give learners a sense of pacing and completion. Estimate the time needed for each section; this will help you plan and execute the program. When you pilot the program, track the actual times and make adjustments.

Provides Appropriate Level of Detail. When scripting the audio portion, do not provide word-for-word text. Scripting the program too tightly reduces spontaneity. Work with the facilitator to develop audio scripting or directions that provide adequate guidance while allowing for innovation and responsiveness.

Lists Supporting Media. Record a description of the visuals you plan to use and the source file names. Tracking the media files in the program script makes it easy to assemble the program, swap out images, and identify missing media.

Matches Objectives to Instruction. Compare the script to the objectives stated in the design document, making sure they agree. This is a good double check for the entire design. Figure 9.13 shows a sample script.

Storyboards

Storyboards have their origins in the production of movies and cartoons. Storyboarding is a technique used to illustrate how a program will unfold. Each

---

Figure 9.12. Benefits of Using a Program Script

☑ Breaks instruction into clear sections.

☑ Provides appropriate level of detail.

☑ Lists supporting media.

☑ Matches objectives to instruction.

Figure 9.13. Sample W/SVC script			
Time	**Audio Directions**	**Visual**	**Media/Files**
Pre-start −5 to 0	Music	Title screen showing course name and start time (what learners who log in before class see)	Title Screen Intro.music/intro.wav
0–2	Instructor welcomes class to New Product Introduction Training. *Ask if everyone was able to locate and read the forum postings on new products.*	Photo of instructor	b_smith.img
	Review objectives and ask for questions.	List of objectives	Whiteboard
2–5	Review features and benefits of CyberTop family of computers.	Pictures of models 300, 500, 700; List of features and benefits	Cyber300.gif; Cyber500.gif; Cyber700.gif
5–9	Ask learners to brainstormproducts that compete with CyberTops.	Online electronic whiteboard	Draw freehand
9–14	Introduce Tom Dowling, product manager, and invite learners to ask questions.	Picture of product manager; Give Tom whiteboard to supplement his talk.	t_dowling.html; Draw freehand

scene is drawn on a sheet of paper and posted on a wall so that the development team and client can follow it. In Web-based training, this technique helps show how the pages of a lesson relate. Figure 9.14 lists the benefits of using storyboards.

Provides Visual of Program Flow. Storyboards are used for linear and nonlinear programs. The same information presented in the script or flow chart is used in the

Figure 9.14. Benefits of Storyboards

☑ Provides visual of program flow.

☑ Enables content to be resequenced.

☑ Highlights gaps in content or dead-end paths.

storyboards but presented visually. Storyboards help a client understand the path through the main menu, sub-menu, content presentation, interactive exercise, summary, and review. The path may be clear in the flow chart, but still hard for clients to envision.

Enables Content To Be Resequenced. While the program is being put into storyboards is a good time to make revisions to flow and content. Resequencing, deleting, or adding sections is easier before time and money are invested in developing the final media elements.

Highlights Gaps in Content or Dead-End Paths. Storyboards also provide an opportunity for the entire development team to view the program at once, highlighting gaps in content, assumptions about how things will flow, and paths that are dead ends.

> **A developer recommends using PowerPoint® and clip art to create storyboards.**
> *I am a terrible artist and don't like to draw, so I use the clip art in PowerPoint® to make my storyboards. It's faster than hand-drawn boards and easier to update.*

The level of detail in storyboards depends on how they are to be used. If they are being used to provide an overview of the flow of the program and a sense of the level of interactivity, rough hand-drawn pieces of paper may work well. If they are being used to communicate details to graphic artists and communicate the look and feel of the program to clients, a detailed drawing created with a sophisticated graphics program may be required.

A simple storyboard created with PowerPoint® software allows the designer to print 8½-by-11-inch visuals and to print multiple visuals on a single page with annotation. These options allow many ways to communicate the design of the program.

The 8½-by-11-inch visuals are large enough for the entire team to see at one time. This makes it easy to walk through with the instructional designer as he or she explains the program, points to elements on the visuals, and clarifies the interactions. Yet another option is to send team members a document that contains the visuals and a brief explanation of what is taking place in each. Figure 9.15 is an example of a simple storyboard created in PowerPoint® that combines visuals and annotation.

PURPOSE: *This worksheet helps you think about ways to enhance the adult learning experience in W/CBT and W/VSC programs.*

Think about how the blueprint for a class to teach job-search skills would differ from a W/CBT program to a W/VSC program. Use the Brainstorming Blueprints Worksheet to list the differences.

Figure 9.15. Sample Storyboard

Visual	**Explanation**

Program title

Screen that displays as Bob Smith introduces himself and explains how to reach him after this class.

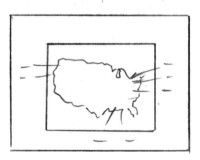

Outline map of the United States. Participants are asked to introduce themselves and to indicate where they are from.

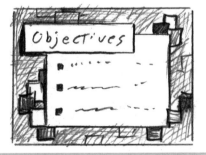

The instructor reviews the objectives and asks the learners if they would like to add any other objectives

✓ Brainstorming Blueprints Worksheet

	W/CBT	W/VSC
How might the goals and objectives differ? Are some cognitive objectives better suited for one type of Web-based training than another?		
Describe the role of the instructor. Describe the activities in which the instructor would be involved.		
Describe the role of the learner. What is expected of the learner?		
List three to five interactions, exercises, or instructional strategies you would use to help adults develop job-search skills.		
How would you test or quiz learners?		

	W/CBT	**W/VSC**
List the resources required to design, develop, and deliver each kind of program. How similar or different are the resources?		
List the deliverables, the items to be given to the client at the close of the project. How similar or different are they?		

Describe the benefits and limitations of a nonlinear program (W/CBT).

Describe the benefits and limitations of a linear program (W/VSC).

Summary

The design document, flow chart, script and storyboard are blueprints that guide the development team. There is a direct relationship between the time and effort put into developing these documents and the quality of the program that is produced. Designers who document the program's goals, objectives, and audience are developing a solid foundation. Clear descriptions of the information presented, learner participation, and the evaluation strategy set client expectations. Detailed navigation and treatment maps guide graphic artists, programmers, and members of the IS staff.

Web-based training programs are resource intensive. Successful programs require cross-functional cooperation among members of the training department, information-systems staff, line managers, field managers, learners, and subject-matter experts. Complex and expensive hardware, software, and infrastructure are required to support Web-based training. It is essential to understand what is required during the design, development, and delivery phases. Test your assumptions regarding the functionality of software and hardware and partner with members of your information-systems group to explore options.

Use these documents as a yardstick against which the development team and client measure success. After the program has been developed, decide whether it achieves what the blueprints specify. Chapter Ten presents techniques and strategies for evaluating programs.

Suggested Readings

Gery, G. (1987). *Making CBT happen: Prescriptions for successful implementation of computer-based training in your organization.* Boston: Gery Associates.

Hall, B. (1997). *Web-based training cookbook.* New York: John Wiley.

Khan, B. H. (1997). *Web-based instruction.* Englewood Cliffs, NJ: Educational Technology Publications.

Morrison, G. R., & Ross, S. M. (1988). A four-stage model for planning computer-based instruction. *Journal of Instructional Development, 11,* pp. 14–16.

Orr, K. L. (1994). Storyboard development for interactive multimedia training. *Journal of Interactive Instruction Development, 6*(3), 18–31.

Reynolds, A., & Iwinski, T. (1996). *Multimedia training: Developing technology-based systems.* New York: McGraw-Hill.

Chapter 10

Evaluating Programs

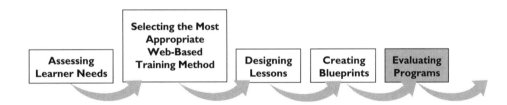

What You Will Learn in This Chapter

After completing this chapter, you will be able to

- Explain the benefits of evaluating Web-based training programs during development; and

- Plan evaluations for all forms of Web-based training.

Benefits of Evaluating W/CBT Programs

It is important to evaluate Web-based training programs during the development process. Designing graphics, laying out HTML pages, writing directions, and building interactive segments are expensive and time-consuming activities. Before much time and money are committed, check that the program will be effective.

Web-based training demands that many elements be brought together to produce an effective learning experience. What appeared to be clear and well-organized in the design document and what flowed well in the storyboards and scripts may not be so clear or well sequenced in the final product. Use the process outlined in this chapter to evaluate content, learner participation, interactions, and the facilitator's role.

First, subject-matter experts (SMEs) determine whether the content of the lesson is correct and complete. Next, rapid-prototype evaluations determine whether the overall design of the program is effective by examining a sample module. In the alpha phase the effectiveness of the entire course is tested. Instructor-led programs (W/VAC and W/VSC) are taught by the developers to focus on the effectiveness of the course.

Beta classes are only used to evaluate instructor-led Web-based training programs (W/VAC and W/VSC). These evaluations assess the effectiveness of the entire course and the clarity and completeness of the instructor directions.

Types of Evaluations for WBT

Evaluation of Web-based training has several phases; each tests a different aspect of the program. All types require subject-matter expert evaluation, rapid-prototype evaluation, and alpha-class evaluation. Instructor-led classes require a beta-class evaluation. Be sure to include time on your milestone chart for each of these phases, as well as time to make changes or corrections that result from the evaluations. Web-based training programs are a form of software programming; therefore, the program *must* be tested prior to shipping. Figure 10.1 shows the phases of evaluation.

Subject-Matter Expert Evaluation

First assess the accuracy of the content by asking a subject-matter expert (SME) to examine it for factual integrity and completeness. Request the help of an SME to

Figure 10.1. Phases of Evaluation				
	W/CBT	**W/EPS**	**W/VAC**	**W/VSC**
Subject-Matter Expert	✔	✔	✔	✔
Rapid Prototype	✔	✔	✔	✔
Alpha Class	✔	✔	✔	✔
Beta Class			✔	✔

evaluate the content as soon as feasible. Avoid spending time and money designing HTML pages and complex interactions that could require major changes. Provide the SME with detailed storyboards, hand-drawn examples of interactions, full-length scripts, content for text screens, and quizzes (provide the correct and incorrect answers). Speed the process by giving SMEs clear directions regarding the kind of feedback you want and the dates by which the material must be reviewed.

If possible, target sections of the program to be reviewed by different SMEs. Ask those most familiar with a specific topic to review the sections related to that topic. Shorten the evaluation process by having several sections reviewed at the same time by more than one SME. If the recommended changes are substantial, ask the SMEs to review their sections again after responding to their comments.

A trainer at a start-up software company recommends that developers tell SMEs what they are and are not expected to review.

A Web-based training developer for a software company recently received feedback from an SME that was of little value and cost the company a lot of money. The SME was a senior network system engineer who was given insufficient directions. He spent a great deal of time critiquing the Website's design, page layout, and the technical optimization of the interactions. Better directions would have focused the SME's attention on the network content; the resulting feedback would have been more valuable

---

Rapid-Prototype Evaluation

The concept of rapid prototyping comes from the manufacturing sector, where it is used to build physical models and archetypes. Prototypes save companies money because they enable people to evaluate physical, three-dimensironal models rather than waiting to evaluate fully functioning machines that take a long time to build.

In Web-based training, rapid prototyping serves a similar function. Developers do not build fully functioning training programs; rather, they create programs with just enough functionality to evaluate the lesson. Developers use prototypes to identify obvious errors in the instruction and to gauge learners' reactions to the program before building the entire course. Evaluating a rapid prototype of a lesson requires a number of steps and many decisions along the way. Figure 10.2 lists the steps.

> **Figure 10.2. Steps for Conducting Rapid-Prototype Evaluation**
>
> 1. Make rapid prototype for one lesson.
> 2. Identify learners.
> 3. Develop a plan to gather feedback.
> 4. Use one-on-one sessions.
> 5. Explain purpose.
> 6. Create comfortable environment.
> 7. Take notes.

Rapid Prototype for One Lesson. The amount of detail in a rapid prototype depends on the tools, audience, budget, and time available for the project. Figure 10.3 illustrates the range of prototypes from abstract, paper-based lessons to fully functioning Internet lessons.

In an ideal world, the prototype should be the way the final training program will appear and function. The most abstract kinds of prototypes are paper-based lessons, pictures of screens on paper described to the learner. Abstract prototypes are easy to build using simple tools such as word processors, PowerPoint® slides, and hand-drawn pictures. More concrete prototypes that look and act exactly like the final training program are more time-consuming and costly to produce.

Although prototypes range from the abstract to the concrete, most are somewhere in between. For example, in a simple W/CBT program that uses only hypertext and images, the prototype may be concrete. In this case it is possible to develop a concrete prototype of the lesson that looks and functions like the final program. In contrast, a complex W/CBT program that uses sophisticated Java applets and sections of compressed video may be evaluated using a more abstract prototype. In this case, the developer would create a series of paper-based drawings to indicate where video or Java applications belonged in the program. During the evaluation, the developer would explain these sections to reviewers.

The complexity and cost of the tools used to build the prototype influence where the prototype falls along the continuum. If the final training program requires the development of Java applets, CGI scripts, compressed video, and Macromedia Shocked® images, it may be too costly to develop a prototype with fully function-

Figure 10.3. Range of Rapid Prototypes

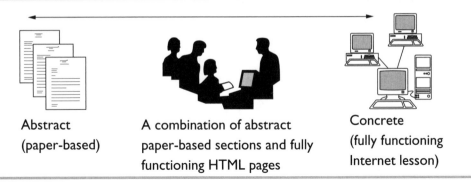

Abstract
(paper-based)

A combination of abstract
paper-based sections and fully
functioning HTML pages

Concrete
(fully functioning
Internet lesson)

ing interactions. In their place, developers can create paper-based screens or simulate the interactions using PowerPoint®slides.

The pilot audience for a rapid prototype will also influence how abstract or concrete it is for review purposes. People familiar with the Web and computer-based training will be more capable of understanding how a paper-based version of the program will work on the Web. Learners who have spent limited time using a browser, the Internet, or CBT programs may have difficulty understanding how a paper-based prototype will work on the Web. Feedback on the clarity of directions, level of interest, and effectiveness of instruction can only be assessed if those reviewing the program understand how the program will operate.

The project's budget and timeline influence the prototype. Developing a concrete prototype may be disproportionately expensive and time-consuming relative

A developer creating a class for nontechnical managers shares her insights regarding the different degrees of detail needed in a rapid prototype.
I have developed many programs for technical people. Quick-and-dirty prototype screens worked well. I was able to use simple graphics as placeholders for detailed diagrams that had not been created and a box with the phrase "Photo goes here" to represent an image or photo. When my learners are technical people familiar with the Web, HTML, and CBT, they understand what my shorthand means. Dealing with less technically sophisticated learners, I found that they were not able to understand my shorthand. These kinds of learners require a more fully developed prototype that uses the real images, icons, working interactions, and functioning navigation.

to the balance of the project. A fully functioning prototype requires that the graphic style be defined and that interactions, quizzes, and images be created. These are time-consuming to design and develop, but if the prototype elements are determined to be effective, these initial items become templates—reusable elements for the final program.

It is difficult for clients to understand that, although the prototype appears to be expensive, it is actually a way to save money. It is less expensive to learn that an icon is confusing or that certain types of interactions are too "cutesy" during the prototype than after the program has been fully developed.

Identify Learners. Work with your client or the organization sponsoring the program to identify learners who are representative of the audience. Find learners who represent the full spectrum of skills and experiences: those who are experienced and inexperienced in the content area and those who are skilled using the Internet and those who are not.

Use a grid like the one shown in Figure 10.4 to select a representative sample. Six to nine users will provide sufficient feedback on the content and the issues related to using a browser.

Your sample audience may not be as diverse as the one shown in Figure 10.4. If you are training in an environment in which Web-based training is new, you may not have any experienced browser users in your audience.

Develop a Plan To Gather Feedback. Develop a plan to collect data from try-out learners. Focus on collecting information regarding the clarity of content and level of difficulty in using the browser. Create checklists or questions that will guide the evaluation sessions, such as the one in Figure 10.5.

Figure 10.4. Identifying Prototype Learners

Familiarity with Browser	Familiarity with Content		
	Novice	**Practitioner**	**Expert**
Beginning User	Tom	Gene	Scott
Intermediate User	Sue	Tim	Terry
Experienced User	Karen	Nora	Jose

Figure 10.5. Sample Questions for Rapid-Prototype Sessions

	Sample Questions
Content	• Are the directions clear?
	• Does the content meet the objectives?
	• Is the vocabulary appropriate?
	• Do the examples add clarity to the lesson?
	• Is there adequate practice?
Browser or software running in browser	• Are the icons clear?
	• Is the navigation intuitive?
	• Are the screen "hot spots" clear?
	• Are pop-up windows confusing?
	• After using a hypertext link, is it easy to return to the program?

Use One-on-One Sessions. After you have prepared the evaluation guidelines, invite the try-out learners to evaluate the prototype during one-on-one sessions in which it will be easier to collect information. Also, if the prototype is abstract, you will be able to explain how interactions, hypertext links, or icons work.

Explain Purpose. Explain the purpose of the evaluation to the learners. Stress that learners' experiences and feedback are valued. Explain that the program is not perfect or error free and that they are being asked for their opinions. Remember that they are the best qualified people to guide the development of the program.

Create Comfortable Environment. Create a comfortable environment for conducting an evaluation. As with one-on-one evaluations for conventional training materials, the role of an evaluator in Web-based training is to be critical of the material being presented. In the context of Web-based training, this role is more complex because the learner must be critical not only of the content and design, but also of the computer interface. Help the learners feel comfortable with the role of evaluator. Do not be impatient with novice browser users. Separate the criticism of the content, design, and interactions from the learners' frustrations with network speed and browser interface.

Take Notes. Keep track of feedback. If you are using a fully developed Web-based training program, print out the screens and take notes directly on the screen prints. This will make it easy to keep track of feedback in nonlinear programs. Use a copy of the navigation map to note navigation problems or interactions that create confusion.

After the rapid-prototype evaluation, make the recommended changes, and develop all of the lessons.

Alpha-Class Evaluation

The purpose of an alpha class is to assess the effectiveness of the changes made as a result of the rapid-prototype evaluation and to determine if the materials can be used as intended (i.e., via the Web as self-paced or via the Web with facilitation). In this phase, the learners are using fully developed materials, including graphics, page layout, interactions, tests, and links to other sites.

The alpha class is the first time the materials are used over the Web as intended. In the case of W/VSC and W/VAC, the developer acts as the instructor. Based on the developer's experience as an instructor, changes are made to the instructor's notes or instructor's guide. These notes can be useful for conducting a train-the-trainer session. Figure 10.6 lists the steps required to evaluate Web-based training programs that are self-paced or instructor-led.

Identify Learners. The learners should be representative of the population for whom the training is being developed. This is the first evaluation of the training program by remote learners of instruction delivered via the browsers. Use a representative sample of learners to provide broad feedback on technical difficulties and instructional issues.

Figure 10.6. Steps To Evaluate an Alpha Class

1. Identify learners.
2. Plan how to gather feedback.
3. Explain purpose of alpha-class evaluation.
4. Help learners feel comfortable and collect data.
5. Compile data and make necessary changes.

Table 10.1. Considerations for Collecting Data	
Planning Data Collection	**Sample Data-Collection Methods**
How will data be collected?	• e-mail • telephone • text-chat • survey sent via postal service
What methods for collecting data will be used?	• Individual interviews • Focus groups
What areas will be assessed?	• Design • Content • Technical functionality • Interactions • Timing

Plan How To Gather Feedback. Identify the data to be collected from the alpha class and create a plan to collect it. Make a list of questions about relevance of content, clarity of instructions, effectiveness of instructional design, and the ease of use of the interface and computer interactions. Table 10.1 lists the considerations for creating a plan to collect feedback.

Determine how feedback will be collected (phone, e-mail, text-chat). Use tools that are familiar to the learners. If they are not familiar with a tool, their feedback may be limited. Think about the methods of collecting data. In some cases you may want to have a focus group, and in others you may want to invite people to contact you by phone or e-mail. If possible, find a try-out learner and ask if you can observe him or her using the program. Observing learners helps you to see the environment in which the program will be used. In addition, observation helps identify frustrations caused by unclear navigation, delays in downloading files, and other issues that may not be voiced in feedback sessions.

Explain Purpose of Alpha-Class Evaluation. Explain the purpose of the alpha-class evaluation to learners. Inform them that the class is being piloted and that their feedback is important. Before the class begins, explain what kind of information you will be collecting so that learners can take notes. Set learners' expectations regarding frequent stops for feedback and the need to complete exercises, to take quizzes, and to participate in text-chat sessions and threaded discussions.

Help Learners Feel Comfortable and Collect Data. Help learners feel comfortable delivering feedback, as well as acknowledging their technical limitations. Much of the data will be collected at a distance via telephone, e-mail, and surveys, which makes it difficult to sort the technical obstacles from the instructional problems. Learners must feel comfortable and be encouraged to provide honest feedback. In some cases, the designer will need to ask follow-up questions to determine which problems are technical and which are educational. If learners are unfamiliar with the browser or if tools such as text-chat and threaded discussions frustrate them, the developer needs honest feedback. Effective feedback from learners regarding unclear directions will lead the developer to improve the directions rather than eliminate the exercise.

Compile Data and Make Necessary Changes. Compile the data and make changes as indicated by the alpha class. Additional changes are still possible, of course. One of the benefits of Web-based training is that minor modifications and changes can be made quickly and cost effectively. Changes to complex elements such as Java applets, compressed video segments, and other multimedia elements can be expensive because they require more effort and access to resources such as programmers, hardware, and software.

If this is a Web/CBT or W/EPS program, it is ready to launch if the content has been checked for accuracy and completeness and the instructional strategies and the program have been tested for completeness and effectiveness. These programs do not require beta-class evaluation because they do not involve an instructor.

Web/virtual synchronous classes and Web/virtual asynchronous classes are now ready for a beta-class evaluation. Beta evaluation tests the effectiveness of directions to the instructor and how well the class runs when delivered by someone other than the developer.

PURPOSE: *This worksheet will help you think about how to select and manage adult learners as evaluators for your Web-based training program.* Think about the role of the adult learner in evaluating a Web-based training program. What are the challenges in selecting a representative sample of learners? What steps will you take to make learners feel comfortable with technology? How will you make learners feel comfortable delivering feedback? Use the Selecting Adult Learners To Provide Feedback Worksheet to reflect on these questions.

Selecting Adult Learners To Provide Feedback Worksheet

1. Use the following matrix to identify learners who will evaluate your program.

Familiarity with Browser	Familiarity with Content of Lesson		
	Novice	**Practitioner**	**Expert**
Beginning User			
Intermediate User			
Experienced User			

2. What challenges are there in selecting a representative sample of learners?

3. How could you overcome these challenges?

4. What steps can you take to help learners feel more comfortable evaluating Web-based training?

5. Draft questions to solicit positive and negative feedback about the program.

Beta-Class Evaluation

The purpose of the beta-class evaluation is to assess the changes made as a result of the alpha class and to use the materials in their intended environment with an instructor. In this phase, a Web/virtual synchronous class is delivered by an instructor who was not part of the development team. Then the development team assesses how clear and effective the directions are. Figure 10.7 shows the steps required in the beta-evaluation phase.

Recruit Full Complement of Learners. Recruit learners who mirror the final population in regard to skill level and number. If the final program is intended for groups of twenty, then the beta class should have twenty. In addition, recruit an instructor who is representative of the instructors who will be delivering the program. Use notes from the alpha class to conduct a train-the-trainer session. If possible, identify the instructors early enough to enable them to participate as learners in the alpha class.

Plan How To Gather Feedback. Develop a plan to collect data from learners and the instructor. Collecting data during the beta class is similar to collecting data during the alpha class. Create a clear plan for the kind of information you want and how you will collect it.

Arrange to collect data from the instructor at two points in time, first, as the instructor is preparing to teach. Ask him or her to talk about how easy or difficult the system tools (text-chat, application sharing, whiteboards, and microphone) are to use and the benefits and limitations of instructor notes (sequencing, chunking, examples). Second, after the class, ask the instructor for additional feedback regard-

---

Figure 10.7. Steps To Conduct Beta Evaluation

1. Recruit full complement of learners.

2. Plan how to gather feedback.

3. Explain purpose of beta-class evaluation.

4. Help learners and instructors feel comfortable.

5. Compile data and make necessary changes.

ing pacing, interactions, and navigation. The instructor's feedback can provide insights into the need for additional resources, interactions, and tools.

Further observations are made by the development team, who sit with the instructor as he or she delivers the program and attend the class as participants. Observations from both the instructor's and the learners' perspectives provide rich data to improve the program.

Explain Purpose of Beta-Class Evaluation. Explain the purpose of the beta-class evaluation to the learners and the instructor. Remind learners that you want to hear about the shortcomings of the program as well as the highlights. Use focus groups to collect data from the participants, asking how exercises involving dialogue, interaction, and collaboration worked from both the learners' and the instructor's perspective.

Help Learners and Instructors Feel Comfortable.
Give learners the freedom to criticize the program without criticizing the instructor. Set expectations of all participants; explain that it is a pilot class and that changes are expected.

Compile Data and Make Necessary Changes. Compile data from learners and the instructor and review your notes for additional data. Based on a synthesis of opinion, make the necessary changes.

Summary
Adult learners should be involved in all phases of development and modification. Use participatory evaluation to encourage them to become actively involved in recommending changes.

Table 10.2 summarizes the four evaluation phases. Each phase provides an incremental assessment of the content, the design, the learners' reactions, and the instructor's ability to use the program. Skipping any step in this process risks overlooking important data.

Evaluation is often eliminated when projects run over budget or the schedule slips. Developers spend so much time conducting the learner assessment, synthesizing data, designing lessons, and creating blueprints that they fail to see potential problems. A thorough evaluation involves learners, technical experts, and SMEs with fresh perspectives.

Table 10.2. Summary of Evaluation Phases

	Purpose	Evaluators	Methods
Subject-Matter Expert	Check the accuracy and completeness of the content.	SMEs in the content or topic area	• Document review • Interview
Rapid Prototype	Check effectiveness of the instructional design, clarity of directions, and ease of interactions, using a single lesson.	Representative learners of high, moderate, and low skill levels	• One-on-one meetings • Interviews • Observations
Alpha Class	Test the effectiveness of the complete course being taught as a stand-alone program or as a facilitated program taught by the developer.	Representative learners of high, moderate, and low skill levels	• Interviews • Surveys • Observations
Beta Class	Assess the effectiveness of the complete course and clarity and usefulness of directions for instructor	Instructor and representative learners of high, moderate, and low skill levels	• Interviews • Surveys • Observation

Suggested Readings

Barksdale, S. B., & Lund, T. B. (1997). Setting standards for evaluating Internet-based training. *Multimedia & Internet Training Newsletter, 4*(11), 4–5, 10.

Brookfield, S. (1990). *Understanding and facilitating adult learning.* San Francisco: Jossey-Bass.

Clark, R. E. (1994). Assessment of distance learning technology. In E. L. Baker & H. F. O'Neil, Jr. (Eds.), *Technology assessment in education and training.* Hillsdale, NJ: Lawrence Erlbaum Associates.

Flagg, B. N. (1990). *Formative evaluation for educational technologies.* Hillsdale, NJ: Lawrence Erlbaum Associates.

Harasim, L., Hiltz, S. R., Teles, L., & Turoff, M. (1995). *Learning networks: A field guide to teaching and learning online.* Cambridge, MA: MIT Press.

Kaner, C., Falk, J., & Nguyen, H. (1996). *Testing computer software* (2nd ed.). New York: International Thomson.

Moore, M., & Kearsley, G. (1996). *Distance education: A systems view.* New York: Wadsworth.

Chapter 11

Ready, Set, Go

What You Will Learn in This Chapter

After completing this chapter, you will be able to

- Determine where Web-based training fits in your overall curriculum;
- Select the topic for your first Web-based training pilot;
- Avoid common pitfalls; and
- Discuss the future of Web-based training.

Web-based training offers four distinct modes: Web/computer-based training, Web/EPS systems, Web/virtual asynchronous classrooms, and Web/virtual synchronous classrooms. This book has presented information about conducting a needs assessment, selecting the most appropriate type of Web-based training, designing lessons, creating blueprints, and evaluating programs. Each of these processes has been discussed in detail and, when possible, guidelines for designing instruction have been presented.

This chapter takes a step back and examines Web-based training in the broader context of an organization's curriculum and gives suggestions on selecting the topic for an initial pilot. The last section of the chapter is devoted to (1) common pitfalls of pilots, based on interviews with practitioners, the author's personal experience, and a review of the literature and (2) a look at the trends in Web-based training and recommendations for practitioners seeking to remain current with the technology.

Where Web-Based Training Fits in Your Curriculum

It is frequently reported (Fryer, 1997; Hall, 1997; Masie, 1997) that training departments are mandated to develop online learning initiatives. Such mandates appear to be based on a technological imperative, a pressing need to use Internet and intranet technology for the sake of technology. In some cases Web-based training is implemented to justify the cost of intranets and connections to the Internet. In others, it is piloted to satisfy management's demand for innovation or to bolster the prestige of the training organization. Training professionals must examine WBT initiatives in the broader context of the organization's curriculum and the ability to fill a gap in skills and knowledge.

Curriculum is defined as the aggregate of courses of study in a given discipline. A training organization can provide a series of courses for the entire company (macro level) and a series of courses for an individual department (micro level). Designing a curriculum requires planning and selecting content, instructional strategies, and delivery methods to create a meaningful learning experience. Using Web-based training as a delivery method requires the trainer to consider three key factors: what is taught, who is taught, and where the teaching takes place.

What Is Taught

As was discussed in Chapter Five, not all goals or courses are appropriate for Web-based training. If the goals of the course are attitudinal or psychomotor, the course may not be suitable for delivery via the Web. For example, you may want to eliminate courses in a workplace safety curriculm such as Using Fire Extinguishers and Testing Fire Alarms because they require practicing psychomotor skills such as pulling, aiming, and spraying. Other courses that teach concepts such as the storage and disposal of hazardous materials may be well suited for web-based training. Figure 11.1 shows which types of workplace safety courses are suitable for WBT versus classroom training.

Who Is Taught

Who is being taught is another factor in choosing training methods. As was discussed in Chapter Four, determining whether Web-based training is the right de-

Figure 11.1. Safety Courses Suitable for WBT

Workplace Safety Curriculum

| Introduction to Workplace Safety | Using Fire Extinguishers | Testing Fire Alarms | Hazardous Material Storage | Hazardous Material Disposal |

- WBT
- Classroom

livery method for your learners and organization is important. The decision to use Web-based training should reflect the preferences of the learners and the culture of the organization. For example, regional managers learning to use a new billing system may be excellent candidates for a WBT program if they are skilled computer users and highly self-directed learners and if the company has a powerful computer network. However, the organization's culture may value the interpersonal relationships that develop as a result of attending instructor-led training at corporate headquarters. The intangible benefits of classroom-based instruction in this case would be the informal exchanges of information at breaks, opportunities for upper management to meet regional managers, and the transmission of corporate culture. The choice of whether to use Web-based training will vary from organization to organization and from audience to audience within an organization.

Where the Teaching Takes Place

Where the class is delivered is as important as *what* and *whom* you plan to teach. Examine the technical infrastructure required to support this delivery method. Find out the capacity and limitations of the network, Internet, and intranet connections as well as the desktop computers. These determine your ability to use the asynchronous interactions described in Chapter Seven and the synchronous interactions described in Chapter Eight.

There is no single answer for when to use Web-based training. Each organization has to evaluate what is being taught, who is being taught, and where the learning is taking place. Figure 11.2 illustrates that only those courses that have appropriate

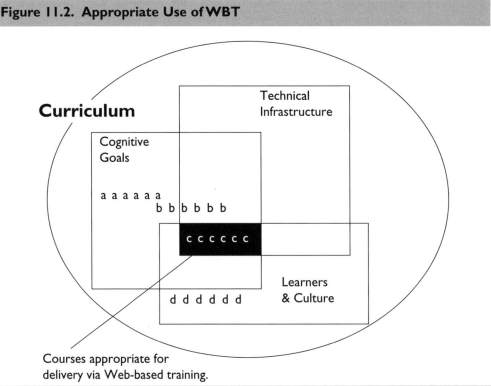

Figure 11.2. Appropriate Use of WBT

goals, can be supported via the existing technical infrastructure, and are suitable for the learners and the organization's culture should be delivered via the Web. Courses that fail to meet all of the criteria should be delivered by other means. After you have identified the curriculum or courses in a curriculum that are appropriate for Web-based training, the hard work of sorting out possible pilots begins.

Selecting the Topic for a Pilot

Selecting the topic for a pilot is one of the most difficult tasks the WBT team must struggle with. The choice is not obvious. Figure 11.3 provides a checklist for deciding on a successful topic.

Fill Gaps in Skills and Knowledge. It is essential to choose a pilot project that seeks to fill gaps in skills and knowledge. It is easy to lose sight of the distinction between communication and education when working on the Web. Most Web pages communicate in that they present information to readers, but they are passive and sim-

---

Figure 11.3. Checklist for Choosing a Topic

☑ Fill gaps in skills and knowledge.

☑ Keep the project within manageable bounds.

☑ Establish clear benchmarks for success.

☑ Choose tools the organization can support.

☑ Find a powerful and visible champion.

☑ Avoid projects with tight deadlines.

---

ilar to a magazine. Web-based training pages provide skills; they provide knowledge transfer and enable the learner to *do* something. Web-based training pages are interactive and similar to self-study books, job aids, and live classroom instruction. Figure 11.4 provides some examples of appropriate and inappropriate WBT pilot projects.

Keep the Project Within Manageable Bounds. After selecting a topic, establish manageable boundaries regarding time and resources. A pilot serves as a way to introduce a new delivery method and as a learning experience for the development team. Develop a course 90 to 120 minutes in length that provides learners with a substantive learning experience. Short courses provide boundaries for development and delivery resources. Allow six to eight weeks for the development and deployment of such a course. Limit the number of learners participating to eight to twelve. The

---

Figure 11.4. Appropriate and Inappropriate Pilot Projects

Appropriate Topics	Inappropriate Topics
Filling out travel and expense forms	Publishing a course catalog
Using a new phone system	Learning to use a high-power drill press
Introducing principles of accounting	Conducting diversity training
Dealing with hostile customers	Announcing the new 401K plan
Managing new accounts	Presenting the company president's speech on the importance of training

---

fewer learners involved, the less time required to install WBT software and resolve network, security, connectivity, and access problems.

Establish Clear Benchmarks for Success. Establish benchmarks for success before beginning development. It is impossible to declare a project a success unless members of the team agree on the criteria. Take the time to draft a list of measurable outcomes that serve as indicators of success. Figure 11.5 lists some sample benchmarks. Each organization must develop its own.

Choose Tools the Organization Can Support. Carefully choose the tool(s) to create a WBT program. The tools selected will determine the level of interaction, ability to track learners, and the level of support required to develop and deliver training. Analyze the support required at three different levels. Figure 11.6 lists the three groups that may require organizational support.

Learners located in remote offices may require assistance installing Web-based training software, downloading plug-ins, locating new versions of browsers, and adjusting the controls for sound, color, and screen size. They may also need simple assistance using a browser or connecting to the Internet. Depending on the tools used to create the program, the level of support can range from minimal to substantial.

Developers may also need assistance. The amount of assistance will depend on the complexity of the software and the hardware and network configuration required. The information-systems staff may be responsible for installing the software required to create the program and making the course available to learners. All WBT programs require some level of support.

Figure 11.5. Sample Criteria for Success

Criteria	Benchmark Statement
Cost	Development costs will not exceed $2500.00.
Time	Project will be developed in 160 hours.
Learner Satisfaction	Learners will rate the WBT experience as 4.5 to 5.0 out of 5.0.
Ease of Development	Minor edits require less than one hour to execute.
Reliability	Under 5 percent of learners report problems accessing.
Usability	Learners require no help-desk assistance to install WBT software.

Figure 11.6. Groups Requiring Organizational Support	
Pilot Groups	**Type of Support Required**
Learners	What support will learners in remote offices require to participate?
Developers	What support will course developers require to use the software to create the WBT course?
Information-Systems Staff	What support will the IS staff require to install and maintain the software development environment, server, and remote users?

Be aware of the support required and choose a software program that your organization is capable of supporting or a software application vendor who offers a service agreement for telephone support for learners, training for developers, and on-site consulting for the IS staff.

Find a Powerful and Visible Champion. Select a project that is significant to a powerful and visible champion. Projects that are supported by someone in upper management have an increased chance for success. A powerful champion can hold people accountable for deliverables, create working relationships between cross-functional groups, and make scarce resources available.

Avoid Projects with Tight Deadlines. Do not agree to conduct the pilot as part of a larger project that must be completed on a fixed date. Failure will result in scuttling the larger project and abandoning the WBT pilot project. Remember, pilot projects introduce new delivery methods and provide a learning experience for the development team. Because the method is new, it is difficult to anticipate all the delays. Some frequent causes for delay are lack of availability of cross-functional team members, inadequate network access at remote offices, extensive bureaucracy, and delays in coordinating the implementation plan (installation of software, configuration of hardware, and identification of learners).

Avoiding Common Problems

No pilot project is perfect. Some common pitfalls encountered by developers who have completed pilot projects are given below.

Moving Content from One Medium to Another

Many organizations are eager to develop a WBT program quickly to demonstrate the viability of the method. Reusing existing self-paced workbooks, computer-based training, and PowerPoint® slides appears to be a way to reduce the development cycle. Although it is technically possible to move existing training materials from one format to another with minimal effort, this should be avoided. Because Web-based training has unique strengths and limitations, development for this medium is unique.

Allow adequate time to move existing content from self-paced workbooks, computer-based training, CD-ROMs, and PowerPoint® slides to a Web-based training format. Make clients aware that redesign may require adding more detail to substitute for the information provided by the instructor, recreating large graphics files to make the program Web ready, resequencing content to take advantage of the nonlinear nature of Web-based training, and creating navigation means. The time and expense required to repurpose will depend on how difficult it is to move the training materials from one medium to another.

Choosing the Software Before Defining Needs

There are a number of reasons why organizations choose software before they have analyzed needs. Sometimes, the choice is made by zealous managers who want to be perceived as being at the cutting edge. In other cases, people are convinced by a persuasive demo or exciting Website visit. The problem is that you must then work in reverse, finding a training problem that can be solved by the software chosen. If an organization selects software to create a Web/VSC program, it must now locate a training problem and audience for which this is an appropriate solution. The designers must start by identifying learners with new computers, reliable network connections, and compatible time zones, as well as a problem that can be addressed using collaborative group learning solutions.

Insist on defining the gap in skills and knowledge and conducting an analysis of the learners before selecting a WBT development tool(s). In the same way that you would not buy groceries before deciding what to have for dinner, do not shop for WBT software before you know what you have to accomplish.

Creating a WBT Pilot Program Single-Handedly

Nothing is impossible, but some things are not advisable. Even if you have the skills and resources needed to develop a Web-based training program without the assistance of others, it is not recommended. Developing a program, delivering it to the field, and maintaining it are labor intensive. One person working alone cannot accomplish multiple tasks at the same time, so the pilot will take longer to complete. It is also more difficult to resolve technical and logistical problems when working alone.

Question your organization's commitment to Web-based training and the need for an ongoing WBT program if you cannot obtain adequate resources for designing, developing, and delivering a pilot program. Demonstrate the advantages of a cross-functional team by comparing the timeline for developing a program alone with the timeline for developing a program as a team.

Adding a WBT Assignment to Your Regular Work Load

Many training organizations are working to full capacity and have reduced staff levels as a result of downsizing. Pilot projects are often seen as assignments that must be accomplished without disrupting the normal work load. Treating a WBT pilot project as an extracurricular activity does not provide a fair evaluation. A pilot requires dedicated resources and realistic time allocations.

Create a project plan that includes a comprehensive list of the team members, a detailed description of what each member is accountable for, and an estimate of the time required. Negotiate to ensure that the pilot project is part of each team member's regular work load and not something that must be done in addition to regular responsibilities.

Underestimating the Complexity

Vendor demonstrations often lull the development team into a false sense of confidence. Each task is manageable, even for a novice training professional, but the overall process is complex. A WBT pilot is an excellent example of a situation in which the total is greater than the sum of the parts. The complexity is due to three factors: the large number of dependent tasks; the politics of working cross-functionally; and the untested assumptions made by team members.

Before launching the pilot project, create a chart that visually displays how tasks are related. Share this display with the entire team to identify additional relationships and contingencies. Manage the politics by communicating decisions, changes, deadlines, and risks and dependencies to all team members. Because Web-based training relies on many people and resources, it is important to clarify expectations and test assumptions. For example, if learners are to be issued laptop computers, clarify who will pay for equipment and how learners will receive training to use the laptop computers.

Dedicating Too Little Time to Instructional Aspects

The learning curve is steep for teams developing their first WBT pilot. It is easy to spend a disproportionate amount of time addressing technical issues such as ordering servers, establishing user accounts, resolving fire wall issues, and learning to create courses using a WBT application. These activities can leave you short on time to address the more mundane issue of developing an educationally sound program.

Leave adequate time to work on the educational aspects of the program. The learners expect that the program will work technically and that it will be reliable. Dedicate the time needed to create programs that accomplish the stated objectives, engage learners, and demonstrate respect for adult learners. Determine the time needed to design and develop a program. If technical issues or logistical problems create delays in the timeline, extend it. Do not compress the design or development dates to compensate for slips in the schedule.

Future Trends in Web-Based Training

Web-based training is evolving quickly due to the fast-paced nature of the Internet. The four major emerging themes are listed in Figure 11.7.

Blend of Technologies

The easiest theme to notice is the blending or blurring of technologies, bringing together not only various forms of instructional technology but also blurring the lines between learning and working, consuming and creating, and being entertained and being educated.

An example of this blending of instructional technologies is the ability to use the Web to replace unique single-function devices. In the past, videoconferences required conferencing systems such as PictureTel® or CLI® systems; audiographic training required telephone systems and bridges to connect groups of learners; and videos required videocassette players. The functions of all these instructional technologies are

---

Figure 11.7. Emerging Themes in Web-Based Training

☑ Blend of technologies.

☑ Learners at disparate skill levels.

☑ Greater complexity of tools.

☑ IS leadership in corporate training.

---

being integrated into WBT applications. New technologies, such as compression algorithms, audio streaming, and DHTML, make it possible to replace old devices.

A second trend in technology is the fusing of education and noneducational events. In the future, training will become seamlessly integrated into working, purchasing, and playing. For example, medical imaging systems will offer technicians just-in-time learning. The imaging systems will be connected to the Internet, and training will be provided as yet another feature. There will be less distinction between when workers are training and when they are working. Consumers will also experience the blending of training and consuming. They will be able to learn about investment options, vacation destinations, and the side effects of medications before making a buying decision.

Learners at Disparate Skill Levels

The ability to train learners at disparate skill levels is a trend worth watching. As a result of very different Internet and computer-skill levels among learners, the demands on developers of Web-based training will vary greatly. Younger workers may be experienced using video games or have logged hundreds of hours on the Internet. Programs developed for them may vary greatly from programs developed for people who have little or no computer experience. In an attempt to address the needs of learners at various levels, customizable user interfaces and training applications that assess a learner's skills and recommend a training path are the next steps.

Greater Complexity of Tools

Another theme is the greater complexity of tools, evidenced in many related trends. As the tools become more complex, they will also require larger budgets for designing, developing, and delivering training. The skills required to use WBT tools will require that trainers have more specialized knowledge of graphic design, programming, network management, and interface design. The organizations providing leadership in Web-based training will be those that have the most infrastructure and Internet/intranet experience related to their core business.

IS Leadership in Corporate Training

The last theme is the increasingly important role played by information-systems professionals in corporate training. The trends to watch are changes in necessary competencies for educators, a focus on technical skills, and new career paths for educators.

Besides knowing and applying the principles of adult education, understanding instructional design, and possessing strong facilitation skills, educators will need competencies related to computer-based training, HTML, and networking. Web-based training will bring the IS groups and training groups closer together in an effort to meet corporate needs. Leadership in training organizations will come from individuals who are able to combine educational and technical skills. It is likely that professionals will move from training into information systems and from information systems into training.

Although the future is far from clear, one thing is certain: Educators in corporations, nonprofit organizations, and academic institutions must invest in their professional development.

Summary

Web-based training is about *training*. This seems obvious, but it is not clear in many WBT programs. It is too easy to be caught up in the hype and hoopla of the technology and to lose sight of designing effective training. As educators, we must realize that this is just another form of instructional technology. It is a means to an end, not an end in itself. It is our role to be advocates for the learner and to apply the principles of adult education and instructional design to Web-based training.

Take the lead in educating your organization about the benefits and the limitations of Web-based training. Invite managers and department heads to attend seminars, conferences, and vendor presentations. Begin to build the alliances and cross-functional relationships needed to implement Web-based training. Take note of changes and improvements in the technical infrastructure, such as improvements to Internet access, standards on browser software, and the functionality of new computers.

Invest in yourself and your subordinates. Identify instructional technology, Web-based training, and computer competencies that will be important in the next twelve to eighteen months. Encourage your subordinates to learn the basics of HTML, WBT design, and Internet skills. Use the resources in the appendix of this book to locate professional organizations, books, journals, and listservs to help you stay current.

Suggested Readings

Diamond, R. M. (1989). *Designing and improving courses and curriculum in higher education: A systematic approach.* San Francisco: Jossey-Bass.

Fryer, B. (1997). Caught in the Web. *Inside Technology Training, 1*(6), 10–14.

Grundy, S. (1987). *Curriculum: Product or praxis?* New York: Falmer Press.

Hall, B. (1997). *Web-based training cookbook.* New York: John Wiley.

Laurillard, D. (1993). *Rethinking university teaching: A framework for the effective use of educational technology.* New York: Routledge.

Masie, E. (1997, December). When your own CEO pushes online learning—get ready! *Lakewood Report on Technology for Learning.* Minneapolis, MN: Lakewood.

Oliva, P. F. (1992). *Developing the curriculum* (3rd ed.). New York: HarperCollins.

Posner, G. J., & Rudnitsky, A. N. (1997). *Course design: A guide to curriculum development for teachers* (5th ed.). New York: Longman.

Appendix A

Tools for Developing Web-Based Training

THIS SECTION provides a list of software applications for creating Web-based training. The list is organized by the type of Web-based training each tool is best suited for creating. Descriptions and comparisons are not included because the technology changes too quickly to provide a meaningful analysis.

No information is furnished on unbundled solutions, those applications that provide a single function such as listserv software, e-mail servers, IRC, threaded discussions, live audio, streaming video/audio, and other functions because they are so numerous.

Use this list as a starting point in your search for tools to create programs. Each month new software applications are introduced and existing programs are improved. The URLs are also subject to change with little notice. This list and the other resources found in the appendices can be used to locate additional applications.

Web/Computer-Based Training

Webmentor

Avilar Technologies, Inc.
8750–9 Cherry Lane
Laurel, Maryland 20707–6208, USA
Tel: (301) 725–7014
Fax: (301) 725–0980
http://avilar.adasoft.com

Course Info

CourseInfo.LLC
409 College Avenue
Ithaca, New York, USA
Tel: (607) 277-3369
Fax: (607) 277-9476
http://courses.lightlink.com/web

Digital Trainer

MicroMedium Inc.
1434 Farrington Road
Apex, North Carolina 27502, USA
Tel: (919) 303–6022
Fax: (919) 303–6011
http://www.micromedium.com

Director/Authorware

Macromedia, Inc.
600 Townsend Street
San Francisco, California 94103, USA
Tel: (415) 252–2000
Fax: (415) 626–0554
http://www.macromedia.com

Docent

Docent Software, Inc.
3180 Porter Drive, Bldg. B, Suite A,
Palo Alto, California 94304, USA
Tel: (650) 813–6200
Fax: (650) 813–6209
http://www.docent.com

Eloquent Presenter! Software

Eloquent, Inc.
2000 Alameda de las Pulgas, Suite 100
San Mateo, California 94403, USA
http://www.eloquent.com

Ignite Courseware Development Systems

Engage Interactive Inc.
921 College Hill Road
Ferdericton, New Brunswick
Canada E3B 6Z9
Tel: (506) 460-1622
Fax: (506) 452-1395
http://www.engageinteractive.com

IntraLearn

OnTour Multimedia
21 Southwest Cutoff
Northboro, Massachusetts 01590, USA
Tel: (508) 393–2277
Fax: (508) 393–6841
http://www.otm.com

LearningSTATE

106 East Sixth Street
Suite 800
Austin, TX 78701, USA
Tel: (512) 322-5730
Fax: (512) 322-5731
http://www.learningstate.com/

Mentor Ware

MentorWare
528 Weddell Drive, Suite 1
Sunnyvale, California 94089, USA
Tel: (408) 541–1714
Fax: (408) 541–1717
http://www.mentorware.com

NetShow

Microsoft Corporation
One Microsoft Way
Redmond, Washington 98052–6399, USA
Tel: (425) 882–8080
http://www.microsoft.com/netshow

PHOENIX

Pathlore Inc.
7965 N. High St.
Columbus, Ohio 43235–8402, USA
Tel: (888) PATHLORE
http://www.pathlore.com

PointPlus

Net-Scene
75 Ahad-Ha'am St.
P.O. Box 14144
Tel-Aviv, 61141
Israel
Tel: +972-3-685–0727

http://www.net-scene.com

QUEST NET+

Allen Communication
Triad Center 5th Floor
Salt Lake City, Utah 84182, USA
Tel: (800) 537–7800
Fax: (801) 537–7805
http://www.allencomm.com

Serf

The Instructional Technology Center
307 Willard Hall Education Building
University of Delaware
Newark, DE 19716, USA
Tel: (302) 831-8164
Fax: (302) 831-2089
http://www.udel.edu/serf/

SyberWorks

SyberNet, Inc.
One Kendall Square, Suite 2200
Cambridge, Massachusetts 02139, USA
Tel: (781) 646–7496
http://www.syberworks.com

TenCORE
Computer Teaching Corporation
1713 South State Street
Champaign, Illinois 61820, USA
Tel: (217) 352–6363
Fax: (217) 352–3104
http://www.tencore.com

ToolBookII
Asymetrix Corporation
110–110th Avenue NE
Bellevue, Washington 98004–5840, USA
Tel: (206) 637–2458
http://www.asymetrix.com

Web Electronic Performance Support Systems

Web/EPSS applications range from simple Web pages that provide steps and procedures to highly sophisticated tools such as agents and knowbots that look for information on behalf of the learner.

Use the Yahoo® search index categories shown below to locate simple WYSIWYG HTML editors and tools for creating Web pages:

Top; Business and Economy; Companies; Computers; Software; Internet; World Wide Web; HTML Editors

The following are two examples of software applications for creating HTML help pages.

HTML Help

Microsoft Corporation
One Microsoft Way
Redmond, Washington 98052–6399, USA
http://www.microsoft.com/workshop/author/htmlhelp

RoboHTML

Blue Sky Software
7777 Fay Avenue, Suite 201
La Jolla, California 92037, USA
Tel: (619) 459–6365
Fax: (619) 459–6366
http://www.blue-sky.com/products

Sophisticated W/EPSS Application Development Tools

Assistware®

Assistware
29 Merrion Square,
Dublin 2
Ireland.
Tel: 353-1-661-9725
Fax: 353-1-678-9392
E-mail info@assistware.ie
http://www.assistware.ie

KnowDev

Innovative Knowledge Products, Inc.
430 10th Street, N. W.
Suite S-009,
Atlanta, Georgia 30318, USA
Tel: (404) 881-1411
Fax: (404) 881-1852
http://www.ikp.net/home.html

OnDemand

1555 Adams Drive
Menlo Park, CA 94025, USA
Tel: (650) 463-6719
Fax: (650) 463-6701
http://www.ondemandinc.com

PTS Learning Systems

1150 First Avenue, Suite 700
King of Prussia, PA 19406, USA
Tel: (800) 387-8878
Fax: (610) 337-2838

The Desktop Support Factory

Usability Sciences Corporation
5525 N. MacArthur Blvd., Suite 575
Irving, Texas 75038, USA
Tel: (972) 550-1599
Fax: (972) 550-9148
http://www.usabilitysciences.com

Web Virtual Asynchronous Classroom

ClassNet

Iowas State University
209 Durham
Ames, Iowa 50011, USA
Dr. Pete Boysen
Tel: (515) 294-6663
Fax: (515) 294-1717
http://classnet.cc.iastate.edu/

Flax

Flax Interactive Courseware
Leicester, England
Tel: +7123 920 325
Fax: +7723 920 610
http://www.cms.dmu.ac.uk/coursebook/flax

Learning Space

Lotus
55 Cambridge Parkway
Cambridge, Massachusetts 02142, USA
Tel: (617) 577–8500
http://www.lotus.com

TopClass

WBT Systems
185 Berry St., Suite 5601
San Francisco, California 94107, USA
Tel: (415) 487 2250
Fax: (415) 487 2251
http://www.wbtsystems.com

Virtual-U

Virtual Learning Environments Inc.
SFU Discovery Park, Multi-Tenant Facility
270-8900 Nelson Way
Burnaby, B.C. V5A 4W9
Canada
Tel: (604) 291-3971
Fax: (604) 291-3987
http://virtual-u.cs.sfu.ca/vuweb/

WebCT

WebCT Educational Technologies
3204 Main Avenue
Belcarra, British Columbia
Canada V3H 4R3
Fax: (604) 224–1192
http://homebrew.cs.ubc.ca/webct

WebFuse

David Jones
Faculty of Informatics and Communications
Central Queensland University
Rockhampton, Queensland
Australia, 4702
http://webfuse.cqu.edu.au/

WebTeach

Chris Hughes
Professional Development Centre
UNSW
Sydney 2052
Australia
Tel: 61-2-9385-4940
Fax: 61-2-9385-5970
Email: c.hughes@unsw.edu.au
http://www.pdc.unsw.edu.au/webteachdemo/welcome.html

Web Course in a Box

MadDuck Technologies
Richmond, Virginia 23298, USA
http://www.madduck.com

Zebu

MC2 Learning Systems Inc.
265, 8900 Nelson Way
Burnaby BC
Canada V5A 4W9
Tel: (800)808-0388
http://www.mc2.sfu.ca/index.html

Web Virtual Synchronous Classroom

BrightLight

Avalon Information Technologies Inc.
1 Kenview Boulevard
Brampton, Ontario
Canada L6T 5E6
Tel: (905) 792–2072
Fax: (905) 792–2594
http://www.atlantis.com/avalon

Class Point

White Pine Software, Inc.
542 Amherst Street
Nashua, New Hampshire 03063, USA
Tel: (603) 886-9050
Fax: (603) 886-9051
http://www.pine.com/products/ClassPont/index.html

ClassWise

Magideas Corporation
3105 Honda Road
Oakton, Virginia 22124-2325, USA
Tel: (703) 620-9191
Fax: (703) 620-0851
http://www.magideas.com/

CONFEREASE 100

OutReach Technologies
9101 Guilford Road
Columbia, Maryland 21046, USA
Tel: (410) 792-8000
http://www.outreachtech.com

CUSeeMe

White Pine Software, Inc.
542 Amherst Street
Nashua, New Hampshire 03063, USA
Tel: (603) 886–9050
Fax: (603) 886–9051
http://www.wpine.com

DataBeam Learning Server

DataBeam Corporation
230 Lexington Green Circle
Lexington, Kentucky 40503
USA
Tel: (606) 425–3500.
http://gw.databeam.com

Distance Learning Server

PictureTalk, Inc.
4234 Hacienda Drive, Suite 200
Pleasanton, California 94588, USA
Tel: (510) 467–5300
Fax: (510) 467–5310
http://www.picturetalk.com

Horizon Live Distance Learning

i/o 360 digital design Inc.
841 Broadway, Suite 502
New York, New York 1003, USA
Tel: (212) 533-4467
http://horizon.io360.com/dsl/horizon/

KMI Stadium

Knowledge Media Institute
The Open University
Walton Hall
Milton Keynes MK7 6AA
United Kingdom
Tel: +44 1908 655761
Fax: +44 1908 653169
http://kmi.open.ac.uk

KoTrain

Kobixx Systems, LLC
51 Gibraltar Drive, Suite 2B
Morris Plains, New Jersey 07950, USA
Tel: (973) 984–2229
Fax: (973) 984–9646
http://www.kobixx.com

MeetingPlace Conference Server

Latitude
2121 Tasman Drive
Santa Clara, California 95054, USA
Tel: (408) 988–7200
http://www.latitude.com/latitude/

LearnLinc

Interactive Learning International Corporation
385 Jordan Road
Troy, New York 12180, USA
Tel: (518) 283–8799
Fax: (518) 286–2439
http://www.ilinc.com

NetMeeting

Microsoft Corporation
One Microsoft Way
Redmond, Washington 98052–6399, USA
http://www.microsoft.com/netmeeting

NetPodium

MetaBridge, Inc.
2101 Fourth Avenue, Suite 310
Seattle, Washington 98121, USA
Tel: (206) 674–6000
Fax: (206) 674–6001
http://www.netpodium.com

Pebblesoft

Pebblesoft Learning, Inc.
2251 Lawson Lane
Santa Clara, California 95054, USA
Tel: (408) 746-7099 or
http://www.pebblesoft.com/content/Home.html

PlaceWare Auditorium

PlaceWare, Inc.
201 Ravendale Drive
Mountain View, California 94043, USA
Tel: (650) 404–9920
Fax: (650) 526–6199
http://www.placeware.com

Symposium

Centra Software, Inc.
430 Bedford Street
Lexington, Massachusetts 02173, USA
Tel: (781) 861–7000
Fax: (781) 863–7288
http://www.centra.com

TALKshow

Quarterdeck Corporation, Inc.
5150-E21 El Camino Real
Los Altos, California 94022, USA
Tel: (415) 254–9000
Fax: (415) 254–9010
http://web.futurelabs.com

VideoLink™ NET

Smith Micro Software, Inc.
51 Columbia
Aliso Viejo, California 92656, USA
Tel: (714) 362–5800
Fax: (714) 362–2300
http://www.smithmicro.com

Appendix B

Training Organizations

DEVELOPING Web-based training brings together the skill and knowledge of many different kinds of educators. Because of the cross-disciplinary nature of the field, many organizations provide resources to developers. The major ones are listed below:

American Association for Higher Education (AAHE)
1 Dupont Circle, Suite 360
Washington, DC 20036
Tel: (202) 293–6440
Fax: (202) 293–0073
http://www.aahe.org/

AAHE's conferences and publications highlight a broad range of issues. They have developed many in-depth, long-term commitments to specific programmatic areas, such as quality, service-learning, teaching/peer review, and technology. AAHE's Technology Projects seek to mainstream the effective use of technology for instructional purposes.

American Society for Training and Development (ASTD)
1640 King Street
Box 1443
Alexandria, Virginia 22313–2043
Tel: (703) 683–8100
Fax: (703) 683–8103
http://www.astd.org/

ASTD's mission is to provide leadership to individuals, organizations, and society to achieve work-related competence, performance, and fulfillment.

Association for Educational Communications and Technology (AECT)
1025 Vermont Avenue, N.W., Suite 820
Washington, DC 20005
Tel: (202) 347–7834
Fax: (202) 347–7839
http://www.aect.org/

The mission of AECT is to provide leadership in educational communications and technology by linking professionals with a common interest in the use of educational technology and its application to the learning process.

British Interactive Multimedia Association (BIMA)
6 Washingley Road
Folksworth
Peterborough
PE7 3SY
United Kingdom
Tel: 01733 245700
Fax: 01733 240020
http://www.thebiz.co.uk/bima.htm/

The British Interactive Multimedia Association was established in 1985 to promote a wider understanding of the benefits of interactive multimedia to industry, government, and education and to provide a regular forum for the exchange of views. Members come from the fields of application development, computer manufacturing, publishing, disc pressing, hardware distribution, programming, and consulting. Membership of BIMA is open to any organization or individual with an interest in multimedia.

CAUSE
4840 Pearl East Circle, Suite 302E
Boulder, Colorado 80301
Tel: (303) 939–0319
Fax: (303) 440–0461
http://www.cause.org/

CAUSE's mission is to be an indispensable partner in enabling the transformational changes occurring in higher education through the effective management and use of information resources: technology, services, and information.

Computer Education Management Association (CEdMA)
Peter Sherman
Chapter & Membership Trustee
Data General Corp
2400 Computer Drive MS G153
Westboro, Massachusetts 01580
Tel: (512) 794–5832
http: //www.cedma.org/

CEdMA's goal is to provide formal and informal forums for education managers to discuss critical training and business issues encountered in high-tech companies. CEdMA also provides opportunities for members to participate in initiatives to shape excellence in education and training.

EDUCOM
1112 16th Street, N.W., Suite 600
Washington, DC 20036
Tel: (202) 872–4200
http://www.educom.edu/

EDUCOM is a nonprofit consortium of higher education institutions that facilitates the introduction, use, access to, and management of information resources in teaching, learning, scholarship, and research. EDUCOM believes that education and information technology (IT) will provide the most significant enhancements for human capability over the coming decade and that IT will have a fundamental impact on education's ability to fulfill its mission.

Information Technology Training Association, Inc. (ITTA)
8400 North MoPac Expressway, Suite 201
Austin, Texas 78759
Tel: (512) 502–9300
Fax: (512) 502–9308
http://www.itta.org/

ITTA's mission is to provide vision, leadership, and opportunity for those involved in learning to enable the effective use of information technology.

International Society for Performance Improvement (ISPI)
1300 L Street, N.W., Suite 1250
Washington, DC 20005
Tel: (202) 408–7969
Fax: (202) 408–7972
http://www.ispi.org/

ISPI is the leading association dedicated to increasing productivity in the workplace through the application of performance and instructional technologies.

Society for Applied Learning Technology (SALT)
50 Culpepper Street
Warrenton, Virginia 20186
Tel: (540) 347–0055
http://www.salt.org/

The society is oriented to professionals whose work requires knowledge and communication in the field of instructional technology. SALT provides a means to enhance the knowledge and job performance of an individual by participating in society-sponsored meetings and through receiving society-sponsored publications. It enables one to achieve knowledge in the field of applied learning technology by association with other professionals in conferences sponsored by the society.

United States Distance Learning Association (USDLA)
P.O. Box 5106
San Ramon, California 94583
Tel: (510) 606–5160
Fax: (510) 606–9410
http: //www.usdla.org/

The association's purpose is to promote the development and application of distance learning for education and training. The constituencies served include K through 12 education, higher education, continuing education, corporate training, and military and government training.

Appendix C

Listservs, Threaded Discussions, Notes Conferences, and Forums

Listservs, threaded discussions, notes conferences, and forums provide an excellent means to join national and international discussions regarding Web-based training, distance education, and development. As a member of these groups, one can participate or just observe the conversation. Whatever level of participation you choose, you will access a rich source of experience and knowledge.

Listservs

A sample e-mail subscription screen for a listserv is shown in Figure C.1. Some helpful commands for managing listserv mail are listed in Table C.1. Remember, to subscribe or to take care of maintenance issues, send e-mail to the listserv with the subject area blank and the signature (if you have one) turned off. See the table for message suggestions.

AAHESGIT

This list is a lively discussion of issues related to teaching, administration, and policy regarding instructional technology in higher education. It is run by Steven B. Gilbert, Director, Technology Projects, American Association for Higher Education (AAHE).

Figure C.1. Sample Subscription Screen for a Listserv

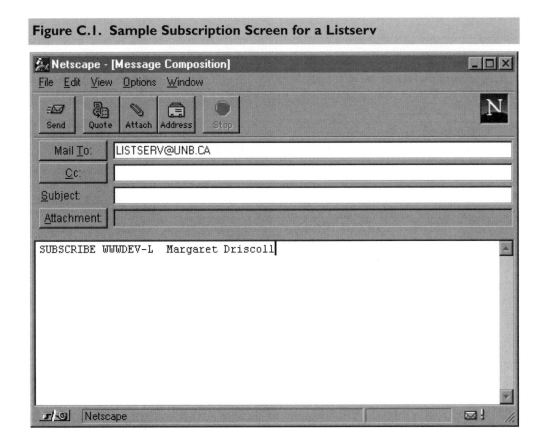

To be included, send e-mail to LISTPROC@LIST.CREN.NET with the following, and only the following, in the body of the message:

SUBSCRIBE AAHESGIT [your name here]

AEDNET

The Adult Education Network list is a broad discussion group of students, practitioners, and academics. The topics center on adult learning and literacy.

To be included, send e-mail to LISTSERV@ALPHA.ACAST.NOVA.EDU with the following, and only the following, in the body of the message:

SUBSCRIBE AEDNET [your name here]

Table C.1. Helpful Commands for Listserv Mail

For the Following Functions:	Put This Message in the Body of the E-Mail:
Subscribe	SUBSCRIBE WWWDEV [your name]
Stop a subscription	SIGNOFF WWWDEV
Stop mail for a limited period	SET WWWDEV NOMAIL
Receive a digest of messages once a day, rather than individually	SET WWWDEV DIGEST
Return to receiving e-mail as it comes	SET WWWDEV MAIL
Obtain a list of subscribers	REV WWWDEV
Find a HELP file	HELP WWWDEV

CYBERPHIL

This list is run by the International Society for Interactive Instructional Technology and sponsors a discussion about interactive instructional technologies.

To be included, send e-mail to LISTSERV@CARINS.CARIBOO.BC.CA with the following, and only the following, in the body of the message:

SUBSCRIBE CYBERPHIL [your name here]

DEOS-L/DEOSNEWS

The American Center for Study of Distance Education sponsors this large, diverse list. This is a good source for book reviews, summaries of research findings, and discussion related to distance education in academic and organizational settings. There are two lists: DEOSNEWS, an electronic journal for distance educators, and DEOS-L, an electronic forum. The purpose of DEOS is to disseminate information and to support international computer conferencing through systems accessible to professionals and students in the field of distance education.

To be included, send e-mail to LISTSERV@PSUVM.PSU.EDU with the following, and only the following, in the body of the message:

SUBSCRIBE DEOS-L [your name here]

SUBSCRIBE DEOSNEWS [your name here]

EDTECH

EDTECH is a moderated list that discusses all forms of educational technology, instructional systems, and multimedia instruction.

To be included, send e-mail to LISTSERV@MSU.EDU with the following, and only the following, in the body of the message:

SUBSCRIBE EDTECH [your name here]

IPCT-L

Interpersonal Computing and Technology sponsors this list. It is focused on Computer Mediated Communication and broadly on teaching and learning.

To be included, send e-mail to LISTSERV@GUVM.CCF.GEORGETOWN.EDU with the following, and only the following, in the body of the message:

SUBSCRIBE IPCT-L [your name here]

MEDIA-L

MEDIA-L is a list that discusses media in education, kindergarten through high school, higher education, and workplace use of media for training and instruction.

To be included, send e-mail to MEDIAL@BINGVMB.CC.BINGHAMTON.EDU with the following, and only the following, in the body of the message:

SUBSCRIBE MEDIA-L [your name here]

NEWEDU-L

New Patterns in Education sponsors this list, which discusses all styles, media, and delivery systems and distance education.

To be included, send e-mail to LISTSERV@UHCCVM.UHCC.HAWAII.EDU with the following, and only the following, in the body of the message:

SUBSCRIBE NEWEDU-L [your name here]

TRDEV-L

The aim of this training and development list is to create a community of scholars and practitioners in training and development by facilitating communications about issues, opportunities, and problems affecting the field in private, public, and government sectors.

To be included, send e-mail to LISTSERV@LISTS.PSU.EDU with the following, and only the following, in the body of the message:

SUBSCRIBE TRDEV-L [your name here]

You will receive an e-mail request from the LISTSERV asking for a confirmation of your subscription within forty-eight hours. If you have any problems subscribing to TRDEV-L, contact the TRDEV-L Manager (*cxl18@psuvm.psu.edu*)

UPDATE/EDUPAGE

Educom sponsors the EDUPAGE list, a short mail summary of educational computing issues, and the EDUCOM UPDATE list, a twice-a-month electronic summary of the organizational news and events.

To be included, send e-mail to LISTPROC@EDUCOM.EDU with the following, and only the following, in the body of the message:

SUBSCRIBE UPDATE [your name here]

SUBSCRIBE EDUPAGE [your name here]

WEBTRAINING-L

This is a moderated mailing list for those interested in delivering training over the Internet or intranet.

To be included in the weekly distribution, send e-mail with the subject or message "Subscribe WebTraining-L" to LISTMANAGER@BRANDON-HALL.COM.

WWWDEV-L

WWWDEV-L is a list that originates in Canada and serves academics and practitioners who are seeking answers to design and development questions related to Web-based training and online learning.

To be included, send e-mail to LISTSERV@UNB.CA with the following, and only the following, in the body of the message:

SUBSCRIBE WWWDEV [your name here]

Threaded Discussions, Notes Conferences, and Forums

The following discussions require that you open your browser and enter the URL to participate in the conversation. Some of the discussions may require that you establish a user name and password.

epss.com!

http://www.epss.com/

epss.com! is a performance support and knowledge management forum. It is a virtual meeting space open to all to discuss topics of interest to performance support and knowledge management practitioners. Use this forum to post questions or provide information you think may be useful to your peers. Each month epss.com has a suggested topic for discussion.

Tech Learn Chat

http://www.masie.com/

Tech Learn Chat is a moderated conference that offers participants an opportunity to post questions, share experiences, and explore trends in instructional technology.

WBTIC Discussion

http://filename.com/wbt/

The Web-Based Training Information Center offers four discussion forums. The Open Forum provides a place to ask about Web-based training and Web-electronic performance support systems. The Design Forum explores instructional design, usability, and graphic design. The Jobs Forum is the place to post an open position or find a WBT job. The Developers Only Forum is for developers who want a virtual space to discuss tools and techniques of creating WBT and W/EPS systems.

TSS Discussion Board

http://www.trainingsupersite.com/tss_link/disboardset.htm

The Training Supersite board is a discussion group that covers the full gamut of training topics. The sponsors are eventually planning to spawn many targeted groups on specific "hot" topics. They have installed a search engine to help users quickly find comments posted by topic.

NovaTRAIN Forums

http://www.onbusiness.net/cgi-local/netforum/training/a.cgi/1

NovaTRAIN offers a forum for posting questions and answers; giving advice; and discussing issues related to training and development. This site offers three discussion groups: Trainers' Peer to Peer Forum, Training and Technology Forum, and Human Resources Forum.

Appendix D

Selected Bibliography

Adult Education

Brockett, R. G., & Hiemstra, R. (1994). *Self-direction in adult learning: Perspective on theory, research, and practice.* London: Routledge.

Brookfield, S. D. (1991). *Understanding and facilitating adult learning: A comprehensive analysis of principles and effective practices.* San Francisco: Jossey-Bass.

Brookfield, S. D. (1995). *Becoming a critically reflective teacher.* San Francisco: Jossey-Bass.

Brookfield, S. D. (1995). *Developing critical thinkers: Challenging adults to explore alternative ways of thinking and acting.* San Francisco: Jossey-Bass.

Candy, P. C. (1991). *Self-direction for lifelong learning.* San Francisco: Jossey-Bass.

Claxton, C. S., & Murrell, P. H. (1987). *Learning styles: Implications for improving educational practices.* Washington, DC: American Association for Higher Education.

Cranton, P. (1994). *Understanding and promoting transformation learning: A guide for educators of adults.* San Francisco: Jossey-Bass.

Cranton, P. (1996). *Professional development as transformative learning: New perspectives for teachers of adults.* San Francisco: Jossey-Bass.

Cross, P. (1992). *Adults as learners: Increasing participation and facilitating learning.* San Francisco: Jossey-Bass.

Flannery, D. D. (1993). *Applying cognitive learning theory to adult learning.* San Francisco: Jossey-Bass.

Galbraith, M. W. (Ed.). (1991). *Adult learning methods: A guide for effective instruction.* Malabar, FL: Krieger.

Jaques, D. (1992). *Learning in groups.* Houston: Gulf.

Knowles, M. (1984). *Andragogy in action: Applying modern principles of adult learning.* San Francisco: Jossey-Bass.

Mezirow, J., and Associates. (1991). *Fostering critical reflection in adulthood: A guide to transformative and emancipatory learning.* San Francisco: Jossey-Bass.

Rothwell, W. J., & Cookson, P. S. (1997). *Beyond instruction: Comprehensive program planning for business and education.* San Francisco: Jossey-Bass.

Schwarz, R. M. (1994). *The skilled facilitator: Practical wisdom for developing effective groups.* San Francisco: Jossey-Bass.

Smith, C. M., & Pourchot, T. (Eds.). (1998). *Adult learning and development: Perspectives from educational psychology.* Hillsdale, NJ: Lawrence Erlbaum.

Tennant, M., & Pogson, P. (1995). *Learning and change in adulthood: A developmental perspective.* San Francisco: Jossey-Bass.

Vella, J. K. (1995). *Training through dialogue: Promoting effective learning and change with adults.* San Francisco: Jossey-Bass.

Creating Web Pages, HTML, and Java

Evans, T. (1996). *10 minute guide to HTML 3.2.* Carmel, IN: Que Corporation.

Flanagan, D. (1996). *Java in a nutshell: A desktop quick reference for Java programmers.* Sebastopol, CA: O'Reilly & Associates.

Harris, S., & Kidder, G. (1996). *Official HTML publishing for Netscape: Your complete guide to online design and production.* Research Triangle Park, NC: Ventana Communications.

Lampton, C. (1997). *Home page: An introduction to web page design.* Danbury, CT: Franklin Watts.

Lemay, L. (1995). *Complete teach yourself HTML kit.* Indianapolis, IN: Sams.net Publishing.

Lemay, L. (1996). *Teach yourself web publishing with HTML 3.2 in a week.* Indianapolis, IN: Sams.net Publishing.

Lemay, L., & Perkins, C.L. (1996). *Teach yourself Java in 21 days.* Indianapolis, IN: Sams.net Publishing.

Lemay, L. (Ed.). (1997). *Laura Lemay's Java 1.1 interactive course.* New York: Waite Group.

McCoy, J. (1996). *Mastering web design.* Markham, Ontario: Sybex.

Pomeroy, B. (1997). *Beginnernet: A beginner's guide to the Internet and the World Wide Web.* New York: Slack, Inc.

Stauffer, T. (1996). *HTML by example.* Carmel, IN: Que Corporation.

Summitt, P. M., & Summitt, M. J. (1996). *Creating cool interactive web sites.* Foster City, CA: IDG Books Worldwide.

Teague, A. C. (1997). *How to program HTML frames interface design and JavaScript*: Emeryville, CA: Ziff Davis.

Tennant, R. (1996). *Practical HTML: A self-paced tutorial.* El Dorado Hills, CA: Library Solutions Press.

Williams, R., & Mark, D. (1996). *Home sweet home page.* Berkeley, CA: Peachpit Press.

Distance Education

Berge, Z. L., & Collins, M. P. (Eds.). (1995). *Computer mediated communication and the online classroom: Distance learning.* Cresskill, NJ: Hampton Press.

Cyrs, T. E. (1997). *Teaching and learning at a distance: What it takes to effectively design, deliver, and evaluate programs.* San Francisco: Jossey-Bass.

Eastmond, D. V. (1995). *Alone but together: Adult distance study through computer conferencing.* Cresskill, NJ: Hampton Press.

Garrison, D. R., & Shale, D. (Eds.). (1991). *Education at a distance: From issues to practice.* Melbourne, FL: Krieger.

Harasim, L., Hiltz, S. R., Teles, L., & Turoff, M. (1995). *Learning networks: A field guide to teaching and learning online.* Cambridge, MA: MIT Press.

Hiltz, S. R. (1994). *The virtual classroom: Learning without limits via computer networks.* Norwood, NJ: Ablex Publications.

Keegan, D. (Ed.). (1993). *Theoretical principles of distance education.* London: Routledge.

Moore, M. (Ed.). (1992). *Distance education for corporate and military training.* University Park, PA: American Center for the Study of Distance Education.

Mantyla, K. & Gividen, R. (1997) *Distance learning: A step-by step guide for trainers.* Alexandria, VA: American Society for Training and Development.

Moore, M. G., & Kearsley, G. (1996). *Distance education: A systems view.* Boston: Wadsworth.

Rossman, M. H., & Rossman, M. E. (Eds.). (1995). *Facilitating distance education.* San Francisco: Jossey-Bass.

Rowntree, D., & Lockwood, F. (1994). *Preparing materials for open, distance and flexible learning: An action guide for teachers and trainers.* London: Kogan Page.

Rumble, G. (1986). *The planning and management of distance education.* New York: St. Martins Press.

Verduin, J. R., & Clark, T. A. (1991). *Distance education: The foundations of effective practice.* San Francisco: Jossey-Bass.

Instructional Design

Banathy, B. H. (1968). *Instructional systems.* Palo Alto, CA: Fearon.

Dean, G. J. (1994). *Designing instruction for adult learners.* Malabar, FL: Krieger.

Bosworth, C., & Hamilton, S. H. (Eds.). (1994). *Collaborative learning: Underlying processes and effective techniques.* San Francisco: Jossey-Bass.

Bruner, J. S. (1966). *Toward a theory of instruction.* Cambridge, MA: Harvard University Press.

Dempsey, J. V., & Sales, G. C. (Eds.). (1993). *Interactive instruction and feedback.* Englewood Cliffs, NJ: Educational Technology Publications.

Dick, W., & Carey, L. (1995). *The systematic design of instruction.* New York: HarperCollins.

Forsyth, I., Jolliffe, A., & Stevens, D. (1995). *The complete guide to teaching a course: Practical strategies for teachers, lecturers and instructors.* London: Kogan Page.

Gagne, R. M., Briggs, L. J., & Wager, W. W. (1992). *Principles of instructional design.* New York: Harcourt Brace.

Hannafin, M. J., & Peck, K. L. (1988). *The design, development, and evaluation of instructional software.* New York: Macmillan.

Jacobs, L. C., & Clinton, I. C. (1992). *Developing and using tests effectively.* San Francisco: Jossey-Bass.

Krathwohl, D., & Bloom, B.S. (1984). *Taxonomy of educational objectives, handbook 1: Cognitive domain.* London: Longman.

Kemp, J. E., Morrison, G. R., & Ross, S. M. (1997). *Designing effective instruction.* Englewood Cliffs, NJ: Prentice-Hall.

Lan, H. R., McBeath, A., & Hebert, J. (1995*). Teaching strategies and methods for student-centered instruction.* New York: Harcourt Brace.

Laurillard, D. (1993). *Rethinking university teaching: A framework for the effective use of educational technology.* New York: Routledge.

Mager, R. F. (1992). *What every manager should know about training.* Belmont, CA: Lake Publishing.

Merrill, D. M. (1994). *Instructional design theory.* Englewood Cliffs, NJ: Educational Technology Publications.

Posner, G. J., & Rudnitsky, A. N., (1994). *Course design: A guide to curriculum development for teachers.* New York: Longman.

Pregent, R. (1994). *Charting your course: How to prepare to teach more effectively.* Madison, WI: Magna Publications.

Resnick, M., & Kafai, Y. (Eds.). (1996). *Constructionism in practice: Designing, thinking, and learning in a digital world.* Hillsdale, NJ: Lawrence Erlbaum.

Rossett, A. (1987). *Training needs.* Englewood Cliffs, NJ: Educational Technology Publications.

Rothwell, W. J. (1997). *Mastering the instructional design process: A systematic approach.* San Francisco: Jossey-Bass.

Smith, P. L., & Reagan, T. J. (1993). *Instructional design.* New York: Macmillan.

Weimer, M., Parrett, J. L., & Kerns, M. (1998). *How am I teaching? Forms and activities for acquiring instructional input.* Madison, WI: Magna Publications.

Multimedia Design

Boyle, T., & Boyle, T. (1996). *Design for multimedia learning.* Englewood Cliffs, NJ: Prentice-Hall.

Dempsey, J. V., & Sales, G. C. (Eds.). (1993). *Interactive instruction and feedback.* Englewood Cliffs, NJ: Educational Technology Publications.

Gassaway, S., Davis, G., & Gregory, C. (1996). *Designing multimedia web sites.* Indianapolis, IN: Hayden Books.

Gayeski, D. M. (Ed.). (1993). *Multimedia for learning: Development, application, and evaluation.* Englewood Cliffs, NJ: Educational Technology Publications.

Gery, G. (1987). *Making CBT happen.* Boston, MA: Weingarten Publications.

Gery, G. (1991). *Electronic performance support systems.* Boston: Ziff Institute.

Giardina, M. (Ed.). (1992). *Interactive multimedia learning environments: Human factors and technical considerations on design issues.* New York: Springer Verlag.

Gloor, P. A. (1996). *Elements of hypermedia design: Techniques for navigation & visualization in cyberspace.* New York: Springer Verlag.

Kommers, P. A. M., Grabinger, S., & Dunlap, J. C. (Eds.). (1996). *Hypermedia learning environments: Instructional design and integration.* Hillsdale, NJ: Lawrence Erlbaum.

Morris, M. E. S., & Hinrichs, R. J. (1996). *Web page design: A different multimedia.* Englewood Cliffs, NJ: Prentice-Hall.

Reynolds, A., & Araya, R. (1995). *Building multimedia performance support systems.* New York: McGraw-Hill.

Web-Based Training/Web-Based Instruction

Brooks, D. W. (1997). *A guide to designing interactive teaching for the World Wide Web: Innovations in science, education and technology.* New York: Plenum.

Corrigan, D. (1996). *Internet university: College courses by computer.* Harwich, MA: Cape Software.

Hall, B. (1997). *Web-based training cookbook.* New York: John Wiley.

Kaplan, H. (1997). Interactive multimedia & the World Wide Web: A new paradigm for university teaching & learning. *Educom Review, 32*(1), 48–51.

Khan, B. H. (Ed.). (1997). *Web-based instruction.* Englewood Cliffs, NJ: Educational Technology Publications.

Porter, L. R. (1997). *Distance learning with the Internet.* New York: John Wiley.

Web Design (Graphics)

Black, R., & Elder, S. (1997). Web sites that work. Indianapolis, IN: Hayden Books.

Holzschlag, M. E., & Lemay, L. (1997). *Laura Lemay's guide to sizzling web site design.* Indianapolis, IN: Sams.net Publishing.

Kristof, R., & Satran, A. (1995). *Interactivity by design: Creating and communicating with new media.* Indianapolis, IN: Hayden Books.

Lopuck, L. (1996). *Designing multimedia: A visual guide to multimedia and online graphic Design.* Berkeley, CA: Peachpit Press.

McCanna, L. (1996). *Creating great web graphics.* New York: MIS Press.

Milano, D. (1997). *Interactivity in action: Case studies of way cool web sites, multimedia masterworks and CD-ROM success stories.* Gilroy, CA: Miller Freeman Books.

Mok, C. (1996). *Designing business: Multiple media, multiple disciplines.* New York: Macmillan.

Sather, A. (Ed.). (1997). *Creating killer interactive web sites: The art of integrating interactivity and design.* Indianapolis, IN: Hayden Books.

Siegel, D. (1996). *Creating killer web sites: The art of third-generation site design.* Indianapolis, IN: Hayden Books.

Siegel, D. (1997) *Creating killer web sites* (2nd ed.). Indianapolis, IN: Hayden Books.

Tufte, E. R. (1992). *The visual display of quantitative information.* Cheshire, CT: Graphics Press.

Waters, C. (1998). *Web concept and design* (2nd ed.). Indianapolis, IN: New Riders Publishing.

Weinman, L. (1996). *Deconstructing web graphics.* Indianapolis, IN: New Riders Publishing.

Weinman, L. (1996). *Designing web graphics: How to prepare images and media for the web.* Indianapolis, IN: New Riders Publishing.

Wurman, R. S., & Bradford, P. (Eds.). (1996). Information architects. Cheshire, CT: Graphics Press.

Workplace Learning

Bowsher, J. E. (1998). *Revolutionizing workforce performance: A systems approach to mastery.* San Francisco: Jossey-Bass.

Chawla, S., & Renesch, J. (1995). *Learning organizations: Developing cultures for tomorrow's workplace.* Portland, OR: Productivity Press.

Forrester, K., Payne, J., & Ward, K. (1995). *Workplace learning: Perspectives on education, training and work.* London: Avebury.

Marsick, V. J., & Watkins, K. E. (1990). *Informal and incidental learning in the workplace.* London: Routledge.

Senge, P. M. (1990). *The fifth discipline: The art and practice of the learning organization.* New York: Doubleday.

Spikes, W. (Ed.). (1995). *Workplace learning.* San Francisco: Jossey-Bass.

Watkins, K. E., & Marsick, V. J. (1993). *Sculpting the learning organization: Lessons in the art and science of systemic change.* San Francisco: Jossey-Bass.

Appendix E

Matrix of Web-Based Training Types*

Matrix of Web-Based Training Types				
	Web-Based Training			
	Web/CBT	**Web/EPS Systems**	**Web/VAC**	**Web/VSC**
Purpose	To provide performance-based training with measurable goals and objectives.	To provide practical knowledge and problem-solving skills in a just-in-time format	To provide group learning in a non-contiguous time environment	To provide group learning in a real-time environment
Types of Learning	Well-structured problems that require transferring knowledge, building comprehension, and practicing application of skills	Ill-structured problems that require analysis and synthesis of elements, relationships, and organizational principles to produce solutions	Less structured problems that require application, analysis, synand evaluation to produce new ideas, plans, or products	Ill-structured problems that require the synthesis and evaluation of information and shared experience to produce new ideas, plans, or products

	Web/CBT	Web/EPS Systems	Web/VAC	Web/VSC
Roles of Facilitator or WBT Designer	*Manager of instruction:* controls, predicts, directs, and assesses the learning outcomes; communicates with learner	*Organizer of content:* locates, analyzes, abstracts, indexes, and classifies information into learning modules	*Facilitator of group learning:* guides instruction, provides resources, evaluates outcomes, and communicates with learners	*Coordinator of learning experience:* participates as a co-learner, recommends learning direction, but does not determine direction or evaluate outcomes
Roles of Learner	Takes active role role practicing new behaviors; receiving feedback; and communicating with instructor.	Takes initiative to direct own learning; determines the level of detail; and assesses the success of instruction.	Guided by facilitator as an individual or as a member of a group; participates in instructional activities; and receives feedback.	Active participant in a collaborative learning process with facilitator and peers, participates in dialogue and reflects on experience.
Methods	Drill and practice, simulations, reading, questioning, and answering	Problem-solving, scientific method, experiential method, project method	Experiential tasks, group discussions, team projects, self-directed learning, discovery method	Dialogue and discussions, problem-solving, and maximum interaction
Interactions	Multimedia, hypertext, hypermedia, simulations, application exercises, e-mail, listserv, and bulletin boards, communication with instructor	Multimedia, hypertext, hypermedia, bulletin boards, notes conferences, modules of Web/CBT, and e-mail access to facilitator and peers	Multimedia, hypertext, hypermedia, bulletin boards, notes conferences, modules of Web/CBT, and e-mail access to facilitator and peers	Synchronous audio- and video conferencing, shared white-boards, shared applications

*Note: There are many variations of these approaches, and different approaches are often used in combination.

Appendix F

Netiquette

Netiquette refers to a set of guidelines for online behavior. The guidelines presented here are general and can be used to help shape the guidelines for your own Web-based training program.

Checklist for Participating in Mailing Lists*

Questions to ask oneself before posting a message to a mailing list or listserv:

1. Is the message being sent to the appropriate destination (the whole list versus one or more selected individual(s)? If your reply is no longer related to the subject of the list, you should send it privately to the person who wrote the original message. Also, if the original sender volunteered to summarize responses, you should generally send your message privately to him or her.

2. Is the subject line descriptive of my message? A descriptive subject line will include specific, concise information about the content of a message.

3. Have I included only enough of any past messages that my message refers to so that other list members know what I am referring to? Delete as much of the original as you can, such as headings, signature files, and any part of the message you are not replying to.

4. Is my message as brief as possible, and have I referred interested parties to a website or other method of getting additional information (or offered to send more information via e-mail for those who want it)? The longer the message, the less chance people will read it.

5. Have I attempted to express appreciation to list members who have made a useful contribution to the list? Send a private thank you message to people who go out of their way to help you.

6. If I have disagreed with someone else's ideas, have I attempted to avoid a personal attack against him or her?

7. Have I attempted to ignore or defuse anything that I consider a personal attack against me?

8. Does my message say something more than "me too"? If all you say is "I agree," do not send your message to the entire list. If you give another example of the point being made, or in some other way add new content, then you can send your message to the list.

9. Have I offered to summarize the replies to any question I asked? Certain questions will elicit many responses, and if you think your question will be of this type, it is easier for readers to use the information if it is provided in one message.

10. Have I signed the message and included my e-mail address in the body? You need to include your e-mail address in the body, because some lists do not include the header with your address.

11. Did I proofread the message? Messages with spelling and grammatical errors can reflect poorly on the writer.

Appendix G

Glossary

Active-X	A programming language used to develop interactive applications that are downloaded and executed from within a Web browser.
Alpha Test	A formative evaluation of a Web-based training program that determines the program's effectiveness after development has been completed.
Applets	Small Java programs that can be embedded in HTML pages.
Application Sharing	The ability for two or more learners to work simultaneously on a shared piece of software, for example, a group of learners working together to create a spreadsheet to be turned in for an assignment.
Asynchronous Learning	Educational events that take place independently in time, that is, a learning exchange between students and

	facilitator(s) that is delayed by minutes, hours, or days.
Attitudinal Skills	Abilities related to teaching learners to behave in a particular manner, such as teaching people to choose to recycle or to reduce the amount of salt they consume.
Bandwidth	The amount of network capacity available to carry files, e-mail, and other materials from one place on the network to another.
Beta Test	A final formative assessment of a Web-based training program by the facilitator who will ultimately assume responsibility for teaching the program.
Browser	An application that enables users to access various kinds of Internet and intranet resources such as HTML files, video, audio, and images.
Bulletin Board Systems (BBS)	A computerized meeting and announcement system that allows subscribers to carry on discussions, upload and download files, and make announcements without the subscribers being connected to the computer at the same time. This is also referred to as a threaded discussion, forum, e-forum, and notes conference.
Bundled Solutions	Software that integrates several features such as live audio, whiteboards, and application sharing.
Common Gateway Interface (CGI)	A small program that takes data from a Web server and performs some action with it, such as putting the content of a form into an e-mail message or turning the data into a database query.

Cognitive Skills	Intellectual abilities such as balancing a checkbook or completing a tax form.
Cognitive Domain	The classification of goals and objectives into six levels of intellectual skills (knowledge, comprehension, application, analysis, synthesis, and evaluation).
Cognitive Loading	The process of putting large amounts of information into a learner's short-term memory. Cognitive loading reduces a student's ability to learn and, therefore, should be avoided.
Critical Reflection	The ability of learners to draw on experience and question underlying assumptions.
Design Document	A detailed plan that provides the development team specifications needed to produce the final product.
Dumbing Down	The process of revising training material by removing sophisticated interactions and complex multimedia segments.
E-Commerce	The exchange of business information using electronic formats, as in the use of e-mail, electronic funds transfer, and other network technologies to conduct business.
E-Zine	A magazine published on the Internet.
Flow Chart	A detailed version of the navigation map that guides the work of the development team.
Forum	See Bulletin Board Systems.
Help Desk	An organization that end users can call for assistance with their hardware or software problems.

Helper Applications

Applications that help the browser deal with file types it does not have the ability to play or read. Helper applications are different from plug-in applications in that they launch a separate window to play or read the file.

HTML

See Hypertext Markup Language

Hypermedia

Any media (text, audio, graphics, video, or animation) that can be chosen by a learner, connected and displayed in a nonlinear manner.

Hypertext

Text or other medium that can be chosen by a learner and that causes another document or medium to be retrieved and displayed.

Hypertext Markup Language (HTML)

A coding language used to make hyper text documents for use on the Web. Using HTML, text or graphics on a Web page can be linked to resources (images, sound, video, and text) on another page on the Internet.

Instructional Strategy

An overview of how the information will be presented and how students and facilitator(s) will interact in a training program.

InterConstructive

A term to describe designing and teaching a Web-based course that allows students to add to the class Web-cluster, drawing their research and interactions into an accumulating hypertext archive of materials.

Interactivity

The ability to provide control, to direct attention, and to coordinate the communication among the students, instructor, and content.

Interface	The screen through which the learner and the computer communicate and access, transfer, add, and exchange information.
Internet	A sub-set of the World Wide Web that is accessed via a graphic browser.
Internet Relay Chat (IRC)	A multi-user, live, real-time, text-based conference via the Internet or intranet.
Intranet	An internal network that can stand alone or be connected to the Internet.
IRC	See Internet Relay Chat.
ISO Standards	Standards published by the International Organization for Standardization (ISO) that define minimum requirements for the implementation of quality systems.
Java	A network-oriented programming language invented by Sun Microsystems specifically designed for writing programs that can be downloaded from the Internet to the desktop and immediately run.
Listserv	A software product that manages distribution lists for e-mail.
Macintosh	A computer made by Apple.
Microsoft On-Line Institute (MOLI)	A Website dedicated to the promotion and delivery of computer-based training.
Multimedia	The use of two or more of the following elements in a computer-based training program: text, images, video, audio, and animation.
Navigation Map	A high-level graphical depiction of how a program is organized.
Netiquette	The etiquette or rules of behavior for the Internet.

News Groups	A discussion group on USENET devoted to talking about specific topics. See also Threaded Discussions.
Notes Conferences	See Bulletin Board Systems.
Off-the-Shelf Programs	Web-based training programs that provide instruction for nonproprietary topics and are offered for sale to the general public.
Opportunity Statement	An explanation of how the training program will improve productivity, reduce cost, and increase profitability for an organization.
Participatory Evaluation	The process of involving the learners in the review of the training program.
Plug-In	A small piece of software that adds features to a larger piece of software. Examples are plug-ins for the Netscape® browser and Web server.
Posting	Writing a reply to a message on an electronic bulletin board, threaded discussion, e-forum, or notes conference.
Praxis	The process of exploring a topic, taking action, and reflecting on the outcome of the action.
Program Script	A detailed plan of the audio, the visuals, and the interactions planned for a Web/virtual synchronous class.
Psychomotor Skills	Skills that combine physical movement and mental activities, such as hitting a golf ball or using a table saw.
Rapid Prototype	A Web-based training program with just enough functionality that it can be assessed for effectiveness before finishing development.

Repurposing	The process of revising training material for use in a different format.
Screen Real Estate	The amount of space available on a videodisplay terminal or screen.
Search Engine	A software application that locates words, phrases, and files on a Website.
Server	A computer processing unit that is shared by a number of users and dedicated to performing specific tasks, such as processing mail and managing print requests.
SME	See Subject-Matter Expert.
Spamming	The act of sending unwanted e-mail to a large number of people.
SQL	See Structured Query Language
Structured Query Language	A specialized programming language for sending queries to databases.
Storyboarding	A technique used to display pictorially how a program will unfold.
Subject-Matter Expert	One who is highly skilled and knowledgeable in a given topic area.
Synchronous	Events that take place in real-time.
Systemic Design of Instruction (SDI)	The process of developing training and instruction using a structured and repeatable technique.
Threaded Discussion	A form of communication that enables learners to carry on an asynchronous conversation by posting notes to an electronic bulletin board with strands or threads of discussions.
Treatment	A description of a program's style and overall approach.

Try-Out Learners	A group of learners who are similar to the intended audience and who will test the Web-based training program.
Unbundled Solutions	Individual software applications that perform a specific function and can be used alone or be pieced together with other applications. They are not integrated into a single interface.
Uniform Resource Locator (URL)	A standard way to address any resource on the Internet or on an intranet.
Web Computer-Based Training (W/CBT)	A Web-based, multimedia method that features drill and practice, simulations, reading, and question and answer.
Web Electronic Performance Support System (W/EPSS)	A Web-based job aid for just-in-time training that focuses on problem solving, scientific method, and experiential methods of instruction.
Web Virtual Asynchronous Class (W/VAC)	A Web-based collaborative learning method that features discussions, problem solving, and reflection as instructional strategies conducted asynchronously.
Web Virtual Synchronous Class (W/VSC)	A Web-based group learning methodology that employs experiential tasks, discussions, and team projects as instructional strategies conducted in real-time.
Webmaster	A person who designs, manages, and maintains an organization's Website.
Whiteboard	An application that enables two or more users to share a Web-based "chalkboard" device.
World Wide Web (WWW)	The electronic, global network of networks.
WYSIWYG	What You See Is What You Get

Index

About the Author

Margaret Driscoll is an instructor in the Instructional Design Program at the University of Massachusetts Boston Graduate College of Education. She also works as a consultant, speaker, and workshop facilitator bringing fourteen years' experience with organizations such as the University of Massachusetts Medical Center, Digital Equipment Corporation, BayBank, Stratus, Interleaf, Compaq Computer, and Fidelity Investments. Her experience as a distance educator in high-tech fields, medical education, financial services, and academic institutions has exposed her to the real-world challenges and opportunities that trainers face.

Ms. Driscoll holds a Master's degree in Instructional Technology from Boston College; an M.B.A. from the University of Massachusetts at Boston; and a Master's degree in Adult and Higher Education from Teachers College, Columbia University, where she is a doctoral candidate studying the design of Web-based training in high-tech environments. Her research papers have appeared in the *Journal of Performance Improvement,* the *Multimedia* and *Internet Newsletter, Technical Training, CommunicationsWeek,* and *The 1998 ASTD Training and Performance Year Book.*